"Oh, Waiter!
One Order of Crow!"

"Oh, Waiter! One

G. P. PUTNAM'S SONS
NEW YORK

JEFF
GREENFIELD

Order of Crow!"

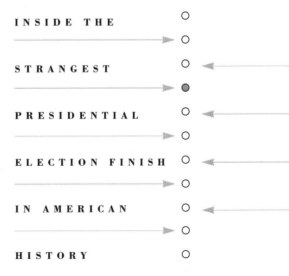

INSIDE THE

STRANGEST

PRESIDENTIAL

ELECTION FINISH

IN AMERICAN

HISTORY

G. P. Putnam's Sons
Publishers Since 1838
a member of
Penguin Putnam Inc.
375 Hudson Street
New York, NY 10014

Library of Congress Cataloging-in-Publication Data

Greenfield, Jeff.
"Oh, waiter! One order of crow!" : inside the strangest presidential
election finish in American history / Jeff Greenfield.
p.   cm.
ISBN 0-399-14776-4
1. Presidents—United States—Election—2000.   I. Title.
JK526 2000h   2001019342 CIP
324.973'0929—dc21

Printed in the United States of America

1   3   5   7   9   10   8   6   4   2

This book is printed on acid-free paper. ∞

Book design by Judith Stagnitto Abbate
and Claire Naylon Vaccaro

For my mother, Helen Greenfield, who taught me to love politics, music, and newspapers; who (perhaps to her own surprise) gave me the courage to take chances . . . and who was always, always there.

"*Victory Has a*

Hundred

Fathers. . . ."

● **M A Y B E   I T   W A S**

Newt Gingrich's fault.

If the Speaker of the House had not misread the Republican congressional takeover of 1994 as a call to revolution, he might not have turned a scrap over budget legislation in 1995 into a confrontation that threatened a government shutdown. When President Clinton called Gingrich's bluff on November 14, the government canceled tours of national monuments, shuttered nonessential government offices, and furloughed workers. The White House itself was forced to use unpaid interns for low-level logistical work. One of those interns, a twenty-two-year-old, working at the White House as a favor to a major Clinton contributor, was dispatched to deliver a pizza to the president of the United States in the Oval Office. Maybe the Earth moved; maybe it didn't. But what happened clearly triggered a seismic shift in the terrain of the 2000 presidential race.

● Maybe it was Ross Perot's fault.

One of the major achievements of the shorthaired, short-fused billionaire's presidential campaigns was the harsh light it shone on the ballot access laws: a collection of two-party protection rules that strangled new political parties in their cribs. No state was more hostile to third-party politics than Florida. In 1996, for example, the Green Party tried to put Ralph Nader's name on the ballot. Under state law, the party needed to collect more than sixty-five thousand signatures—an impossible task for a party with no money and no foot soldiers. Two years later, a broad coalition of reform groups succeeded in putting Amendment 11 on the Florida ballot. Its aim: to "grant equal ballot access for independent and minor parties." It was approved by a nearly two-to-one margin. Now, all a minor party needed to do was to pay a small filing fee.

The result? In November 2000, ten different tickets qualified for the Florida ballot: not just Gore, Bush, Nader, and Pat Buchanan, but the Natural Law Party, the Socialist Party, and the Workers' World Party.

All this clutter worried local election officials, such as Theresa LePore in Palm Beach County, who'd been working in the field since the age of sixteen. She'd seen firsthand what could happen with a cluttered ballot. In a very close 1988 Florida race for the U.S. Senate, the candidates for that office were buried on the bottom of the first page of the punch-card ballot booklet. Some one hundred seventy thousand Floridians overlooked that highly competitive race. Moreover, LePore knew her constituents. There were so many old folks in Palm Beach County that even the STOP signs featured supersized letters. There was, LePore concluded, only one way to put all those presidential candidates on the ballot with type big enough for her voters to read easily. She decided to put the names on *both* sides of the page, with the punch holes in the middle. Most other local election officials in Florida rejected that idea; they even talked about it among themselves when they met in September in Tampa for their big annual meeting. LePore did not hear the conversation; she was out of the room at the time (the group that met was the Urban and Large County Election and Registration Supervisors: ULCERS).

In Duval County, which includes Jacksonville, voting officials decided on a different approach—they put the presidential candidates on *two* pages, rather than one. No one took much notice of the change—including local officials of the NAACP and the Democratic Party, intent on getting out the African-American vote for president and for U.S. senator. Their mailings and leaflets all urged voters—many of them first-time voters, who had never seen a ballot before—to "punch every page" on their ballots. Those instructions assumed that the ballot this time would be like the Duval County ballots in the past—one office, one page.

On Election Day, the confusion spawned by the "butterfly

ballot" in Palm Beach County and the "caterpillar" ballot in Duval County cost Al Gore thousands of votes from his two most loyal constituencies. Gore lost the state of Florida by 537 votes. Because he lost Florida, he lost the White House.

● Maybe it was Tom Connolly's fault. If the longtime Maine Democrat hadn't stumbled upon a twenty-five-year-old police report, the public would never have learned that George W. Bush was once stopped by Maine police and cited for "Driving Under the Influence"—certainly not five days before Election Day. Voters would not have gone to the polls knowing that the governor had concealed this story for all of his public life. Karl Rove, who oversaw the Bush campaign strategy from start to finish, thought the story cost Bush anywhere from half a million to a million votes, enough to make him the loser in the national popular vote.

● Or maybe you'd rather blame Senator Tom Daschle and House Minority Leader Richard Gephardt. If they'd marched up Pennsylvania Avenue in August 1998 and told President Clinton that his self-indulgence and mendacity required his resignation, Al Gore would have been an incumbent president, embracing the record of peace and prosperity, instead of edging away from it, for fear that it would tie him to scandal. How about New Jersey Governor Christine Whitman, and a handful of unidentified California Republicans? Late in the campaign, buoyed by surprising poll numbers, Whitman urged Bush to make a stop in New Jersey; California Republicans beckoned the candidate westward. Bush spent precious time in those states; further, he spent over $10 million in California. That time and money might have made all the difference in Wisconsin, Iowa, Oregon, and Pennsylvania—which would have made Florida a matter of brotherly pride for Jeb Bush, rather than the key to the presidency for George W.

"Victory has a hundred fathers, and defeat is an orphan," President Kennedy said famously after the collapse of the Bay of Pigs invasion. The campaign we have lived through invites an amendment: A presidential deadlock has a thousand second guesses.

Our political history as a nation is studded with evidence that history turns on a dime. If a paranoid political rebel named Giuseppe Zangara had arrived five minutes earlier at a Miami Beach park in 1933, with a better line of sight at the vacationing FDR, there would have been no New Deal. Had it rained in Dallas on November 22, 1963, a bulletproof bubble top would have covered the presidential limousine, and JFK instead of LBJ would have decided whether to widen the war in Vietnam. If John Hinckley's bullet had hit an inch or so to the right, the Reagan administration would have lasted seventy days instead of eight years. This time, fate had another twist to display. That dime never turned; when it hit, it landed right on its edge.

In statistical terms, what happened in this election was inevitable, like that infinite number of monkeys banging away at typewriters who would sooner or later produce all the works of Shakespeare. Sooner or later, a combination of bad numbers, computer glitches, human folly, and hubris would turn the easy assurance of Election Night projections into a slapstick farce. Sooner or later, a presidential election with a hundred and one million voters would come down to a single state,

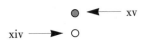

where six million votes came down to a (highly questionable) margin of 537—a statewide difference of five one-thousandths of 1 percent of the total. That margin was so small that the single wisest words about Florida were delivered not by a pundit but by mathematician John Allen Paulos, who wrote, "Whatever happens, the margin of error is greater than the margin of victory or defeat." Sooner or later, the rickety voting machinery that routinely produces a couple of *million* lost, spoiled, miscast, and miscounted ballots would play a decisive role in determining the next president. Sooner or later, we would once again see a candidate win the presidency even though more Americans voted for the other guy. This time, every one of these highly improbable possibilities all happened at the same time.

For all the results of Election Night, for all the never-before-seen-on-any-American-stage spectacles of those thirty-seven days, perhaps the most astonishing event was one that did not happen: an authentic, no-hype-necessary battle over the identity of the next president; a battle that threatened our political stability. There was much talk over those thirty-seven days of a "Constitutional crisis." Maybe there was seductive power in the alliterative crunch of the phrase. And no, there was never the possibility (to borrow a cliché that sprang from a thousand talking heads) of "tanks in the streets," or warring camps battling over control of the nation's airwaves. But imagine it is January 6, 2001, again, and this is what we faced:

The presidency will be determined by the electors of one state; two different slates claim to be the rightful electors. The Republican slate has been chosen by the Republican state legislature, and certified by the Republican governor, in defiance of the supreme court of his state. The governor happens to be the brother of the candidate he certified. The Democratic slate has been certified by the Democratic attorney general, following the mandate of the state supreme court, all of whose members were appointed by a Democratic governor. When the Congress meets in early January to cast final judgment on the nation's electoral vote, a conflict arises. The Congress retreats to the House and Senate. The Republican House votes to accept the Republican slate of electors. The evenly split Senate deadlocks, with the tying vote cast by a senator who is also the Democratic nominee for vice president. The tie is broken by the vote of the presiding officer of the Senate—who also happens to be the Democratic nominee for president. In such a deadlock, federal law says the slate certified by the executive of the state shall prevail. But the state's highest court has already said that the governor acted in defiance of the state's highest legal authority.

Tanks in the streets? Of course not. A Constitutional crisis? Sure. How close did we come to this? A switch of one Supreme Court vote might well have done the trick.

It is not my intention here to take you through a minute-by-minute replay of the weeks that followed this deadlocked election. You will not find extensive talk of chads—hanging, swinging, dimpled, pregnant, or virgin. Nor will you find a detailed account of the legal and political ploys of the players. Newspapers and newsmagazines have already chronicled much of the story; later, many of the principals will surely tell their own tales. I am aiming elsewhere here. I want to convey as closely as I can what it was like to watch this incredible Election Night unfold from a ringside seat—and to realize, at one and the same time, that you are part of one of the most exciting, and embarrassing, Election Nights ever. I want to tell you the kinds of thoughts (many of them decidedly inappropriate for air) that pop into the head of a journalist armed with a live microphone and a limited amount of self-control. I also want to look back at the 2000 campaign, and suggest how these two candidates came to deadlock. The postelection battle was so compelling, so riveting, that it overshadowed almost everything that had come before it. Still, the events of that campaign are in themselves compelling, especially when they are filtered through the prism of the voters' own explanations of why they chose as they did.

From this portrait, at least one fact emerges that (in my view) is simply not open to doubt: One of the figures most central to the election outcome, and even to the fight that followed, was President Bill Clinton. In a sense, much of the campaign turned on who and what he was. Was he the brilliant, energetic president who brought us the peace and prosperity of the millennium, handing the baton to his chosen successor? Or was he the living embodiment of the excesses and self-indulgence of the '60s and '70s, a coarse and coarsening figure his partner in government failed to repudiate? On this question, the election results suggested, the country could not make up its mind. When the vote deadlocked, the absolute conviction of the Republicans that they were about to have the election stolen from them was in substantial measure a testament to what they believed President Clinton had done to them, without any real consequence. In fighting as hard as they did to keep Al Gore out of the White House, they were fighting one last battle against their worst, most skilled, enemy.

The Election Night divisions were striking: We were divided by race and by gender; by where we lived and how we lived; by how and whether we prayed. But we were not *deeply* divided. Partisans were, of course: They often sounded as Teddy Roosevelt did when he tried to recapture the White House as a Bull Moose Progressive in 1912: "We stand at Armageddon, and we battle for the Lord." As for the country? Most Americans were watching a spectator sport, intriguing enough but without any of the passion they might have thrown into a fight over a new major-league stadium in their community. Why this indifference? It reflected, I believe, a broader indifference to politics itself that stemmed from disparate sources. A decade of peace and prosperity meant we did not mean to attend as closely to the affairs of government; their decisions no longer held the power to determine whether we would prosper or falter, much less whether we would live or die. A generation of jaded coverage and commentary by the press and the late-night comics had taught us to assume the worst of everyone in public life; the public misbehavior of public officials validated much of that cynicism. In our media, politics was now a lounge act, instead of occupying center stage, as it had through the first half-century or so of instant mass communications.

In this sense, maybe we got lucky. Suppose, for example, that the election of 1968 had ended as the 2000 election did. Suppose the battles in canvassing boards and courtrooms would decide not simply who would occupy the White House, but whether we would try to win a divisive, prolonged war or stop it. Suppose it had been 1980, with a candidate like Ronald Reagan, who aroused enormous hope among his supporters, and enormous fear among his opponents. Instead, the fight between Gore and Bush was a battle waged in the middle of the playing field, where the consequences of the outcome seemed marginal.

"Whoever wins, half the country will look on the president as illegitimate," went one of the refrains of postcampaign coverage. Instead, most of the country seemed to be saying, *"You know, it was pretty much a tie, we'll never really figure out*

who won, it doesn't make a whole lot of difference anyway, so please figure it out before Christmas, okay?" We may, of course, look back on this judgment some years from now and think, *How could we possibly have been so stupid, so ignorant? Why couldn't we have seen what was coming . . . ?*

Years from now, we or our children will know whether the election deadlock and the fight that followed were a passing curiosity or one of those quirks of fate that can change the course of the country. One lesson we have already learned is that some of our bedrock assumptions about our system were badly, and rightly, shaken. All it took to turn Election Night into a thirteen-hour-long free fall, and a thirty-seven-day trip down the rapids, was for a few random events to fall together in just the right—or wrong—way. Even before the first bells and whistles started sounding, we had a clue that this might not be your typical Election Night—which is a little like saying that Dorothy Gale heard there might be a breeze blowing through her little town in Kansas.

JEFF GREENFIELD | *Oh, Waiter! One Order of Crow!*

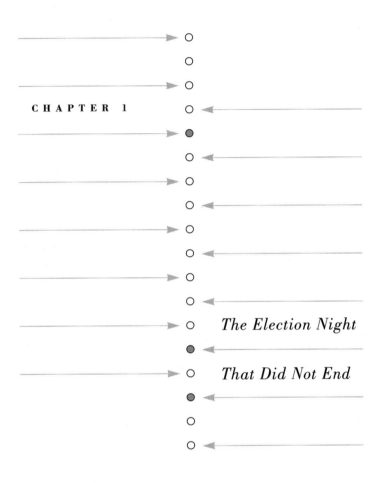

CHAPTER 1

The Election Night

That Did Not End

● A T T W O M I N U T E S

after five o'clock on the

evening of November sev-

enth, 2000, Judy Woodruff

turned to me on the anchor

set at CNN's World Head-

quarters in Atlanta for my

first words of wisdom.

"Jeff Greenfield, our se-

nior analyst, this is the kind of

election those of us who love

politics have been living for."

"Judy, and folks out there," I said, "if you've ever longed for those nights that you've heard about, when people waited late to find out who their leader was, pull up a chair—this may be it."

Who knew?

Well, to be honest about it, we did—sort of. We just didn't know quite how late it would be.

We knew because, in one sense, every Election Night is a ritual of concealment. Hours before the networks take to the air, the first wave of exit polls starts flowing into the headquarters of Voter News Service, then to the television networks, and then—almost instantly, in flat violation of solemn contractual pledges—into the ears of every decently connected campaign operative, journalist, campaign contributor, and kibitzer from one end of the country to the other.

("No kidding . . . a wipeout in Illinois? And the whole California rumor was nothing, right? What about Ohio? . . . Yeah, I figured that. . . .")

For the last twenty years, those early exit polls had pointed to a decisive outcome—sometimes in striking contrast to the last preelection surveys (Reagan romping over Carter in 1980), sometimes reflecting those surveys (Reagan demolishing Mondale in '84, Clinton putting away Bob Dole in '96). So, by the time the TV networks hit the air, every anchor, reporter, and analyst knew what the voters had done—not only nationally, but in most cases state by state. The rules of the game, however, strictly forbade us from reporting to our viewers and listeners the facts that all of us knew, thus turning the whole Election Night into something of a dramatic re-creation—a little like reporting the World Series *after* learning how every key moment of the game would turn out.

"You know, Bernie, I'd keep a close eye on Bill Buckner

down at first base in the late innings; he's not the best in the world at picking up a slow ground ball rolling right at him— just the kind of nubber a guy like Mookie Wilson could hit."

For an analyst like myself, this early-warning system had clear advantages; back in 1992, for example, the sure and certain knowledge that Bill Clinton was going to win New Jersey provided plenty of time for remarkably thoughtful instant analysis of Clinton's ability to lure suburban Jerseyites back to the Democratic Party, thus ending the Republicans' string of six consecutive triumphs in that state. Long before sunset in that same year, we had prepared our comments about the Reagan Democrats in Michigan, secure in our understanding that Clinton had reclaimed Michigan as well—because the exit polls had told us so while the sun was still high in the sky.

But this time? This time the exit polls were telling us exactly what we had been reporting all weekend long: This one was up for grabs.

At 4 P.M. on Election Day, a few dozen staffers jammed into a conference room in the Executive Corridor, one floor above the cavernous CNN newsroom in Atlanta—a 16,500-square-foot room jammed with 136 workstations, thirty-five edit bays, fifty-two computer pods in the satellite-feed areas, and close to 200 people, all of which forms the background behind the Atlanta anchor desk. Bill Schneider, the owlish, genial academic-turned-TV-analyst, sat at one end of the conference table, armed with a yellow legal pad.

"Well," he said with a small smile, "remember we told you it would be close? It's going to be very close." How close? Well, the national popular vote was splitting right down the middle—48 percent to 48 percent.

Some parts of the picture were clear: Bush's late sweep through California, which had cost him seven days and more than ten million dollars in television and radio advertising, had been a fool's venture—Gore was going to win California without breaking a sweat. He was winning comfortably in New Jersey as well, another state where Bush had made a late foray, on the heels of reports that he was "closing fast." And Illinois, once considered a key battleground, was also safely in hand for the Democrats. In other states that Gore desperately needed, however, there was potential trouble brewing. These were the "Dukakis" states—half a dozen won by the hapless 1988 Democratic presidential nominee, and assumed during the early stages of the campaign to be solidly in Gore's column.

("If *Dukakis* can win a state," the mantra went, "no Democrat can lose it.")

Now, it was clear, that assumption was in doubt. Yes, New York, Massachusetts, Hawaii, the District of Columbia, these were safely in Gore's column. The only way that Gore could lose any of those would be to appear on national TV with horns sprouting out of his head, chanting "All praise to Satan!"—and even then, New York would only shift to "Undecided." But some of those "Dukakis" states were precisely those where Ralph Nader could be costing Gore precious votes—Wisconsin, Iowa, Minnesota, Oregon, Washington. No, Nader would not be getting that 5 percent of the national popular vote, which would entitle his Green Party to millions of dollars in future federal funds—but he could still turn out to be a key player. And then there was West Virginia, a reliably Democratic state, but one where a lot of Democrats mined for coal and hunted with guns. Here, Gore's passion for the environment evoked images not of pastoral hills and valleys, but of shuttered mines and food stamps. West Virginia was in play on this Election Night, and in a race this close, even those five electoral votes could be decisive.

And what about Florida? Too close to call, Schneider said, but Gore does have a three-point lead in the exit polls.

"We may be up late with that one," he said. By the way, he added, almost as an afterthought: Hillary Clinton is going to be the next United States Senator from New York. *Some afterthought: the first lady of the land elected to the United States Senate from a state she'd never lived in, less than two years after her husband was impeached for being sexually serviced by a young woman just outside the Oval Office—and in large measure, because of what her husband had done. Helen of Troy may have possessed the face that launched a thousand ships, but Monica . . .*

Forget it: another entry in the "Book of Thoughts You Will Never Hear From Me on National TV."

Bill Schneider's briefing ended with a quick survey of what we *did* know, which did reveal one intriguing example of newsroom partisanship, although not the sort that media critics might assume. When he announced that Democrat Jon Corzine would likely win the open U.S. Senate seat in New Jersey, there were groans of unhappiness. Corzine, a onetime Wall Street whiz, had been banished from the executive suites with some four hundred million dollars. He'd decided to spend as much of it as he and his cost-plus operatives thought necessary to win a Senate seat—some sixty-two million dollars, as it turned out. The spending was so extraordinary, so record-shattering, and at times so duplicitous, that it raised the eyebrows of a press corps whose usual response to such excess was that of a Gallic shrug at reports of widespread marital infidelity.

(My favorite example: Corzine had showered some $650,000 on churches and community organizations during the primary season; a fact he had stoutly denied at the time. When the facts came out, shortly before the November election,

Corzine explained that *he* hadn't given any money to these organizations—his *foundation* had done it.)

Finally, someone asked Schneider, what of the possibility, much talked about in the last week of the election, that Governor Bush could win the popular vote, but lose in the Electoral College.

Actually, Schneider answered, the popular vote is so close, and there are so many states in play, that either of these guys could win the popular vote and lose the Electoral vote. And with that, we adjourned, for the more urgent task that awaits anyone of middle age preparing for a long night in front of the camera: makeup.

● The Electoral College? Could This Be the Election When . . . ?

Among those of us who have spent our lives immersed in covering American politics, every election brings with it a fantasy or two. I am not talking about the fantasy where a stunningly attractive campaign worker or reporter knocks on your hotel door late of an evening, clad only in high heels, garter belt, and fur coat, clutching a bottle of Champagne and murmuring, "You know, I find you oddly yet compellingly attractive." At this point in my life, my late-night hotel room thoughts in Iowa or New Hampshire drift more toward fantasies of late-night room service.

No, I am talking about fantasies of political upheaval, high drama, even melodrama. Early in the process, during those first caucuses and primaries, when half a dozen candidates crowd the race, the fantasy goes like this: *Maybe two or three candidates will battle it out all through the primary season; maybe there'll be no clear front-runner, and we won't know even when the last primary ends in June; maybe we'll go to the convention without knowing who the nominee will be, and there'll be rules challenges, and credentials fights, and bitter arguments and motions from the floor, just like in 1952, and we'll go to a second ballot, and . . . and . . .*

And then the spring comes, only one candidate is left standing, and we start guessing who the vice-presidential nominee will be.

For me, and for a handful of others, Election Nights past have brought with them a different fantasy: *What if one guy wins the popular vote, and the other guy wins in the Electoral College? What if the country wakes up to find out it doesn't really pick the president at all?*

I have a vivid memory, back in 1976, when I was still working as a political operative, of looking at election returns and realizing that *My God, Carter is a million votes or more ahead, but if Ford can pull it out in Ohio and Mississippi, he's going to win the White House!* I remember, in 1988, looking at the early exit polls and thinking, *Bush is winning the South by a landslide, but if Dukakis had run just a few points stronger in Pennsylvania, Michigan, Illinois, and California, he could have won the Electoral vote. Imagine how crazed the country would be if that ever happened. Imagine what would happen if a few of those electors decided to go their own way.*

And then Carter won Ohio and Mississippi, or Dukakis lost all the close states, and the fantasies went away for another cycle. Well, a few years ago, I did turn one set of fantasies into a political novel, but in that account, I simply killed off the newly elected president, leaving the electors free to go their own way. Hollywood even came calling but, in the end, decided that the idea of an Electoral College gone amok was simply too far-fetched to turn into a movie. I thought of that rationale this year, when I saw *The Contender*. The plot of this widely praised film turns in part on the eagerness of an incumbent president to nominate for vice president a confirmed atheist who has expressed open contempt for organized religion. Further, the nominee—to the complete amazement of the crack White House staff and FBI investigators—had been at the center of a widely publicized sex scandal while in college, and had had a widely publicized aldulterous affair with her Senate campaign manager. *Much more plausible, guys.*

In past years, whenever I would raise this fantasy of a split popular/Electoral vote with the number crunchers in a network polling unit, one of the cooler heads would be dispatched to explain to me, in a tone not unlike that of Al Gore talking Medicare with senior citizens, why my fantasy was so unlikely to become reality.

It's a matter of statistical probability, they would say. Once you get past one or two points in the popular vote spread, it's highly unlikely that a close state will break for the popular-vote loser. Maybe if we fell back into a kind of regional politics, where the vote in the South was at wide variance with the national vote, it could happen, but as long as the popular vote isn't close to a tie, it's just not going to happen.

But you know what? This time, this fantasy was being taken very seriously in two other places: the campaigns of Al Gore and George W. Bush.

Not publicly, of course. Publicly, the two campaigns were dismissing the likelihood of anything so bizarre happening. On the day before Election Day, CNN's Jonathan Karl asked Gore on camera about this possibility.

Said Gore, "I think it's unlikely to happen . . . but in all such cases, we are fortunate as a people to have a Constitution that resolves all doubt as to what would happen in that situation."

Gore had good reason to praise the machinery of the Electoral College. It was the strong conviction of his inner circle that Election Night could well end with the vice president winning a majority of the Electoral vote, while finishing behind Governor Bush in the popular vote. In fact, days before the vote, Jack Quinn—a former chief of staff to the vice president—had flown down to Gore headquarters in Nashville, Tennessee, at the request of Campaign Chair Bill Daley. Quinn came armed with a binder filled with materials covering just such an outcome. Quinn's materials included background facts prepared by the Congressional Research Service of the Library of Congress that explained the workings of the system. He also brought state-by-state rules on whether electors in the key states Gore needed were or were not bound by state law to vote in accordance with their pledged intentions. (They were, one source says, particularly concerned about states with Republican governors and legislators, where the laws did not specifically bind the electors.)

Quinn also had with him a list of electors in many states. A near-universal reaction to that list from within Gore's inner circle was: "I never *heard* of these people—who are they?"

In all this preparation, there was one contingency that no one in the Gore camp ever raised. As one insider put it, "There was *no* thought—*none*—given to the possibility that Gore might *win* the popular vote, and *lose* the Electoral vote."

That possibility of a "split decision" was very much alive in the Bush camp—not publicly, of course. Karl Rove, the Bush campaign's top strategist, was a strong advocate of the "inevitability" school of campaigning. The more you could project an image of serene confidence, the more likely it was you could pick up voters who wanted to be with a winner. On the TV talk-show circuit, he was predicting a margin of about five points in the popular vote, and a "minimum" of 320 Electoral votes. Bush's late swing into California and New Jersey was part and parcel of his "inevitability" strategy. Even if Bush had no real chance in those states, the sight of the campaign dumping millions of dollars into a Gore stronghold would at least demoralize the Democrats. ("If those guys are spending that much money in California, either they know something we don't know, or they're so confident of winning elsewhere they're willing to spend millions of dollars just to make the local Republicans feel good.")

On Saturday, November fourth, three days before the election, Rove appeared on CNN's *Evans, Novak, Hunt, & Shields*—one of the few television programs that sounded as if it should be a prominent New York law firm.

Asked about the possibility of an Electoral-vote loss despite a popular-vote win, Rove—who possesses a near-encyclopedic knowledge of American political history—dismissed the possibility.

"I just don't think it's going to happen at all. I mean, the last time that it happened was 1888, and what it took to make it happen was an extraordinary set of circumstances. You had a highly polarized election, where the northern states voted for the Republican candidate and the southern states voted overwhelmingly for the Democrat candidate . . . [this year] I think this is all hogwash. It's not worth the time."

However, added Rove, in what would prove to be a major theme of Bush's post–Election Day argument, "if all we cared about was the popular vote, then the presidential candidates would not campaign in a broad number of states. They would campaign in large metropolitan areas in the big states, and we wouldn't have a truly national contest."

Backstage, however, the Bush campaign was looking very hard at just such a possibility. The week before Election Day, on November 1, New York *Daily News* columnist Michael Kramer reported that some senior Bush advisors were seriously considering a postelection challenge to Gore in the event that he won in the Electoral College while losing the popular vote.

"The one thing we don't do," said one of Bush's senior aides, "is roll over. We fight." We will, the aide said, hit the radio talk shows hard, arguing that such a victory would be illegitimate—"We'll have ads, too—and I think you can count on the media to fuel the thing big-time. Even papers that supported Gore might turn against him because the will of the people will have been thwarted."

The point? To put pressure on Gore electors from states with a strong Republican presence—exactly the scenario the Gore campaign was trying to arm itself against.

In the days after November seventh, the Bush campaign would dismiss Kramer's article.

"I saw it," said Bush spokeswoman Mindy Tucker, "and I couldn't find a single person in our campaign who had talked to the reporter."

Maybe she wasn't looking all that hard. On Election Night, the networks summon to their cameras a wide assortment of commentators and analysts—some, like myself, the soul of detachment and fairness, others who are specifically booked because of their identifiably political leanings. These commentators often check in with the campaigns they support in search of "talking points"—themes of the day, compelling statistical or anecdotal nuggets, persuasive turns of phrase. At least two conservative commentators were specifically briefed by the Bush campaign shortly before taking to the airwaves about the line of attack to be taken in the event that Bush wound up losing the Electoral count despite a popular-vote lead. And that line of attack was clearly pointing to a post–Election Day challenge to the legitimacy of a Gore victory.

"It was part of the talking points," Ken Duberstein says. A former White House chief of staff, and one of the best-connected Republicans in Washington, Duberstein recalls that by Election Day, "They did think they were going to win the popular vote; they were concerned about the Electoral College. It wasn't something that they thought they could win, but they could certainly make an issue of moral authority."

Why the concern? Because by Election Day the Bush campaign knew, in the words of one top aide, "It was clear we were in a deteriorating situation. We were seeing deterioration in the key states, and clearly in the national polls. We suffered some damage on the basis of the DUI [the late-breaking story about Bush's old drunk-driving arrest]. And we did not close as strongly as Gore did. Gore did a better job of closing, working twenty-four hours a day. That had clear impact on the markets where he went."

◉ There is no single way to prepare for eight or ten or twelve hours of continuous coverage. Some of my colleagues spend Election Day working the phones, calling old contacts around the country and inside the campaigns. Others assemble enough research material to complete a doctoral dissertation on the campaign. (My colleague Judy Woodruff invariably arrives on the anchor set with a mountain of five-by-eight cards that contain the names, ages, family and political histories, and blood types of every candidate for every office in the land. Then the live coverage begins; someday, she has promised me, she will actually get to look at one of these cards while we are on the air.) My own practice is to go over as many facts and anecdotes as I can possibly cram into my head. Once they are more or less locked in, I reduce them to a word or two that I can jot down on a note card next to the name of a state. I then list the states in order of their poll-closing times, and go over this list so often that I don't need to look at the written notes once we hit the air.

On some Election Nights, all the preparation in the world won't provide more than a moment of genuinely interesting analysis, except for the hard-core political junkies—the folks who watch C-SPAN 2 for erotic arousal. In 1996, for example, the Clinton-Dole race—and I use that term loosely—never really changed from April to November. Viewed over time, the polling data looked like an EEG of a brain-dead patient, as flat as the Kansas horizon. But on this Election Night, I had come loaded for bear. You want historical ironies? On an election night in 1970, exactly thirty years earlier, the fathers of *both* Al Gore and George W. Bush had lost their races for the United States Senate. You want a dramatic contrast? On his fortieth birthday, Al Gore was a United States senator who had competed in the presidential primaries and was a clear contender for future national office. On *his* fortieth birthday, George W. Bush was a moderately unsuccessful businessman with a losing race for Congress behind him who awakened to the knowledge that he had a drinking problem.

I also came prepared to drop in short "factoids" about each state, once we were able to project a winner—little gems to illuminate the greater meaning of the numbers, preferably within ten or fifteen seconds. My producer-assistant Beth Goodman and I gathered these items under the "iceberg" theory of preparation. Just as eight-ninths of an iceberg never appears above the surface, the great majority of what I gathered would never see the light of day—but you could never tell before the fact what elements would be useful. Here's part of what my checklist had to offer:

- No Republican has ever won the White House without winning Illinois.
- No Republican has ever won the White House without winning Ohio.
- Missouri has voted with the winner in every presidential election in the twentieth century, except for 1956 (it went for Stevenson that year by two-tenths of 1 percent of the vote); Delaware has voted with the winner ever since 1952. These two states have a legitimate right to be considered bellwethers. (I also checked *Safire's Political Dictionary* to make sure I knew what the hell a bellwether was—it's a male sheep, who leads his flock into and out of pastures—often wearing a bell around his neck.)
- If Gore in fact lost Tennessee, that would make him the first candidate to lose his home state since George McGovern lost South Dakota to Nixon in 1972. If he won the presidency despite that loss, he'd be the first victor to lose his home state since

Richard Nixon in 1968 (who claimed New York State as his residence then).

- If Gore won Michigan, talk about the classic New Deal–New Frontier state, the place where Democrats once began every fall campaign in Detroit's Cadillac Square, where blue-collar union workers rallied to the cause. Democrats lost the state to Nixon in '72 over busing, lost to Reagan in '80 over recession and inflation and crime. Bill Clinton regained it for the Democrats, and if Gore holds on, note the power of good economic times. Remember to mention that the United Auto Workers' contract made Election Day a paid holiday from work. If Gore lost Michigan, have that quote handy from his 1992 book *Earth in the Balance,* where he calls for the elimination of the internal combustion engine—and note how many of those UAW members liked to hunt.

- And speaking of guns, note how much money the National Rifle Association spent on issue advertising in places like Michigan, Ohio, West Virginia; note how energetically NRA President Charlton Heston campaigned in those states.

- For the Senate races, too, there was ammunition ready to fire at the drop of a projection. When Hillary Clinton was declared the winner in New York—something we would probably do the moment the polls closed at 9 P.M.—have ready the story of Eleanor Roosevelt. Shortly after FDR died, one of his closest aides, Interior Secretary Harold Ickes, had implored Mrs. Roosevelt to move back to New York and run for the United States Senate. She declined. Now, more than half a century later, aided by the son of Harold Ickes, the First Lady, who was said to have communed with the spirit of Eleanor Roosevelt, was about to claim that seat for herself.

- When Jon Corzine was projected as the winner in New Jersey, talk about the successes and failures of deep-pocket candidates of the past, and note how a twenty-four-year-old Supreme Court decision about campaign-finance laws encouraged the emergence of multimillionaire candidates, past and present. In Minnesota, department-store heir and perennial loser Mark Dayton looked like he would win a Senate seat; in Washington, dot-com millionaire Maria Cantwell might knock off Senator Slade Gorton. (If that happened, give a capsule history of Gorton's career—he won in 1980, lost his seat in '86, won the *other* Senate seat in '88, cruised to reelection in '94, and lost in '00—the first politician ever to win and lose *both* Senate seats in his state.)

- If seventy-nine-year-old Delaware senator William Roth fell to Governor Tom Carper, talk about the rhythms of political life: Roth had won his Senate seat thirty years ago because the incumbent senator, John Williams, had retired at age seventy, having advocated a Constitutional age limit on senators—a plan Roth had strongly supported. Now, his age was his undoing; a fact dramatized when he had briefly passed out in front of the TV cameras while campaigning.

- And then there's Missouri, where Senator John Ashcroft might wind up losing to a dead man: Governor Mel Carnahan, killed in a plane crash just three weeks before the election. The acting governor has promised to appoint Carnahan's widow, Jeanne, to that seat if more people vote for Carnahan than Ashcroft, and she has agreed. Ashcroft had built a small lead in the closing weeks of the campaign, but how the hell do you run against a widow who has just lost a husband and a son? Missouri was also the state where almost twenty-five years earlier, a young Congressman named Jerry Litton, on his way to claim victory in a Senate primary, was killed along with his family in a plane crash.

There were other matters to consider as Election Night began. Some were of great moment—past elections filled with Electoral-vote melodrama, like the John Quincy Adams—Andrew Jackson battle of 1824 (the last time the son of a former president had won the White House). Some were of a more personal nature. For instance, I took great satisfaction from the fact that Larry King would be along every hour for a short interview segment. Not only was he the most familiar and popular personality on CNN, but those segments would afford ample time for a bathroom break, and/or a chance to bolt down food or drink. Speaking of which: Once again I had neglected to bring a change of shirt and tie with me—an omission that made any attempt at refreshment during the night an excursion into danger. I happen to be the victim of a condition that renders me at times all but incapable of bringing food from plate to mouth without a substantial fraction of sustenance winding up on my clothes. And these times generally coincide with moments when I am about to appear on camera.

One short vignette from my past will illustrate this: In 1985, I was one of a group of ABC News reporters assigned to produce pieces during the three-hour-long Super Bowl pre-game presentation. A few days before the event, we were told to come to the stadium wearing the outfits we'd be sporting on game day, in order to record the opening shots for the pregame show. On my way to the stadium, I spotted a colleague enjoy-ing lunch at an open-air Mexican seafood restaurant. I joined him, carefully covering myself with so many napkins that I re-sembled a papier-mâché dummy. I finished my meal, paid the bill, removed the protective covering—and spotted one last tempting bite of seafood enchilada. I picked it up, put it in my mouth . . . and World War III exploded. Only the providential presence of a nearby While-U-Wait dry cleaning establish-ment prevented me from appearing on national TV disguised as a Jackson Pollock painting.

(One of my exasperated producers once said to me, "Greenfield, the next time we have a lunch break during a shoot, either order melba toast or bring along a full-body con-dom.")

There was, finally, one other question on my mind: Just how long would we be here? We were committed to staying on the air until we knew who the president would be, and what the makeup of the new Congress would be; but the House and Sen-ate were both in play, and we might well have to wait until the West Coast results were in to know how those battles would come out. Similarly, with the presidential race up for grabs, we might well have to wait until Oregon and Washington reported in to learn who'd won. In the last close presidential contest, the Ford-Carter race in 1976, the networks had to wait until after five o'clock in the morning, when Mississippi finally went for Carter by fewer than fifteen thousand votes, until signing off. That wouldn't work for me at all; my plan was to get off the air, get back to my Atlanta hotel, throw my things together, and catch a 6:30 A.M. flight back to New York. Why? So I could join my friends for our regular Wednesday lunch. No one can accuse me of lacking a sense of priority. As I sat down to join Bernie Shaw, Judy Woodruff, and Bill Schneider at the faux-oak anchor desk, I hoped we would know the outcome well before five o'clock in the morning.

As I said: who knew?

● As a matter of fact, even with the exit polls telling us that the election was up in the air, even with so many states way too close to call, we knew a pretty fair amount before we ever went on the air. Given what happened with and to the television networks on Election Night, this may sound silly—but in the first hour or so of reporting, before the polls in any of the states had closed, there was a lot of first-rate reporting and analysis going on that gave viewers a remarkably good picture of what to watch for. It's just that it kind of got washed away in the later hours, when we began awarding Florida to everyone except Kathie Lee Gifford.

Consider, for example, the first reports from the competing camps. John King, CNN's senior White House correspondent, had been following Vice President Gore on his attempt to re-create the Bataan Death March in the campaign's final days. It had ended at 1 A.M. on Election Day in Tampa, Florida, "because Florida may well be the state that decides the outcome of this election. . . . If Florida goes Republican," King concluded, "the vice president would have to win most of the remaining late-campaign battlegrounds: Washington and Oregon in the West; Iowa, Minnesota, Michigan, Pennsylvania, Wisconsin, and West Virginia in the heartland. . . . We started this campaign saying the big battleground states would decide it; we might end it looking at some of the very small states making the difference."

Candy Crowley, who had been following George W. Bush for the better part of a year, noted that he had spent twenty-four of the last forty-eight hours of the campaign in Florida, but emphasized another part of the schedule; the journey to Florida, she said, "was bookended by stops as symbolic as they were electorally significant: Tennessee, Al Gore's home state, and George Bush's last stop of Campaign 2000: Bill Clinton's Arkansas."

A few moments later, NAACP President Kweisi Mfume and Christian Coalition President Pat Robertson appeared, to talk about their organizations' respective "get-out-the-vote" operations. Mfume pointed to big increases in black turnout in Pennsylvania, Michigan, and Florida. Robertson spoke of massive efforts by the Christian Coalition, triggered by his group's concerns with "the moral climate of our nation, and the things that have happened in the White House . . . many people admire Clinton for his brilliance in government. But nevertheless, the personal life is repugnant." Their efforts, he said, would have special impact in states like Tennessee, Arkansas, Missouri, and West Virginia.

Even at this early hour, both Mfume and Robertson were striking two of the most important notes of the election. If Mfume was right, if African-American turnout was going to be much higher than in past elections, it meant that the preelection polls would have reflected a fatal error. The accuracy of any poll number rests on whether it is actually measuring the intentions of *voters*, which is one reason why the numbers vary so much; how vigorously are polls weeding out those unlikely to vote—or, in the jargon of the business, how "tight" or "loose" are the voter screens? As a rule, turnout in black districts is lower than in white districts, so pollsters understandably "weigh the sample" to reflect that likelihood.

But if Mfume was right, if large numbers of black voters were showing up in Philadelphia, Detroit, Chicago, and Miami, then those polling estimates would be thrown into a cocked hat. If the early exit polls were right—and they were causing hope in the Gore camp and gloom in the Bush camp—that was exactly what was happening. And if they were wrong, what would that say about Gore's decision to leave Clinton off the campaign playing field?

Now think about what Pat Robertson was saying: Tennessee . . . Arkansas . . . Missouri . . . West Virginia . . . all border states carried twice by Bill Clinton . . . all states with a relatively conservative cultural climate, and where some of Al Gore's political positions—on gun control, on the environment—would not play very well. These were also states where Bill Clinton's personal behavior would not be easily forgiven—but would voters look at Al Gore, a man with an absolutely unblemished personal life, and punish *him* for the sins of Clinton? If voters in these key states were looking with disfavor on the president, then what did *that* say about the Gore campaign's decision not to ask Bill Clinton to come out and campaign?

Beyond demographics and geography: What did the voters across the country think about the man who was about to leave the White House after eight years—or, as the Republican surrogates invariably put it, "eight long years"? (This is one of those compulsory verbal constructs in politics—if you are the opposition party, the incumbent's reign must always be described in terms that evoke the desert wanderings of Moses and his people. "After eight long years . . ." "After four long years . . ." "After two and a half long weeks . . .") Was the country about to say, "Well done, thou good and faithful servant!" and reward him by crowning his designated successor? Or were they about to say, "Don't let the door hit you on the way out, Bub—and by the way, would you mind zipping up your pants?"

The Clinton conundrum was part of a broader question. For months, Bill Schneider had been looking at the polls, and finding the same schizophrenia week after week. "In most elections," he would say on an almost weekly basis, "you find one of two themes that dominate: 'You never had it so good,' or 'Throw the rascals out.' This time, the voters seem to believe both things simultaneously—which is why this is likely to be so close."

As we waited for the first votes to come in, I tried to add to this free-flowing fountain of wisdom by suggesting seven key questions we'd be trying to answer throughout the night:

FIRST—BIG GOVERNMENT

One of Bill Clinton's signal successes—as candidate and president—was that he had redefined Democrats as the party of competence, rather than the party of free-spending boondoggles presided over by petty bureaucrats who spent their lives making government regulations and the IRS forms both indecipherable and draconian. Governor Bush had tried throughout the fall to paint Al Gore as just such a big-government type. For his part, Gore wanted the voters to see George W. Bush as a classic country-club type who would turn the safety nets of Social Security and Medicare into confetti to be thrown at the party celebrating massive income-tax cuts for the yachts-and-Gulfstreams crowd. Were the voters buying either idea?

SECOND—THE GENDER GAP

For more than twenty years, men had been voting with the Republicans, and women with Democrats. Why? For some analysts, it's a simple matter of choice—specifically, freedom to choose an abortion. That view is a massive oversimplification of the gender gap, especially when you consider that the abortion issue, heated as it is, never shows up as a key voting issue for most Americans. (In October, one of our polls asked voters what they thought was "the most important problem facing this country today." One percent listed abortion.) Rather, the answer to the gender gap rests beneath the broad category of gender. Some of it is a matter of economics: Single women, particularly single mothers, are much more likely to be in lower income categories, and less-affluent voters much more likely to vote Democrat than better-off citizens. In part, Democrats were seen throughout the last years of the Cold War as more risk-averse, less eager to use force than Republicans. And while it may sound too simplistic, women (perhaps because they bear and raise the children who are sent off to war) are more risk-averse than men. This also explains why women tend to be less enthusiastic than men about the easy availability of guns. (It also may explain why women are much less likely to go out to a bar, knock back a dozen beers, and then attempt to drive home at sixty miles an hour with their headlights out.)

For presidential candidates, the goal is not to eradicate

the gender gap, but to mitigate it. In 1988, for example, George Bush the Elder had battled Governor Dukakis to a virtual tie among women; his sixteen-point margin among men propelled him into the White House. Bill Clinton *lost* the male vote to Dole in '96, but he only lost among men by one point. His sixteen-point winning margin among women accounted for his entire eight-million-vote plurality. How would it break this time?

THIRD — THE SOCIAL ISSUES

"The Gore campaign had argued months ago," I said, "that the environment and gun control and abortion would play for them. It may be that in states like Pennsylvania and Michigan and West Virginia, issues like gun control and the environment will work against Al Gore. We're going to find out."

FOURTH — WAS IT "THE ECONOMY, STUPID"?

When Clinton campaign maven James Carville placed that sign on the wall of his Little Rock office in 1992—in answer to the question "What is the big issue in this campaign?"—he added a new catchphrase to political conversation. But in 2000, that phrase raised a question of its own. Never in modern history had a presidential campaign been waged during a time of such unalloyed economic good news. The federal budget that had been running deficits for more than thirty years was now in surplus; every month brought new estimates of a multitrillion-dollar surplus over the next ten years. Is that what voters would be thinking about as they made their choices? Or would they be looking at, say, the cultural and moral health of the nation, about which there was a broad sense of pessimism?

Of course, Americans are *always* pessimistic about their cultural and moral health. Back in the summer of 1952, a time that most cultural pessimists now look back on as an Edenic paradise of innocence and abstinence, Cleveland *Press* editor Louis Seltzer composed an editorial that asked: "What is wrong with us? It is in the air we breathe. The things we do. The things we say. Our books. Our papers. Our theater. Our movies. Our radio and television. The way we behave. The interest we have. The values we fix.

"We are, on the average, rich beyond the dreams of kings of old. Yet something is not there that should be—something we once had."

The editorial was reprinted all over the country, and triggered an urgent national conversation—as did our anguish over sadistic comic books and juvenile delinquency in the first years of the 1950s, our fear of rock and roll in the last half of the decade, our concern with our educational rot after the Soviets launched Sputnik in 1957, our night sweats over the generational divide in the latter half of the 1960s, our well-founded fear over the jump in crime that began in the early 1970s, and the three-decades-long debate over abortion, divorce, secularization, the breakup of the family, and periodic spasms of public violence.

Well, by century's end, what the cold numbers told us was that this widespread pessimism had little to do with reality. By every conceivable measure, after eight years of a president whose personal moral behavior had become a cross between a national scandal and a national punch line, we were regaining our social and cultural health. Crime was down more than 27 percent, and in big cities like New York, Chicago, and Los Angeles, the homicide rates had fallen to levels not seen since the early 1960s. Divorce was down by 5 percent; we were shocked by the Columbine slaughter, but youth violence was actually down 3 percent. There were on average 100,000 fewer abortions per year under this pro-choice president than in the best year under the pro-life presidencies of Reagan and Bush. Back in 1993, former Education Secretary and Drug Czar Bill Bennett had created the "Index of Leading Social and Economic Indicators," purporting to measure the non-economic health of the nation. To measure by this staunch conservative's yardstick, America under Clinton had become far happier and healthier than it had been under his far less priapic predecessors; yet so convinced was the country of our steady descent into Hell in a handbasket that Governor Bush's most guaranteed applause line was his promise that his in-augural oath would also symbolize his promise "to return honor and integrity to the White House." The next eight hours or so would test the political potency of the public's perennial pessimism.

FIFTH—THE CLINTON FACTOR

All through the last phase of the campaign, the question hung in the air: *When will President Clinton be sent out to rally the troops? Would that help or hurt Al Gore?*

For some longtime Democrats, the answer was obvious: *Get him out there now!* Ed Rendell, the general chair of the Democratic National Committee and the former mayor of Philadelphia, was hearing the demand everywhere: not just from African-American politicians in St. Louis and Cleveland and Detroit, but from Democrats in culturally conservative areas as well.

"I was in West Virginia, and the elected officials were all over me—'Where's Clinton?' " he recalled a month after Election Day. "I heard from Paul Kanjorski—a congressman from Wilkes-Barre in Pennsylvania, classic conservative Democratic area. 'You've got to get them to bring Clinton in here!' It got to where Nashville [the Gore campaign headquarters] thought *I* was agitating on my own!

"Look," he went on, "as far as I could tell, the logic was that maybe the undecided voters will punish Gore because Clinton wanted Gore to win. So, by not having him campaign, does that voter *forget* that Gore was Clinton's vice president for eight years? My belief—no. And yes, it was a hunch. Now—if Bill Bradley had won the nomination, then Bill Clinton could have been a problem for the ticket—because Bradley would not have any association with Clinton. But to Gore's credit, he always stood by him.

"And at the least," Rendell said, "at the *least* have Clinton campaign in Arkansas that last week."

So the Clinton factor was obvious; he would have been a big, perhaps decisive, weapon for Gore—except that shortly before the campaign ended, I had a conversation with one of Gore's closest, most devoted aides, who was just as certain that bringing Clinton into the campaign would be a disastrous mistake.

"I'm not talking about some psychodrama stuff," said the aide. "You know—'Gore wants to win it on his own.' If we thought Clinton would help, we'd ask him in a minute. But you know what? Go back and check your polls, and see what's happened every time Clinton has taken political center stage in the last six months. If your polls are like ours, you'll see that *every single time* Clinton's dominating politics, we go down in the polls. And it won't work just to put him in black neighborhoods; your cameras will bring him into every living room in America."

So who was right?

SIXTH—THE NADER FACTOR

Four years ago, Ralph Nader had permitted the Green Party to place his name on the ballot as its presidential candidate, but had refused to spend more than $5,000—a number that put a substantial crimp in his ability to campaign. This year, Nader had thrown himself into the battle with enthusiasm, gleefully using most of his energy to bash Al Gore from one end of the country to the other. The only difference between Gore and Bush—or, as he labeled them, "Gush and Bore"—"is the velocity with which their knees hit the floor when big corporations come calling." (For some reason, every time I heard this line, I thought Nader was attempting subconsciously to evoke the image of Monica Lewinsky.) After spending most of the campaign season dismissing Nader's impact, the Gore folks had slowly awakened to the fact that in half a dozen states, Nader was polling 6, 7, 8 percent of the vote—enough to make the difference between winning and losing. These were "Dukakis" states, where reform impulses ran relatively strong, and where populist, anticorporate rhetoric had demonstrated persistent appeal:

•Minnesota, where an independent candidate, a former professional wrestler, had shocked the political world two years earlier, and where Senator Paul Wellstone had won a Senate seat with an aggressively leftist, anti–big boy pitch;

•Wisconsin, home of "Fighting Bob LaFollette," who had won 16 percent of the national vote as a third-party presidential candidate in 1924, and—to be slightly more relevant—of Senator Russ Feingold, who had won reelection two years earlier despite an absolute, potentially crippling refusal to accept any money from political-action committees, or from any "soft-money" campaign funds;

•Washington, where antiglobalization protesters had shut down the city of Seattle a year before, and where Nader's calls for strict environmental and regulatory limits on corporate power had special appeal;

•Oregon, where some years earlier a bar owner with a cheerfully antipolitical pitch had gotten himself elected mayor of Portland, and where, a generation earlier, maverick Senator Wayne Morse—a Republican-turned-independent-turned-Democrat—had distinguished himself by being one of only two senators to vote against the 1964 Gulf of Tonkin Resolution that opened the door to open-ended escalation of the war in Vietnam; and

•Maine, where a second independent was serving as governor, and where in 1992 Ross Perot had gotten 30.4 percent of the vote, coming in a few hundred votes ahead of President Bush—his single best showing in the country.

For Nader, the arithmetic was simple: If he got 5 percent of the national popular vote, the Green Party would earn millions of dollars in federal campaign subsidies for its next national run. For the Gore campaign, the arithmetic was equally simple: A Nader voter was more than twice as likely to vote for Gore as for Bush. Switching those votes became a major Gore message in these states, with radio and television appeals by liberal stalwarts such as Wellstone, Ted Kennedy, and Jesse Jackson.

SEVENTH—WHAT KIND OF LEADER WAS THE COUNTRY LOOKING FOR?

Seldom have American voters been faced with two major party candidates who so completely matched each other's strengths and weaknesses. In one corner, a man who had been immersed in the business of the federal government for a quarter of a century, elected to the Congress before his thirtieth birthday, to the Senate before his fortieth, to the vice presidency before he turned forty-five, and a man so ill at ease in his own skin that his boss once wondered aloud, *It's incredible that Al Gore has come as far as he has in politics, considering how much he dislikes it.* In the other corner, a man of immense ease and charm, skilled from young manhood on at the art of making friends, putting folks at ease; a man frankly, openly bored with the details of governance that always made Gore's heart beat faster, a man who as governor worked a nine-to-five-thirty schedule, with plenty of time carved out in the middle of the day for a brisk run and a challenging game of computer solitaire.

It was almost as if the current occupant of the White House had been cleaved in two for this campaign. It was Clinton's unique gift to fuse cognitive intelligence and emotional intelligence, so that at one moment he could be recalling every fact, every number, every detail from a fifteen-year-old report on international currency fluctuations or national forestry policy, while at the same time convincing every person in the room that he was attending only to him or her.

JEFF GREENFIELD | *Oh, Waiter! One Order of Crow!*

With Al Gore, you got the cognitive intelligence, overlaid with the sense that he was always, always trying to convince you that he knew so much that he had to be taken seriously. Perhaps it was the curse of having been the son of a famous and revered political figure, of having entered the political arena as a very young man, with the sense of unease that results in someone painfully self-contained, every hair in place, every seam perfectly creased, every fact at his fingertips. *"An old person's idea of what a young person is like,"* writer Michael Kinsley had called him once, and that description perfectly drew the line between Gore and the man who had picked him as his running mate. In July of 1992, when the two baby boomers had left the Democratic Convention in New York City and embarked on a triumphal bus tour of the Northeast and the industrial Midwest, they encapsulated energy, youth, even hunkiness—"Heartthrobs of the Heartland," the Washington *Post* had called them—they seemed twin harbingers of change. Launched on his own, Gore seemed drained of those political pheromones that connect a figure like Clinton to the voters.

"He's handsome," a colleague of mine said, watching Gore campaign in New Hampshire, "but he's not *sexy*." No one ever said that about Clinton. Indeed, almost every woman I know who has been in Clinton's presence—all right, we exempt Mother Teresa—has said after meeting him, "You know, I think he was coming on to me." Given his track record, they may have all been right. On the other hand, most of the men I know who have been in his presence have felt that same force, that overwhelming sense that they were being courted, seduced, *attended to,* by someone who was determined to win them over by any means necessary. Clinton was that rare figure who could recount the history of health-care reform state by state, while draping a large, inquisitive hand on your thigh—figuratively or literally.

Gore, by contrast, could recite that same history—emphasizing his own indispensable role in it—with a manner that seemed so calculated it could set your teeth on edge.

I had seen Gore in action for the very first time back in 1988, when he was running for president for the first time. He was campaigning briefly in New Hampshire, before abandoning the state for a southern strategy that came up short, and he was appearing at an evening coffee in the living room of a supporter somewhere around Manchester. It was weeks before the primary, and back then it was still possible to witness a candidate unaccompanied by the dozens of reporters and video technicians who would now crowd into a living room, their boom mikes threatening every piece of glassware in the room, as well as half the audience.

On this evening, it was impossible for anyone to ask Gore about an issue of which he had not been on the cutting edge: ". . . as you may know, I cosponsored the first congressional resolution on the greenhouse effect. . . ." "I chaired the subcommittee on pension-fund portability, and one of the interesting conclusions we reached . . ." ". . . when I traveled to Europe some years ago on our Senate fact-finding tour . . ."

Then, one questioner asked about the current state of the U.S. economy by noting, "Senator, the stock market today dropped eighty-eight points—"

"—eighty-eight point sixty-three," Gore interjected.

Watch Bill Clinton in action and you think of Harold Hill in *The Music Man,* who could make you believe that there would be a band with 76 trombones and 110 cornets marching down Main Street by next week; watch Al Gore, and—as nine out of ten baby-boomer analysts had it—you thought of Eddie

Haskell, the oleaginous suck-up from *Leave It to Beaver*, ingratiating himself with the elders (*"That's a* lovely *dress you're wearing today, Mrs. Cleaver"*) while backstabbing friend and foe alike.

Was this dreadfully unfair to Gore? Probably. Was it his most deadly political weakness? Absolutely.

As for George W. Bush . . . I first saw him early in the campaign year at the Des Moines airport, as he strode from his private jet across the tarmac to speak to a knot of reporters waiting for him behind the chain-link fence. What I saw was best captured, months later, in a *New Yorker* magazine article by Malcolm Gladwell—an article that had nothing at all to do with politics. It was about the power, the enduring power, of the first impression, that precognitive sense you get when you see someone for the first time. In other contexts, it can be called "love at first sight," or "lust at first sight," or "repulsion at first sight," but its significance, Gladwell explained, goes far beyond mating issues. He cited a study by Harvard University psychologist Nalini Ambady, who found that subjects who have had a two-or-three-*second* glimpse of a teacher in a classroom produce the same evaluation of the teacher made by students who have spent an entire semester in that teacher's classroom.

"The power of first impressions," Gladwell wrote, "suggests that human beings have a peculiar kind of prerational ability for making searching judgments about others"—judgments that are probably governed not by detailed thinking, but by something more instinctual.

Whatever the source of this quality, George W. Bush had it, in spades. He is conventionally handsome, but there is something else he possesses when he is relaxed, something that is missing even in many politicians who make it to the top—a sense of ease, of comfort in his own skin. Jimmy Carter never had it; neither, for that matter, did George Herbert Walker Bush, at least not when he was campaigning. With Bush the Younger, there was a sense of playfulness, a sense that he was not taking himself all that seriously. John Kennedy could convey that sense with a quick smile at a press conference; Robert Kennedy often revealed that playfulness when he was running for president. (Once in 1968, as the door to his campaign plane was about to open for an airport rally stop at a small town, he peeked out of the window, leaned back into the aisle, and announced to the press, "The crowd is estimated at about seventy-five thousand." The door opened, he gave a quick wave, ducked back into the plane, and announced, "And they all squealed with pleasure!") And when he worked a room, Bush was every bit the equal of Bill Clinton, absent only the sense that he was on the verge of whisking every attractive woman in the place out for a more private conversation. The hand on the shoulder, the eye contact, the body language that said, *I'll be here talking with you as long as it takes for you to feel comfortable with me*—these were gifts that Bush had to spare.

"When he comes into a room," says one of his oldest friends, "it lights up. Whoever he's talking to, that person feels there's nobody else in the room. His memory for kids, family, past conversations is scary." With Gore, as Nicholas Lemann put it in a memorable *New Yorker* article last year, "you can see Gore read a situation, pause while the script flashes, formulate his response—and then react."

But then there was the George W. Bush whom no one would possibly mistake for a Republican Bill Clinton: the Bush who stood at a lectern, delivering a formal speech, or answering policy questions from the press. Here was the Bush made famous during the campaign by Will Ferrell on *Saturday Night*

Live, the face tightened by tension, the brow furrowed, the eyes closed to a near-squint, the words scrambled like some poorly played board game ("We have to make the pie higher"), subjects and predicates often in awkward misalliance. ("Is our children learning?")

On January twenty-seventh, Bush was appearing at a public elementary school in Nashua, New Hampshire. He sat amid a group of children and watched a series of songs and sketches, then talked to the children. A banner in the schoolroom proclaimed that it was "Perseverance Day" . . . and the governor began talking about the need for "preservation." As the press began exchanging knowing looks, and his aides began a careful examination of their shoes and the floor, it began to dawn on Bush that he was wandering into a rhetorical thicket. The litany of "it's important to preserve . . ." gradually, painfully elided into a plea for "perseverance." He had scrambled back from the cliff, but the cuts and scrapes were obvious.

For voters looking for experience, for a president with a firm grasp of policy, these misadventures with the language would serve as a symbol of their discontent. From the very beginning of the campaign, however, Bush's aides saw a different picture. Yes, they believed, the governor would have to demonstrate enough grasp of substance to erase the sense that he was nothing more than a fortunate son, gliding to the presidency on a path that had been greased by good connections and good fortune. Beyond that test—a test they privately believed would be made easier by the stereotype of Bush-the-Dope—they saw an electorate that would choose the president for very specific reasons.

"This election will *not* be decided on the issues," one of his senior advisers said to me on at least three different occasions, with virtually the same phrase. "It will be decided on questions of character and leadership." Whether consciously or not, they were resting their hopes for Bush on a conviction that the first impression he offered—a steady, reliable, centered but not self-centered man—would carry him through, and that voters would decide based on *who* they wanted the next president to be. Just as surely, the Gore partisans believed that if voters went to the polls thinking about *what* they wanted the next president to do, they would decide that this pleasant young man from Texas was simply not up to the tasks they wanted accomplished.

On this last question we were posing to our audience, the choice was absolutely clear: If most voters decided to go on the basis of experience, Al Gore would win; if they decided to go on the basis of character and leadership, George W. Bush would win. It was equally clear that they would choose between two glaringly different weaknesses: between a candidate who spoke to us as if English were *his* second language, and a candidate who spoke to us as if English were *our* second language.

When I had finished listing these seven questions, I offered this model of uncertainty: "We think, if we get the answers to these questions, we might know who the president is. But I'll tell you something—if it's as close as it looks now, we could still answer these questions and say: 'Your guess is as good as ours.' "

Who knew?

● As I look back on those first two hours of Election Night, I keep coming back to the smart things my colleagues and I said, because we said a number of not-very-smart things, even before the first polls in Florida had closed. And when I say "we," I very much include "me." Moreover, some of those early pieces of misinformation led at least one important Republican officeholder to raise the specter of deliberate media bias.

The first piece of misinformation cannot be laid at the feet of any one network or journalist; in fact, it is so predictable a part of Election Day that it almost shouldn't count—it's a little like a local newscast reporting that the circus "brings delight to children of all ages," when the fact is that a working majority of kids and parents can't wait to get the hell out. It's about . . . turnout.

Every Election Day, as early as late morning, all-news radio stations begin reporting that "voters are defying the experts today, and are turning out at the polls in huge numbers." These reports are based solely on anecdotal evidence: The reporters see long lines at the polls as they drive by; they call local election boards, who report long lines at the polls. And so, they report that there's a huge turnout. This is almost always nonsense.

The reasons for the long lines at the polls in the morning are, a) many senior citizens vote early in the day, and they take longer to vote; b) the people who man local election precincts are well-intentioned folk, but rarely the sharpest knives in the drawer; and c) the combination of elderly voters and day-hire election workers produces a stately pace no matter what kind of ballot is used. Add to this mix one often-overlooked reality that would become quite the topic of conversation in the days and weeks to follow: Election machinery, used once or twice a year at the most, is often susceptible to malfunctions. Most of the year, the machinery lies locked away in warehouses. Neither the mechanics, nor the election workers, nor their supervisors are familiar with the machinery. Nor is anyone all that familiar with the administrative machinery, the way a worker would be who showed up five days a week, fifty weeks a year, at an office or data-processing center. Put simply, once-a-year work does not produce efficient working procedures.

So what happens? Reporters, setting out to visit the polls, discover lengthy lines; word filters back to newsrooms, and to political headquarters, that the polls are jammed with voters. And thus the stories blare out on the all-news radio stations, and on the all-news-all-the-time cable networks, and on the local broadcast stations during their noon newsbreaks: "Voters today are defying the experts, and going to the polls in heavy numbers. . . ."

By the time the first talking heads appeared in the first hours of Election Night coverage, this drumbeat had become accepted wisdom. In Larry King's first cut-in, shortly after 6 P.M., he asked Bush Communications Advisor Ari Fleischer, "What about the turnout: surprisingly high, low, what?"

"Very high," Fleischer replied, "and I think that's a good sign. It's probably helping both candidates. It's a good sign for the country. Looks like a high turnout."

A moment later, Gore campaign spokesman Doug Hattaway enthused, "We got optimistic early today by the unusually heavy turnout early in the day. . . . The pundits were saying voters weren't interested. I think we're seeing the voters had something else in mind entirely."

Well, not exactly. In 1996, at the end of one of the least interesting campaigns in history, a campaign whose outcome had been clear for weeks if not months, when the return of the incumbent was assured, a little more than 49 percent of voting-age Americans went to the polls: the lowest turnout since 1924. In 2000, as it turned out, at the end of one of the most closely contested elections in history, a little more than 51 percent of the voting-age population turned out—one of the five lowest percentages of the twentieth century. (The ability of the Gore campaign to turn out its base *was* important; indeed, it is the reason Gore wound up winning the national popular vote.)

This misinformation about voter turnout was of little consequence; indeed, it can be chalked up to the inherent desire of political junkies to believe that the entire nation has become swept up in our obsession. We are, in this sense, much like those who believe the big bands are coming back, or that the return of the transatlantic ocean liner is just around the corner. Less benign was a different kind of misinformation that we began disseminating as soon as the 7 P.M. hour rolled around.

And I'm not even talking about Florida—yet.

Even in a tight election like this one, there are plenty of states where a network can make a call the instant the polls close. In fact, were it not for the fear of an infuriated political community—very much including the Congress, which still happens to hold regulatory power over broadcasting—we could call plenty of states the instant the first exit polls roll in around lunchtime. For that matter, in almost every election we could call roughly half the states by Labor Day, without a hint of fear. Call me madcap, but if a presidential candidate never sets foot in a state, it's a pretty good indication that he either has the state in the bag or does not have a snowball's chance in Hell of carrying it. (Yes, a candidate may travel to New York or California, regardless of the polls, but such a trip is made strictly on a cash-and-carry basis—carry the cash from your big-money supporters back to headquarters.)

The most partisan Democrat in the country would have had nothing to complain about had we begun our general election coverage on Labor Day by assigning just about all of the mountain West and the cotton South for Bush. The rockiest of rock-ribbed Republicans would nod his head if we colored in Massachusetts and New York State for Gore before the first leaf in New England fell from a tree.

We do not do this. Instead, we wait for the polls to close—or, in the phrase that is now so fateful post-Florida—"for the polls in the vast majority of the state to close." When they do, the boys (and girls) in the back room take a look at the first vote totals that arrive from "sample precincts." These are *not* "key precincts"; they are simply chosen at random. Most of the time, indeed almost all the time, the "sample precinct" votes from safe states simply reconfirm exit-poll numbers. Those numbers, in turn, usually reconfirm the no-brain-surgery common-sense understanding of everyone who has spent more than forty-five minutes looking at American political history. (Anyone, for example, hovering around an Election Day computer who proclaimed: "Gee! Utah's going for Bush! Far out!" would be thrown bodily from the room.)

Sometimes, however, the numbers simply do not permit an early call. They may be late in arriving. They may contain an anomaly that needs checking—perhaps an unexpectedly large or small plurality wildly at odds with the history of a sample precinct. Maybe those numbers are saying that a number of voters had a last-minute change of heart. Maybe an errant computer, or a nearsighted human vote-counter, produced a false total. Whatever the cause of such numbers, it means that a network is not yet ready to make a call. What it does *not* mean—at least, not necessarily—is that a state will wind up being very close when all the votes have been counted. Once the numbers come in from a reliably Republican or Democratic state, it's extremely likely that the margin of victory will be solid—ten points or more.

Unfortunately, CNN's graphic, and our reporting, chose to characterize any state where an early projection could not be made as "too close to call" instead of "cannot yet be called." This may not seem like a big distinction, but in the hands of an analyst too eager to find Significant Meaning where none might lie—in other words, in *my* hands—this difference turned into a highly misleading series of observations. They were more than misleading; they also helped fuel long-standing suspicions on the Right about the fairness of the major news networks.

At 7 P.M. Eastern time, polls closed in half a dozen states— including *most* of the polls in Florida. (Because that state's Panhandle extends hundreds of miles to the west, that part of the state runs on Central, not Eastern time, so polls stay open an hour later.) Based on the numbers at hand at that hour, we reported that Georgia and Virginia were both "too close to call."

"Bernie," I said, "Virginia has not voted for a Democrat for president since Lyndon Johnson in 1964. It is the heart of the Republican base in the South. They should have this one going away."

Well, the history was right, and so was the idea that Virginia is a solidly Republican state. The only small problem here was the implication I left that there was a dogfight going on—either there or in Georgia. Bush wound up winning Virginia by seven points—a bit closer than we expected—and he took Georgia by twelve points. Days later, Louisiana Republican Billy Tauzin was asking pointedly *why* the networks were able to call Gore states so quickly, while waiting for an hour or more to call states that Bush wound up winning handily. The prosaic answer was, "That's what the numbers were telling us," but the inaccurate gloss that we were putting on those numbers—a gloss that made it seem as if Bush was in big trouble on his own turf—made that explanation very hard to swallow.

Indeed, when we *did* call Virginia for Bush some twenty minutes later, I offered what now appears to be a laughable explanation.

"It may well be," I said, "that we just want to see that we are not being—you know, we're being cautious enough so that *we know what we're doing.*"

And that's exactly what we responsible, cautious, accuracy-obsessed networks would do—for the next twenty-eight minutes.

We were, in those heady, pre-Florida-for-Gore moments, demonstrating the proper use of that much-maligned device, the exit poll. In fact, we were using it the way it was meant to be used. As soon as the polls in West Virginia closed at 7:30, analyst Bill Schneider noted that Gore was being badly hurt in that state by his environmental stand. How could Schneider know all this so early? How could he, and the analysts at other networks, provide this insight with such confidence? They were, of course, using exit polls. In this case, those exit polls showed West Virginia voters far more concerned with economic growth than with the environment. That kind of rapid, revealing look at why voters chose as they did is why these polls are so invaluable to political journalism. It also makes what was about to happen that night especially ironic. Our most prized tool was about to blow up in our face.

A BRIEF DIVERSION: ON THE SOFT UNDERBELLY OF EXIT POLLS — OR: FLORIDA, AN ACCIDENT WAITING TO HAPPEN.

A little more than 2,800 years ago, in the Greek town of Delphi at the foot of Mount Parnassus, a shepherd began to notice that his goats were driven into a frenzy whenever they neared a particular chasm in the ground. He looked in, and promptly began muttering incomprehensible words and phrases. The scientific explanation is that a series of earthquakes had cracked the ground open, releasing noxious gases. His friends and neighbors, on the other hand, decided that these were, in fact, messages from the gods. They turned the site into the Temple of Apollo, and a woman, called the "Pythia," was appointed as the person who would interpret the divine messages of the oracle. On special days, the Pythia would purify herself by bathing in the nearby Castalian spring; she would then inhale the smoke of barley flour and laurel leaves, and go into a trance. At this point, those petitioners seeking to learn the future would present an offering to the male priests at the temple, and the priests would sprinkle water over a sacrificial goat (in honor of the animals who had first stumbled upon the site). If the goat trembled, that was a sign to the priests that the moment was right for an oracular consultation. The Pythia would sit on a three-legged stool placed over the chasm, and would answer questions—often in an elliptical manner—that the priests would then interpret.

The Pythians were not always clear about just what it was they were predicting. When Croesus, the king of Lydia, asked whether he should go to war against Persia, the oracle replied: "Croesus, having crossed the Halys River, will destroy a great realm." So he went to war, and he did destroy a great realm— his own. Despite the occasional hitch, the oracle became a magnet for supplicants from all over the known world, who traveled to Delphi and showered the Temple of Apollo with gold, silver, and jewels in the hope of peeking into the future. The Delphic oracle became a powerful political and social influence in the Greek empire, and it remained so for nearly a thousand years.

Today, of course, we are far too sophisticated to rely on Delphic oracles, sorcerers, chicken entrails, tea leaves, or tarot cards for predictions. Today, we have polls. They do not speak elliptically or in riddles, but in the hard, cold numbers that reflect a quantifiable reality. And on Election Day, we have the exit poll—regarded almost universally as the most reliable, trustworthy poll of all—at least, up until 7:50 P.M. on the evening of November seventh. But why? Why did we proceed into the unknown with such confidence in these numbers?

To begin with, exit polls by definition are free from the biggest challenge of preelection polls—*finding people who will actually vote*. Pollsters have always known that if their numbers include a lot of people who will not vote, they will produce a flawed result—nonvoters tend to be younger, poorer, blacker or browner, and less educated than the voting population, which usually means they're more likely to be Democrats than Republicans. So pollsters always try to build a "screen" to keep nonvoters out. But that creates problems. For instance, it doesn't help much to ask people, "Do you plan to vote this year?" People aren't fools. They know when a question has the making of a civics quiz, and they know what the right answer to this question is. That's why voters tell pollsters just before an election that they are planning to vote in what would be record high numbers. It's the same kind of answer people give when they're asked what they want to see more of on TV ("More documentaries! More high-quality dramas! More Shakespeare!" Very few people ever say, "I want more Jerry Springer! More *Smackdown!*"), the same kind of answer people give about their food choices ("I eat lots of broccoli, other cruciferous vegetables, and brown rice"). Moreover, thanks to the huge rise in the use of answering machines, cell phones, and faxes, it takes a lot of effort to get real live potential voters on the other end of a telephone. (My hunch is that the infestation of dinnertime calls from telemarketers may have something to do with the increasing difficulty of reaching voters by phone.) When I worked in politics more than a quarter-century ago, roughly a third of pollsters' phone calls went unanswered. Today, the rate is closer to two-thirds.

So what? This high refusal rate means that pollsters must invest a lot more time—and money—to find anyone who will talk to them. The temptation is great to trim costs by cutting the size of the sample—say, from one thousand likely voters to eight hundred, or six hundred, or less. The smaller the sample, the bigger the chances that the poll is going to be wrong. And when I say "wrong" I mean "way, way, wrong." When a poll with a small sample reports that its margin of error is "plus or minus 4 percent," here's what it's really saying:

"Okay—we have Bush leading Gore 52 to 48. But that '52' might be as high as 56—or it might be as low as 48. And that '48' for Gore might be as low as 44—but it might be as high as 52. So when we say 'Bush has a four-point lead,' maybe he does—or maybe it's a tie—or maybe Bush has a twelve-point lead—or maybe Gore has a four-point lead. And since our 'plus-or-minus' assertions are about 95-percent right, there's a 5-percent chance that we're off by a lot more than we're saying."

What's true about the "horse race" questions is true as well about the "issues" questions that are asked in the pre-election polls. Maybe voters like Gore's education ideas better than Bush's—but maybe they don't. (And maybe they haven't spent five seconds thinking about either of their ideas, but don't want to say so.) Moreover, as every pollster can tell you, the way a question is asked can often skew the answers. Do you list the candidates *and* their party affiliations? Do you give them the candidates first, or do you first ask if they've made up their minds? Do you ask them if they're sure about their choice, or do you "push" them to say how they're leaning? Depending on what you do, your "undecided" total will vary wildly.

If you ask voters: "Do you favor cutting entitlement programs?" an overwhelming majority will say "yes"—because "entitlement" sounds like welfare. If you ask voters, "Do you favor cutting Social Security?"—the biggest federal entitlement program by far—an overwhelming majority will say "no," because they think of Social Security as something they earned. Ask voters, "Do you favor a government-run health care program?" and an overwhelming majority will say "no," because it evokes the image of a doctor's office run with the compassion and efficiency of the New York City Department of Motor Vehicles. Ask them, "Do you favor Medicare?"—a government-run health-care program—and they'll say "yes!" because most Americans want the burden of health care in old age lifted from their shoulders.

Finally, even the best preelection poll can't really measure what voters will do on Election Day. They can't possibly measure whether a sudden illness, or a turn in the weather, or an onslaught of sloth or lust will keep a likely voter from the polls in pursuit of more immediate gratification. They can't measure whether some lingering doubts will morph into a full-blown change of heart on the way to the voting booth. But the exit polls? We went into Election Night secure in the knowledge that here is a tool designed to turn even the greenest neophyte analyst into a master craftsman.

First, and most obvious, exit polls survey actual voters. An army of interviewers, some 1,400 Voter News Service interviewers at precincts in all fifty states and the District of Columbia, will interview more than 140,000 voters *as they leave the polls.* If you're looking for a "tight screen" to make sure you're talking to voters, you're not going to do much better than that. (Of course, there's a built-in assumption that people leaving the polling places have actually cast their votes and had them counted—but why would anyone possibly question that assumption?)

Second, the answers to the questions are far more reliable than those from ordinary polls, since the votes of the respondents—and the reasons why they voted—are fresh in their minds. For instance, they know whom they voted for; not a tough question, you might think, except that polls taken a week or so *after* the election usually show a much bigger margin for the winner than was actually the case. More significant, they know *why* they voted the way they did, *when* they made up their minds, and *what* issues they thought were most important to them and the country. And, since there's only one set of questions being asked, the result is much more likely to reflect the real sentiments of American voters. That's why the real value of these polls lies *not* in their ability to measure the results of the votes, but in the profile they provide of the mind of the voter.

Of course, that's a little like those signs that used to be posted on truck-stop vending machines that dispensed condoms in the days when birth-control devices were illegal in many states. The signs read: "Sold for the Prevention of Venereal Disease *Only.*" You bet; nobody's buying those rubbers to prevent pregnancy. In the case of exit polls, their use on Election Night as a device for calling election results is the reason why the television networks and the Associated Press spent some thirty-three million dollars to fund the Voter News Service. This single organization gathers these figures for AP, ABC, CBS, CNN, Fox News, and NBC. Before we ever take to the air, the exit-poll information is shaping the coverage—alerting us to close races, letting us know that we had better start boning up on Smith rather than Jones, or that we can begin flogging the story of a very close election.

Later in the evening, these exit polls, combined with votes from sample precincts that are called in directly to the Voter News Service, form the basis for the calls that often occur the instant the polls have closed in a state. While VNS is the sole source of the information, it is the responsibility of the networks themselves to make the calls. And why do they do it?

In part, it is ego; a vestige of the days when networks competed with one another to see who could be first to project the winner of a race. Not that long ago, the network public-relations departments trumpeted every first call, and the nation's TV critics in the print press dutifully reported this result as a measure of which network had "won" the Election Night race. This "whose-is-bigger?" battle has waned considerably, since everyone is now using the same information. Still, no television network would even consider dropping exit polls, banning all projections, and waiting until the raw votes were counted until declaring who had won a race. Why not? Because every viewer with a grasp of the remote-control device would have long ago switched to a network that was using exit polls and projections. Is this a question of overweening arrogance? No, it's a question of basic journalism. We don't wait for government announcements to report appointments to high office or new initiatives. We don't wait for officials to act before revealing threats to road safety, or to clean air or water. And we don't keep viewers up until three o'clock in the morning if we can tell them who's been elected, once we know with certainty what has happened. (There's a separate question of whether the calls we make early in the evening have an impact on voters in the western United States. I'm going to defer that question for a while.) We've always tried to report the winners and losers as quickly as possible, whether through the telegraph, the radio and TV, even the first generation of computers. (The very first time I was allowed to stay up late on an Election Night, in 1952, CBS produced a room-sized computer called "Univac," that pronounced early in the evening that the odds were 100 to 1 in favor of an Eisenhower victory. Deprived of a late bedtime on a school night, I have remained a computerphobe ever since.)

And here is one of the real keys to what happened on Election Night. We were sure about these projections, because they had compiled an almost perfect track record. Only once in the last decade had the networks ever gone on the air with a "call" they had to retract: That was in a New Hampshire race for the U.S. Senate in 1996, which was called for Democrat Dick

Swett. Senator Bob Smith wound up winning a narrow reelection; Voter News Service went under the hood, tinkered a bit, and pronounced the defect cured. Other than that glitch, the system worked fine. George Bush's narrow California victory in 1988; Bill Clinton's razor-thin wins in Kentucky in '92 and '96; Gore's close win in the New Hampshire primary against Bill Bradley—the projections were right every time. We were as confident in the technology and process of Election Night projections as NASA was in the technology and process of space-shuttle launches when they sent up *Challenger* in 1986—and for the same reason: There was no reason for doubt to stay our hands.

But, of course, there were plenty of reasons—generally, and more specifically, in what we had already heard about some of the numbers.

In the first place, exit polls and projections have the same capacity for human and mechanical error as any other poll. Someone can hit the wrong keystroke on a computer, and thousands of votes can disappear—or votes can appear that in fact were never cast. (This dilemma, as we shall soon see, is no hypothetical example.) Much more worrisome is that while exit polls obviously deal with voters, *they do not deal with all of the voters.* By definition, absentee ballots are outside the reach of those 1,400 pollsters waiting outside the polling places. The number crunchers try to factor this in, of course. In California, Oregon, and Washington State VNS did a preelection telephone poll to find absentee voters. Unfortunately, VNS did not conduct a similar poll in Florida, but relied instead on past patterns in absentee voting. (They generally tilt Republican, since they're likely to have jobs or money that require or permit travel.) What may have escaped their attention is that absentee balloting has become much more common than in the past. States have loosened their laws; political parties, beginning with California Republicans in the early 1980s, mail out preprinted request forms to make the process easier. In California, as much as 24 percent of the total vote now comes from absentee ballots, and in other states, the numbers have climbed dramatically. In Washington State, 50 percent of the total vote comes from absentee ballots. Further, states across the country have moved to early voting; in Texas, for example, you can go to your local board of elections and cast your vote as early as seventeen days before Election Day. You can do the same thing in thirteen other states. And in Oregon, there are no polling booths at all; everyone votes by mail.

In other words, the exit poll, much like a magnificent beachfront home under which the sand is slowly eroding, was resting on a foundation less and less secure. It looked sturdy enough, but under the right—or wrong—combination of circumstances, it was susceptible to collapse. A combination that could include, say, a vote that was a virtual tie; significant voter confusion in areas that heavily favored one or another candidate; or a computer glitch or two that produced false numbers at precisely the wrong time.

Welcome to Florida.

● There was something wrong about Florida.

At Bush campaign headquarters in Austin, Texas, the bad news was that African-Americans were turning out in huge numbers. Two years earlier, Jeb Bush had been elected governor on a theme of inclusion; he'd campaigned heavily in black neighborhoods, something Florida Republicans rarely if ever did. But in 1999, an anti–affirmative-action proposal by Bush turned the African-American community solidly against him.

"We will take our case to the polls," warned Representative Corrine Brown. "We will let people understand the message that the Bush family has delivered to Florida." Now that promise seemed more like prophecy. Moreover, the Bush folks knew full well that Bill Clinton had almost carried Florida in 1992. In fact, the president had always kicked himself for not putting more resources into the state. Four years later, Clinton had actually carried Florida against Bob Dole. This time, the presence of Joe Lieberman on the ticket was bound to encourage a heavier Jewish turnout ("A heavier Jewish turnout? Impossible!" longtime political reporter Hal Bruno maintained. "Every Jew who can *move* votes. I think it's the eleventh commandment.") In 1996, blacks made up 10 percent of the total vote; if that percentage increased, so did the chances that Bush would lose the state he had once assumed would be his.

In the Gore camp, the worry was what was going on in Palm Beach—one of the heaviest Democratic areas of the state. "The polls opened at 7 A.M.," one Palm Beach Democrat recalls, "and the first call came in to our headquarters eight minutes later. People were saying it was terribly confusing, that they thought they'd voted for Buchanan by mistake." Randy Schultz, an editor at the Palm Beach *Post*, says, "We were getting calls at eight in the morning on Election Day, from people worried that they had miscast their vote, complaining. And it just built from there." While Democrats in Palm Beach began increasingly urgent calls to national headquarters, it wasn't until 5:30 P.M. that Senator Joe Lieberman went on local radio, talking with talk-show host Randi Rhodes in an effort to get every last voter to the polls. When Rhodes asked him about the ballot, Lieberman said, "I just heard as I was listening and waiting to come on, and that's the first I heard about it."

"But it was probably too late by then anyway," the aide said. "Seniors—they vote first thing in the morning."

On his first Election Day as chairman of the Palm Beach County Canvassing Board, Judge Charles Burton, the forty-two-year-old chairman of the board, was expecting a highly uneventful day.

"The only reason I was named chairman in the first place was because they had to have a judge who'd been elected without opposition," he recalled a few weeks later in his ninth-floor office in the modern, sandstone-and-glass Palm Beach County Courthouse. "When they said I'd be chairman of the board, the only thing I asked was, 'What's a canvassing board?'" Before Election Day, Burton remembers, the board had met a few times to go over the rules and regulations— "strictly routine, by-the-book stuff."

But shortly after Election Day began, Burton dropped into the Supervisor of Elections office in a nearby building, and found a distraught Theresa LePore with a sample butterfly ballot, which she handed to him.

"Take this, and see if you can vote for Gore," she asked him. He did.

"We're getting calls about the ballot," she said. "People are saying it's confusing." She decided to send out an advisory to clear up the confusion, and let worried Democrats get it to the polls before turnout began to spike up again in the late afternoon.

The advisory read:

"Attention all poll workers. Please remind all voters coming in that they are to vote for one (1) presidential candidate and that they are to punch the hole next to the arrow next to the number next to the candidate they wish to vote for. Thank you."

In Atlanta, we knew little if anything about the Palm Beach troubles. What we did know was unsettling enough: that the Voter News Service was reporting trouble with some of its early numbers from a series of states when its first exit-poll numbers came in at one o'clock in the afternoon.

"We've got a lot of 'bads,' " Bill Schneider had told the group jammed into the CNN conference room in midafternoon. Schneider was not trying to imitate a homeboy; he was talking about precincts where the exit-poll data seemed at odds with past track records, or with preelection polls. (The early numbers, for instance, pointed to a clear Bush win in Pennsylvania, a state Gore would wind up winning by four percentage points). In each key state, exit polls are taken in about four dozen precincts; if two of those precincts produce "bads," the number crunchers can go about their work with a fair measure of confidence. On this Election Day, roughly 10 percent of the precincts were showing up with shaky numbers. At 4:47 P.M., VNS sent out a reassuring alert to subscribers: "The problems with the state survey weighting are cleared up. We have cleaned out the bad precinct problems." This was not all that reassuring to CNN co-anchor Judy Woodruff, who was openly uneasy about a vote-gathering operation—the *only* vote-gathering operation—deciding in the middle of Election Day that its model might have a bug or two in it. It was, said another colleague, like looking out the window of a jumbo jet ten minutes before departure time, and noticing a group of mechanics huddling around engine number 4 shaking their heads and flipping through the maintenance manual.

So at 7 P.M., when most of the polls in Florida closed, none of us in front of the cameras was surprised that the numbers were showing the state "too close to call."

But less than a half-hour later, in a room in New York City jammed with computers and people, a group of analysts was looking at numbers that were pointing very clearly to a call: the numbers that Voter News Service were dumping into computers were saying that Al Gore was going to carry Florida.

The men and women were part of a "Decision Desk" assembled by Warren Mitofsky, one of the Founding Fathers of modern political analysis. On this day, he was simultaneously working for CNN and CBS News, communicating with both networks through an open telephone line. Similar teams were at work for the other broadcast news divisions and cable networks. But *every one* of these teams was looking at exactly the same data at exactly the same time: the information popping up on the computer screens programmed by Voter News Service.

What were these numbers saying? And why were they so wrong?

- The first exit-poll numbers from forty-five survey precincts showed Gore leading Bush by 6.6 points. When the actual votes for those precincts came in, they were measured against the exit-poll numbers, to see if they were different enough to suggest the poll data were flawed. The first indications were that the so-called "sampling error" was not out of line. Only when all the votes were counted did the truth become clear: the exit poll contained a pro-Gore skew.
- Gore's lead in the exit polls could not be analyzed without an attempt to weigh the impact of absentee

ballots—ballots that would likely tilt toward Governor Bush. The VNS Florida model was estimating that the absentee vote would make up 7.2 percent of the total vote; and that the absentee vote would be 22.4 points more Republican than the Election Day vote. That last estimate was pretty close—the absentee ballots turned out to be 23.7 points more Republican. But instead of being 7.2 percent of the total, they turned out to be *12 percent* of the total. What the Decision Desk did not know, in other words, was that there were 300,000 *more* absentee ballots—heavily Republican absentee ballots—than their computer model was estimating.

- At 7:48 P.M., NBC called Florida for Gore, an act that raised the competitive juices at the other networks. As the Decision Desks looked at the VNS data, they saw six precincts where the exit-poll data could be matched against actual reported votes. Those numbers suggested that the exit polls were actually *underestimating* the Gore vote; in fact, those early numbers turned out to be misleading—the statewide exit poll was *overestimating* the Gore total.

- VNS numbers, a blend of the exit polls from forty-five precincts, past voting patterns, unofficial votes collected by VNS workers, and the tiny amount of tabulated raw votes, were all pointing to a Gore victory. The odds of a mistake, the numbers also suggested, were less than 1 in 200 (assuming, of course, that the numbers were right).

· · ·

● So it was that CNN Political Director Tom Hannon, at 7:50 P.M., opened the microphone to the anchor desk and announced in our ears, "We are calling Florida for *Gore*—Florida for *Gore*."

("I was surprised by the early call for Florida," Hannon said, weeks later. "But it's like a laboratory situation. You look at the numbers, the models, the percentages. There was no reason to assume there was a problem.")

Judy Woodruff announced our call at the instant the commercial break ended.

"A *big* call to make. CNN announces that we call Florida in the Al Gore column. This is a state both campaigns desperately wanted to win."

"This is a roadblock the size of a boulder to George W. Bush's path to the White House," I said. "They had counted these twenty-five electoral votes from the moment George Bush entered the campaign, before he was even nominated. . . . whether it was Social Security, the turnout, Joe Lieberman, now George W. Bush has to look to Michigan, Pennsylvania, Ohio, and those smaller states really become critical."

And for the next two hours, our coverage focused on one question: Could George W. Bush win the White House without Florida? What we did *not* do was assume that Gore had the race won. What we *did* do was assume the accuracy of our call, even as the Bush campaign and its partisans were loudly questioning the call—and question it they did—loudly, urgently, almost desperately. In Austin, Bush political strategist Karl Rove was calling correspondents and news executives alike, with one message: *Your Florida call is wrong! The polls in the Panhandle are still open! You're gonna have egg all over your faces!*

Other Bush operatives were getting the same message out,

both to on-air journalists and to Bush surrogates serving as Election Night analysts and commentators. It wasn't just Florida they were so concerned about, although they genuinely believed the Florida call for Gore was premature. No, what petrified them was the impact the call would have on the psychology of the millions of voters who had not yet cast their votes.

Ed Gillespie, a veteran of Republican Party wars going back three decades, was on the phone from Austin to as many network players as he could find.

"I talked to Dottie [Lynch, director of polling for CBS], to Mark Halperin [ABC News political director], and to [Bob] Novak, on the set of CNN. First, because absentee ballots are so critical in Florida, we just felt that Florida was in play. So we felt they called Florida and Pennsylvania early. And meanwhile, West Virginia and Ohio hung out there forever. I would call and say, 'When are you gonna call Ohio? When are you gonna call West Virginia?' We were worried about the West, absolutely. Because for two weeks, voters across the country had been told that whoever wins Florida wins it all. And when you called Florida for Gore, that was it—you could feel the air go out of our headquarters. I mean, you could feel it go out of Republican voters in California and New Mexico, and places like that."

Even if Florida did wind up for Gore, the Bush campaign knew there was still a chance for an electoral victory, but only if all those swing states in the Midwest and West went for Bush. The campaign was desperate for two pieces of news to reach those voters. First, that Florida was not lost; second, that Bush was winning some critical states like Ohio and West Virginia, to keep Republican hopes alive. If a "bandwagon mentality" swept through the tens of millions of viewers, if they believed it was all over, then Republicans would stay home in later-voting states—and it *would* be all over.

Did anyone at the networks take these complaints seriously? No. After all, what were partisan voices against the cool, objective certainty of the numbers and the models and the system that had worked so well for so long?

Go Challenger, *up full throttle!*

CHAPTER 2

Florida: We That

Giveth Taketh Away

. . . and Giveth . . .

and Taketh . . .

and . . .

● **WITHIN TEN MINUTES**

of the Florida call, just after

8 P.M. on the East Coast, Al

Gore was looking very much

like the next president of the

United States. As the polls

closed in sixteen more states,

the networks called Michigan

and Illinois for Gore. Illinois

was no surprise—the Bush

campaign had more or less

conceded the state days ago;

but in the sweep of big industrial states from New York to the Mississippi River, only Ohio was more central to their hopes than Michigan. This was the state where lunch-bucket union Democrats first began slipping their moorings decades ago. First came the culture wars: School busing and crime helped give segregationist Alabama Governor George Wallace a big win in the 1972 Democratic presidential primary. That fall, Richard Nixon blew away George McGovern in Michigan by more than half a million votes. The industrial recession of 1980 put the state squarely in Ronald Reagan's camp; the defection of union members gave rise to the label "Reagan Democrats." Eight years later, George Bush's portrait of Michael Dukakis as a soft-on-crime, soft-on-patriotism boutique liberal kept the state Republican. Then in 1992, helped by economic hard times and his own tough-on-crime, pro–death penalty, welfare-reform message, Clinton brought Michigan back into the Democratic column—by a narrow margin—for the first time in sixteen years. He won it comfortably in 1996. This time, Republicans thought, they could capture the state by wrapping Al Gore's tree-hugging environmental message tight around his neck. Hadn't he written that book that called for "an end to the internal combustion engine"? Shouldn't that petrify the autoworkers of Michigan? Wouldn't his position on guns shake the loyalty of those same workers, for whom the opening of hunting season was a religious holiday?

Nope. In Michigan, the health of the economy was a trump card for Gore, as was a provision in the contract between the United Auto Workers and the major car manufacturers. For the first time ever, the automakers gave the union a paid holiday on Election Day. The result? Union households made up 43 percent of the voters in Michigan—and they broke almost two-to-one for Gore. The booming economy was of special significance in Michigan, where consumer confidence means full employment and overtime on the automobile production lines. Fifty-five percent of the state's voters said their financial situation was better under Clinton, and Gore carried those economic optimists by two to one. And despite the Bush campaign's hope for an anti–gun control turnout among Democrats, the state's voters backed tougher gun laws by a substantial margin. All this was enough to give the state to the Democrats, and with Florida now in hand, that was two-thirds of the so-called "trifecta" of Florida, Michigan, and Pennsylvania that would, by unanimous preelection agreement, give Gore the White House.

● In the first minutes after we had called Florida and then Michigan for Gore, one question kept popping up in my mind: *What are the other guys doing?* In the barely controlled chaos of Election Night coverage, none of us at the anchor desk has any notion of what is happening on the other networks; it's tricky enough trying to follow our own coverage, while responding to the cues coming from the control room. *("We've got Senator Lott waiting. . . ." "We're ready to make a call in the Delaware Senate race. . . ." "We need to get to commercial. . . .")* It's especially tricky when you're trying to provide some thematic consistency. Earlier in the day, we'd designed a series of graphics based on those seven "Keys to the Election" I'd recited when we first went on the air; every time Bill Schneider had exit-poll numbers to report, I'd be trying to figure out whether we'd learned an answer to one of those keys ("The Clinton Factor," "The Nader Factor," "Was It—'The Economy, Stupid'?"). Each of the questions had a number; so when I heard something that fit, I'd hold up a number—making sure I was off-camera, so it did not look as if I were mimicking an Olympic gymnastics judge—to let the control room and the executive producer know I had a point to make. Under these circumstances, trying to follow the competition's coverage was a dandy prescription for a nervous breakdown. Besides, our colleagues in the cavernous newsroom, and in the control room, had their eyes on the competition.

Still, there was a powerful curiosity to check out the other guys—especially since the Florida call was so important. Moreover, while I knew vaguely that all the networks subscribed to the same single source of data but I did not fully understand that every pair of eyeballs, whether they belonged to Warren Mitofsky (CBS and CNN), or Carolyn Smith (ABC), or John Ellis (Fox), or anyone else, was staring at the exact same numbers. Each network had the power to make or withhold a call, of course. But once the data on those screens indicated a statistically clear call, it would be an eccentric notion indeed to say: "No, my gut tells me this could be wrong." Without this understanding of statistical probability, I wanted to see for myself.

At CNN's Atlanta headquarters, this was no easy task. The anchor desk sits in the middle of a space big enough to stage a basketball game. The television monitors sit on "pods" all over the newsroom, and a bank of monitors runs several feet along the walls. The only way for me to get a glimpse of the action was to lean as far back in my chair as possible, crane my neck, swivel my head to the right, and squint, hoping to catch an Electoral College map. Even then the view is through a glass, darkly—not to mention the danger: If I leaned back far enough, it was entirely possible that I might wind up tipping the chair completely over, thus reappearing after a commercial break with only the soles of my shoes peering over the anchor desk.

By executing this challenging maneuver through a series of commercial breaks and programming segments, I was able to see that we were not alone: The other nets had all called Florida for Gore. I also realized that, in a peculiar sense, I was seeing the last twenty years of my life pass before my eyes.

● *There was a tape of Joe Lieberman on NBC. . . .*

I'd met Joe Lieberman in 1964, when we were first-year students at Yale Law School. He was a notable figure even then. As an undergraduate, he'd turned out a paper on Connecticut Democratic boss John Bailey that was published as a book: *The Power Broker.* As a budding writer, I looked with admiration and envy on anyone who'd published a book in his early twenties. Lieberman himself was a politician-in-the-making; his eyes were so clearly fixed on public office that his friends nicknamed him "Senator." There was also, however, something appealing about Joe. His puckish sense of humor earned him membership in a highly informal group that met weekly in an upstairs dining room at Mory's. We called the group "Ladies' Lunch," for reasons best left in obscurity.

Lieberman and I, along with the rest of the group, participated in one of the last examples of campus hijinks before the more somber mood of the late sixties settled on Yale. In the Fall of 1966, Yale University's rare book library had acquired "The Vineland Map," a thousand-year-old document purporting to show that the Vikings had beaten Columbus to the New World by centuries. This map, understandably, stirred up intense anger in New Haven's Italian-American community. As Columbus Day approached, we in "Ladies' Lunch" decided this would be a perfect occasion for a demonstration of solidarity. On the appointed day, we threw up a picket line in front of the library, with signs reading "How Would You Like Your Daughter to Marry a Viking?" I gave one of my first public speeches, proclaiming, "Forgive them—for they know not what they drew." The rally ended with a burning of the map—okay, a reproduction—and the match was lit by a beaming Joe Lieberman. (When I dug out an old wire-service photo of the event and displayed it on CNN's *Inside Politics,* the Lieberman campaign responded with ever-so-slightly-nervous good humor.)

If Yale was Lieberman's launchpad into politics, it was also mine. In my last year of law school, I was desperate to join a highly selective seminar. The professor said, well, I'm oversubscribed, but if you show up and participate effectively, I'll let you in. I was primed the next day, and turned in a performance never equaled before or after. As it happened, a few days later the professor was called by a classmate now working for Robert Kennedy. I'd applied for a position on his staff; and Kennedy's aide was told, by an appropriately dazzled professor, that I was the real deal. (Had the call been made a few weeks later, the reaction might have been very different.) And that's how I wound up on the Senate staff, and then the campaign staff, of Robert Kennedy. As for Lieberman . . . well, at our thirty-year law school reunion, I was asked to say a few words about our class.

"Life is full of surprises," I said. "We all knew that Joe Lieberman would be a U.S. Senator. But a *respected* U.S. Senator?"

. . .

JEFF GREENFIELD | *Oh, Waiter! One Order of Crow!*

● *There was Dan Rather, on CBS. . . .*

In 1979, Rather was a star correspondent for the *CBS Evening News* and *60 Minutes* when I started as the media critic for *Sunday Morning* with the late Charles Kuralt, armed with a fantastic contract ("Four hundred and fifty dollars a week—it's scale—take it or leave it"). Kuralt was the most luminous writer for the ear I have ever heard. His simple eloquence was the product of the Red Smith School of Journalism.

"Writing is easy," Smith had once said. "You just sit at your typewriter and open a vein." Watching Kuralt at work was the one time the off-camera man differed from the on-camera persona. On TV, Kuralt was avuncular, at ease, the clear, concise language seeming to emerge as a casual observation. At work, he was a bundle of nerves, hair askew, his feet buried under mounds of crumpled yellow paper, his face wreathed in smoke from the cigarettes that helped kill him at sixty-two.

Back in 1980, a few weeks before the Republican National Convention, CBS News President Bill Leonard and Executive Vice President Bob Chandler called me down to their offices.

"We've got Bill Moyers and James Kilpatrick as part of our analysis team," Chandler said. "We need a third. We'd like you to do it."

It was a turning point in my life. When the conventions were done, thirteen years after my law school graduation, my mother called me and said, "All right. Maybe it's okay you didn't take the bar exam."

● *There was Peter Jennings on ABC. . . .*

In 1983, I'd left CBS for ABC, prodded by the new CBS

News president, Van Gordon Sauter. We want you to stick to media coverage, he said; we're up to our ass in politics.

But what about the stuff I did in 1980? What about all those nice words from the critics?

"Bored my ass off," Sauter said. *(Here's a hint for you young journalism students out there: When your boss tells you your work bores his ass off, it's a good time to update that résumé.)* Sauter would later find himself engaged by politics—literally. He married Kathleen Brown, daughter of one California governor and sister of another, who was a rising star herself until she ran against Governor Pete Wilson in 1994 and was buried in a GOP landslide. I always thought she would have done better had she kept the name she'd used during her first marriage: Kathleen Brown Rice. How could you lose in California with a name like that? But I digress.

ABC made a happy home for me at *Nightline,* where anchor Ted Koppel and executive producer Rick Kaplan presided over the happiest home a broadcast journalist could hope for. We had an anchor of extraordinary intelligence who is a *mensch* to boot; an executive producer with a huge appetite for risk; a spectacular staff of producers, editors, researchers, and assistants; and an absolute commitment to do it right. (I often thought the 11 A.M. conference calls should have been transcribed and made compulsory reading at every journalism school in the country.) Covering national politics for *Nightline* was a joy, undercut only by the fact that in 1984, I had been left off the team covering the national conventions. On the last day, ABC News President Roone Arledge spotted me in the makeshift newsroom, came up to me, and said flatly, "We made a mistake with you this time. We won't make it again next time."

I gave the comment the same weight I would have if a casual acquaintance had passed me on the street and said, "We must do lunch soon." But four years later, I was on the floor of the 1988 Democratic convention in Atlanta with a microphone in my hand and a ludicrously oversized pair of headphones clamped to my ears. I'd fantasized about this since I'd heard the 1952 conventions on a tiny radio in my grandfather's summer cottage, the same way I'd fantasized about playing rock and roll guitar while sitting in the balcony of the Brooklyn Paramount theater in 1956, or roaming center field for the New York Yankees as a child in midcentury,

I'd learned early enough that turning these latter fantasies into reality was highly unlikely—a matter of talent. But now, after more than a quarter-century of toil in the vineyards of politics and journalism, I was where I'd always wanted to be.

Unfortunately, by the time I showed up, the story I had come to cover had gone away.

The floor reporters of TV's early days were chasing *news*. Conventions then were where the parties came to pick their nominees, and as often as not, no one knew with any certainty who that nominee would be, or what shape the battle for that prize would take. How would New Jersey vote on that credentials challenge to the Texas delegation? Would the governor of Michigan release his delegates on the second ballot? Would the chair permit a floor vote on the platform fight over civil rights or the United Nations? As late as 1976, when Gerald Ford and Ronald Reagan were fighting it out in Kansas City, CBS News graciously permitted the embattled Mississippi delegation to use one of its trailers for a caucus, slipped a news intern into the trailer to provide "logistical" help, then debriefed him on the air to learn that Mississippi had decided to stay with Ford, thus ensuring him of the nomination. And even in 1980, the networks still provided gavel-to-gavel coverage, and there was still a fair amount of drama. This time Reagan and Ford were negotiating an unprecedented deal for Ford to run as Reagan's vice president; the news that the deal had collapsed, and that George Bush was the choice, exploded onto the convention floor on Wednesday night.

That was the last year anything close to the unexpected happened. By the time I arrived with microphone and headphones, coverage had been cut back to two hours a night; the political parties had begun to script conventions into minute-by-minute infomercials, and the idea of finding breaking news on the convention floor was like hunting for the hottest topless bar in Teheran.

This turned out to be a big break for me. Bereft of anything of great moment to report, I was deployed by the bosses at ABC News as a free safety, charged with wandering through the hall in pursuit of political wit and wisdom. The idea worked; the critics were kind. When the 1988 conventions ended, I found myself occasionally subbing for Koppel as a *Nightline* anchor, and a proud member of a club that included Koppel, Kuralt, and Tim Russert—Guys Who Make a Good Living on TV Even Though They Don't Look Like It Would Be Possible. (Tom, Dan, Peter—eat your hearts out.)

If only the audience for politics hadn't been shriveling to the point where the *combined* network coverage of the conventions attracted barely 10 percent of the viewing audience. By the 1996 conventions, the networks had pulled back to little more than an hour a night. Those of us on the floor knew that when Peter Jennings called on us, and we drew our breath for our first words of lucid, penetrating observation, we would within five seconds hear a producer's voice in our ear: *"Wrap!"*

· · ·

● Every time I leaned back in my chair and swept my eyes across the bank of monitors, I would see another part of my life: people I'd worked with, laughed with, fought with, broken bread with, shared a bed with; every one of whose lives had been shaped in one way or another by a central driving premise: *Politics matters; it is enterprise of weight and significance.* And whatever our political outlooks, every one of us had come to this premise for good and sufficient reason: There was an international totalitarian force to be resisted; there was a purposeless war to be stopped; there were barriers of race and gender to be torn down; there was a breakdown in moral authority to be repaired; there was a compelling political battle to be chronicled and explained. Now, somewhere in the middle of our journeys, we had all been granted a platform from which to speak—at the very time our listeners had developed a historically powerful indifference to the political arena. A dispassionate observer, surveying this same bank of screens, might have mistaken us for a crowd of merchants at some bazaar, beseeching customers to sample our goods as they swept by us with scarcely a backward glance.

● In Nashville, Tennessee, and in Austin, Texas, where the combatants had come to ground to await the returns, news of the Florida call for Gore had hit with predictable force. Among Gore's campaign team, there was a near-universal assumption that with Florida and Michigan in hand, a win in Pennsylvania—the completion of the "trifecta"—would lock the election up.

"I know the scenario you were all playing out on the air," says one key aide about the notion that Bush could win without Florida, "but I didn't believe it for a minute. For one thing, I was absolutely sure Gore would carry Tennessee in the end. For another, there just weren't enough other states for Bush to get him to two hundred seventy."

Elaine Kamarck had an even stronger intimation of impending victory. For more than a decade, Kamarck has been one of the major players in the Democratic Party's ideological wars. After the Dukakis debacle of 1988, she coauthored an influential paper, "The Politics of Evasion," detailing how and why the party had drifted from its core message of opportunity and responsibility, abandoning white-working-class Democrats to the Republican themes of cultural breakdown and values. She worked for Gore in his abortive 1988 campaign, joined his vice-presidential staff in 1993, and helped drive the "reinventing government" initiative. In this presidential campaign, she had spent months working on policy themes for a Gore transition, looking at every department of the executive branch to see how Gore's themes would translate into action. On Election Day, she wandered between the Loew's Vanderbilt Plaza Hotel and the inner sanctums of campaign headquarters—the "boiler room" and the "kitchen"—returning to her office where a suitcase full of transition books sat waiting. Even after the first exit polls were released, Kamarck had no idea whether those countless hours of work would become the building blocks for the next administration, or curiosities in a file drawer.

"We're getting the exit polls," she recalls, "and there's no pattern to them. They're here and there. They're jumping up and down. You have no earthly idea."

By 8 P.M., Kamarck was at the nearby Tennessee Club, where many of Gore's big contributors and key supporters were watching the returns. It was there she learned that the networks had awarded Gore the trifecta—Florida, Michigan, and

Pennsylvania. Now, she thought, all those books filled with detailed accounts of the gears of government, matters to make a C-SPAN junkie nod off, were about to be the marching orders of the next president. What made the sense so real was that a leading figure in the National Education Association, the biggest teachers' union in the country and one of Gore's earliest supporters, tracked Kamarck down in the club and asked her to meet him in Washington the next Monday.

"My husband and I started to laugh," she says. *It's started already. Everyone's getting their agendas ready—here we go.*

In Austin, the Florida call for Gore came as a special shock to some twenty close Bush friends and family members who had gathered on the ninth floor of the Four Seasons Hotel. It was an optimistic group; the final polls, the campaign assured them, pointed to a comfortable victory. According to the schedule, Bush would dine at a restaurant next-door to the hotel with his parents and brother, Florida Governor Jeb Bush, and come over to the hotel about 7:45 (Central time) to celebrate. But when the networks called Florida for Gore, everything changed. Jeb Bush was "in tears, very, very emotional," one intimate remembers. Bush called Campaign Chair Don Evans, and said simply, "I have to take my family back to the mansion."

For Karl Rove, Bush's senior strategist, the calls in Florida and Pennsylvania spelled a potential disaster even beyond the likely loss of these states. The Bush campaign had known for weeks that Florida was in doubt; that it was at least possible that Bush could lose Florida *and* Pennsylvania *and* Michigan.

They knew by midafternoon on Election Day that Gore's turnout operation had carried the day in Michigan and Pennsylvania, perhaps even in Florida.

"They did the best job of getting out the vote that they ever did," acknowledged one of Bush's closest advisors. "We had a huge operation, seventy-two million pieces of direct mail, thirty thousand volunteers walking precincts in California, but their ground game in places like Michigan and Florida was significant." But they also believed that there was at least a chance that Bush could pull out an electoral victory even with those states in Gore's column. The task was daunting; it seemed incredible that anyone could win the presidency while losing New York, New Jersey, Pennsylvania, Florida, Michigan, Illinois, and—almost surely—California. But it could be done *provided* Bush took every other state that was up for grabs. *If* he won all the border states Clinton had won twice—Arkansas and Tennessee, Kentucky and Missouri and West Virginia— and *if* he won a chunk of the "Dukakis" states where the race was close—Wisconsin, Iowa, Minnesota, Washington, Oregon—there was a way to win. But that could only happen if Bush supporters in the Midwest and West, where the polls were still open, realized the race was still in doubt. If these early network calls convinced them that there was no reason to vote, then those states would fall to Gore as well, and six years of Karl Rove's life would turn to so much dust.

Was Rove right about the impact of television's early calls on later voters? Maybe not (we'll get to that). But he and others in the Bush campaign clearly believed that the impact could be fatal. Almost immediately, Rove and other aides began calling the TV correspondents to challenge the call.

The Bush campaign did not have to wait for the networks to put Rove or other official campaign representatives on the air. Every network had partisans of the two candidates ready to offer commentary throughout the evening; these partisans, in turn, had telephone access to the campaign headquarters. So at 8:24 P.M., barely twenty minutes after CNN called Florida for Gore, Mary Matalin was armed with her talking points when CNN put her and Mike McCurry on the air. After McCurry credited the selection of Joe Lieberman and the Social Security issue as the decisive factors in Florida, it was Matalin's turn:

"I'm going to go out on a limb here," she began. "We have early data. The spread is two percent. The raw total is four thousand votes at this point. If it continues at this pace, there are a half a million absentee ballots out there. I'm just telling you, this reminds me of Deukmejian in California [referring to a very close 1982 race for governor that was decided by absentee ballots]: lost on Tuesday, won on Thursday."

"What are you suggesting, Mary?" asked Judy Woodruff.

"I'm suggesting," replied Matalin, "that when the real count is in, the absentee ballots are counted, that they're—they are extensive in there, and that state's going to flip. I really feel that way." There was, she added, a way for Bush to win without Florida, but those absentee ballots were going to make the difference.

McCurry demurred, but was unwilling to claim victory for the Democrats. He had another point to make.

"There is something important," he said. "The closeness of the numbers so far and as we are reporting it and talking about it, and reflecting on it, is surely driving that turnout in the West. Because people out West, who in past elections have been told that their votes aren't going to count, are suddenly realizing that there are very large stakes here, it's a very close election, and nobody's running away with it.

"This may have a real significant impact on turnout out in the Pacific Northwest especially."

This was a point that would dominate the commentary for the next hour and a half: The election *wasn't* over, Bush *could* win, the turnout in the western half of the United States *would* be crucial. And, if the widespread assumption about media influence was correct, these early calls should spur a Republican turnout in the later hours—unless, of course, Karl Rove's fears were realized, and the calls persuaded discouraged Republicans to stay at home. As it turned out, the impact of these early projections validated the skeptics among us—present company included—who doubted that they had ever had any discernible impact. When all the votes were counted, there was *no* geographic pattern to increases or decreases in voter turnout. In New York, for example, voter turnout was up almost three points from 1996; in neighboring New Jersey, it was down slightly. Both states had competitive Senate races. In Washington State, voter turnout was up by more than two points; in California, it was up by a fraction of a point. Turnout was down in Idaho, Kansas, and Louisiana; it was up in Vermont, Tennessee, and Nevada.

As for Mary Matalin's argument that Florida might still flip to Bush? Well, we had heard such whistling in the dark on every Election Night. Even when a landslide is in the making, there is always some forlorn campaign spokesman standing in the middle of a funereal "victory party," bravely reminding us that "it's still very early, and we're confident that we've been getting our message out in the final days of the campaign." Still, nobody wanted to rain too heavily on Matalin's parade—so Bill Schneider provided some light sprinkles.

What about her point about absentee ballots? Judy Woodruff asked.

"Well," Schneider said, "when we do call the state, we've taken the absentee ballot count into account. When we call the state, we're pretty sure that that state is going to go for the winner."

"But this is a critically important point," your ever-helpful analyst interjected. "If you're just using exit polls, by definition, you can't count absentee ballots. But when we call a state, or anybody else calls a state, they've weighed that into the equation."

"That's right," said Schneider.

"—which doesn't mean we can't be wrong," I added. *Might as well throw a bone to the Bush folks, even though we've never had to call a state back—ever.*

Even when Pennsylvania fell for Gore at 8:48 P.M., completing the trifecta, we still weren't proclaiming Al Gore the winner—but from the Bush camp, the sound of crepe being unpacked for the hanging was unmistakable.

"At some point," Candy Crowley reported from Austin, "you run out of electoral votes that are there, particularly when you realize that California has always seemed like safe Gore territory, despite a Bush effort there [*an artful way of noting that our exit polls were projecting a big Gore win in California, even though we were unable to say so, since the polls out West would be open for two more hours*] . . . it comes to a point where George Bush is going to have to run the table if he's going to stay in this game."

A few moments later, at 9 P.M. on the East Coast, we turned to another story. The polls in New York had closed, and so we were able to report what we had known for hours: Hillary Clinton was going to be the next senator from New York. So obvious was our imminent descent into political hyperbole that I had toyed for days with a historical footnote I was sure nobody—and I mean *nobody*—was going to report. Only a rare outburst of self-restraint kept me from reporting:

"An epochal moment in American political history, Bernie and Judy—for the first time since 1958, New York State has elected a Protestant to the United States Senate."

Even without that remarkable insight, there was plenty to report about the First Lady's victory: the sympathy vote in the wake of her husband's behavior; the fading of the "carpetbagger" issue after her year-and-a-half-long trek through the state; the impact of Al Gore's huge, 1.7-million-vote plurality. And while our eyes were fixed on New York, Florida was starting to look a little weird.

Sometime after 9 P.M., Larry Rosen, one of the people at Warren Mitofsky's Decision Desk in New York, began to notice that the raw, county-by-county vote in Florida was starting to indicate a probable win for Bush. In the VNS system, there are half a dozen statistical models that project a state race's likely outcome. They factor in everything from geographic patterns to past voting history to actual votes from sample precincts. Now, the county vote—the so-called "CORE estimator"—was pointing to Bush. Tom Hannon, CNN's political director, recalls that "the news about the county vote *electrified* us. It's like the green lights on a NASA control panel—when one of them suddenly goes red, you pay attention." And when Rosen saw that the numbers were pointing to Bush, "everybody on the decision team dropped what they were doing, and asked, 'My God, what's going on?' "

For Hannon, the news did *not* suggest an immediate recall.

"My first thought was that, if they're in doubt, we'll wait on a 'recall' until we know that the 'winner' has in fact become the loser. Because otherwise, you're just adding to the confusion."

That restraint seemed prudent at 9:20, when Gore picked up twenty thousand more votes. That increase in Gore's lead made the projection look much more solid—except that these were *phantom* votes, the result of a computer glitch tallying the numbers from Duval County. Once that error was caught and corrected, CNN and every other network knew the truth: The exit polls from Florida had *overestimated* Gore's actual vote total. The absentee vote was *much* larger than the VNS projection had assumed; the current VNS projections were showing a dead heat.

On the anchor set, we knew nothing of the drama building in the control room. In fact, at about 9:50, we were chatting again with Mary Matalin and Mike McCurry. And Matalin was still insisting that Florida—and for that matter, Pennsylvania—was in play.

"I want to reiterate the competition in Florida and Pennsylvania isn't over, but as the Bush campaign looks west to the states you're looking at, there is a way to add thirty-three states up to two hundred seventy plus. . . . It's threading the needle, as we say, but they see their way there and again are not giving up on Pennsylvania and Florida."

A few moments later, Bush himself sought to rally the troops; the campaign permitted cameras into the governor's mansion, where he and Laura were watching the returns.

"This was Governor [Tom] Ridge calling when you came up, and he doesn't believe the projections. He believes there are votes outstanding. . . . We're getting the same report out of Florida as well. The networks called this thing awfully early, and people who are actually counting the votes have a different perspective, so . . ."

Time for a little perspective, I thought.

"I think, in fairness, these projections are not infallible. There are times when the networks have to eat a hearty portion of crow. It happened to Senator Bob Smith in New Hampshire in 1996. The networks called it for his opponent, had to bring it back."

This would have been a perfect time to stop. But no-o-o-o-o-o . . .

"But I think, Bill, and you're the maven on this one, that generally networks do not call unless they have a pretty high degree of assurance, correct?"

"That is correct," Bill Schneider said. "We have a pretty high degree of assurance that Florida and Pennsylvania have gone for Al Gore."

About fifty seconds later, as Schneider and I were discussing likely recriminations among Republicans for the coming presidential loss, Tom Hannon opened his key to Bernie Shaw, and Shaw took over.

"Stand by, stand by," he said. "CNN right now is moving our earlier declaration of Florida back to the too-close-to-call column. Twenty-five very big electoral votes and the home state of Governor Bush's brother are hanging in the balance. This is no longer a victory for Gore."

And I blurted out the only thing I could think of that fit the moment:

"Oh, waiter! One order of crow!"

CHAPTER 3

"And We Are Here

as on a Darkling

Plain . . ."

● I M A G I N E   Y O U   A R E

driving on an unfamiliar road, across terrain you have never seen. You are nonetheless serenely confident, because you are being guided by a satellite navigation system that has never failed before. It even comes complete with voice commands that tell you exactly when and where to turn. Then, suddenly, with no warning, bells and whistles and sirens go off, and an urgent, disembodied voice begins to blare: *"System Error! System Error! Guidance Mechanism Has Failed! Revert to Manual Operations!"* The car starts wildly gyrating all over the road. You sit bolt upright, grasping the wheel, as two thoughts simultaneously pop into your mind:

First: *This is one hell of a ride.*

Second: *I wonder if we hit anything or anybody back there.*

Welcome to Election Night 2000, 10 P.M. to 2:18 A.M.

In the first moments after Florida was pulled back from Gore, we had to deal with one stark fact: Every assumption we'd been making for the last two hours was now, in the words of President Nixon's press secretary, "inoperative." If Florida wound up in Bush's camp, it would represent a shift of *fifty* electoral votes; the twenty-five Gore would lose, and the twenty-five Bush would win. And that meant that all those "Dukakis" states where Gore had been struggling through the campaign, and where the outcome was clearly hanging in the balance, would now become for Gore a matter of political life and death. West Virginia, Minnesota, Iowa, Wisconsin, Washington, Oregon—Gore might need every one of them to make it to 270 electoral votes if Florida was lost.

Moreover, as soon as Florida had become a state of suspended animation, two other states that had already been called began to take on heavy political significance. Bush had prevailed in Ohio, and no Republican had ever won the White House without it. Except for perennially Republican Indiana, it would be the only state in that wide swath of big industrial states between the eastern seaboard and the Mississippi River that he would win. And at Gore campaign headquarters in Nashville, the anger of Democratic National Chair Ed Rendell was so thick you could cut it with a knife.

Ohio bordered Rendell's Pennsylvania, another battle-ground that Gore had won with a huge turnout of African-American and labor votes. ("If you had told me before Election Day that Gore would carry Philadelphia by a bigger margin than Clinton had, I'd have said you were crazy," Rendell said much later. "But he did.") Ohio, Rendell believed, could be won with the same strategy at work in Pennsylvania: *Fire up the base. Get the president into the black neighborhoods of Cleveland, into the labor strongholds like Akron, and turn to the most popular and trusted of Democratic voices.*

Long before the election, Rendell had called former Ohio Senator John Glenn, who'd retired in 1998 after four terms. Would you do radio ads for Gore? Yes, said Glenn. Rendell let the Gore campaign know. He was told: "This looks good—we'll poll it."

"They'll *poll it*?" Rendell recalled incredulously. "They're *polling* about whether they should put the biggest Democratic vote-getter in Ohio on the air?"

Weeks later, Glenn called to see if the campaign wanted him to cut those ads; he'd heard nothing. Ultimately, radio ads with Glenn were cut but never used; nor was Glenn ever even asked to make TV ads.

"The campaign didn't believe in 'tailoring,' " Rendell said. "They were much more aimed at national messages. And to be fair, I didn't have the full picture of their financial situation. Maybe they just didn't have the resources."

That also may explain why the campaign sharply reduced its advertising budget for Ohio from one million dollars to two hundred thousand dollars in the last week of the campaign. With poll numbers showing an uphill battle, with the race so close in so many other states, the Gore campaign folded its tents.

There was a reason why the Gore forces may have retreated from Ohio. It is the most culturally conservative of all the traditional Midwest battleground states; less cosmopolitan, more fundamentally conservative in its outlook—befitting the home of the Tafts. One example: Fully 40 percent of the voters were opposed to stricter gun controls, and they broke almost three to one for Bush.

There was a more telling measure of the state's mood, one that foreshadowed what would happen to Al Gore for the rest of the night: how they felt about the president. In its judgment about Clinton, Ohio was a near-perfect reflection of the nation as a whole. Fifty-six percent approved of the job Clinton had done as president, but *61 percent* rated him unfavorably as a person. Not surprisingly, these voters were likely to cast their ballots for Bush over Gore; it's just that, in Ohio, they did so with a vengeance. Bush won 70 percent of the votes of those who frowned on Clinton as a person. Elsewhere in the industrial battlegrounds—in Pennsylvania, Michigan, Illinois—a massive turnout among African-Americans and labor-union members was enough to overcome the anti–Clinton sentiment. But not in Ohio; African-Americans made up just 9 percent of the electorate there, compared to 11 percent in Michigan, which Gore carried narrowly, and 14 percent in Illinois, which Gore won handily. The Ohio vote was a harbinger of what was going to happen in a raft of other, smaller states that Clinton had captured twice—states where voters appeared to be taking aim at the president's personal misconduct, and scoring a direct hit . . . on Al Gore.

Just forty minutes before the networks pulled Florida back from Gore, Tennessee had fallen to Bush. Tennessee, of course, was Gore's home state, the state he'd represented in the House and Senate for sixteen years, the state his father had served for three terms as a United States senator. Candidates for national office aren't supposed to lose their home states; in fact, it hadn't happened since George McGovern lost South Dakota in the Nixon landslide of 1972. Nevertheless, the Bush camp sniffed out a possibility here, and their candidate had hit the state in the last days of the campaign. Bush himself had taken a deft swing at Gore the Insider by arguing that he'd heard Gore bragging that he was going to win his home turf.

"Well," Bush had said, "he may win Washington, D.C., but he's not gonna win Tennessee." In fact, two-thirds of the voters said it mattered either very little or not at all that Gore hailed from Tennessee.

What they said about Clinton was much more consequential. The president's job-approval rating stood at only 50 percent—substantially lower than his national ratings. Those who viewed him unfavorably as a person—62 percent—broke massively for Bush, by more than three to one. Well before the election, the polls were showing Gore in trouble at home; even so, Joe Lieberman would say weeks later, the loss "felt like a punch in the stomach."

So even before Florida was taken off the boards, the night was turning chilly for Gore, with these early clues that the border states might be slipping from his grasp. Those clues grew more damning than the blood on O. J.'s glove when Missouri and its 11 electoral votes went for Bush a few minutes past 10 P.M. This was a state that had gone with the winner in every election of the twentieth century but one. Like Kentucky and Tennessee, Missouri had a strong touch of the South in its cultural as well as geographical makeup. It was a state where a lot of Democrats owned guns, went to church regularly, and found Clinton's personal behavior not just disappointing, but infuriating. Clinton's personal-unfavorability numbers in Missouri were no worse than his national average—but those who *did* feel that way broke three to one for Bush. More unnerving for Gore's camp was the fact that blacks had turned out in big numbers here, as well; in fact, our reporting earlier in the evening focused on a judge's decision to keep polling places open late in heavily black districts in St. Louis, a decision that enraged Republican Senator Kit Bond. He called it "the biggest fraud on the voters of this state and on this nation that we've ever seen." In the end, even that big increase in black turnout couldn't save Gore—although it almost certainly tilted the Senate race to the late Governor Mel Carnahan over incumbent Senator (now Attorney General) John Ashcroft.

Just a few minutes later came another hammer blow for Gore: West Virginia was called for Bush. It is a small state—only five electoral votes—but the message it was delivering to Al Gore would have awakened the dead. Over the past half-century, it had taken a Republican landslide to shake West Virginia loose from the Democrats—and sometimes even that wasn't enough. It was one of only six states that had stayed with President Carter in the Reagan landslide of 1980; it had gone for Dukakis in 1988. But tonight, it was rejecting Gore. Gore's environmental stand was one big reason. In this perpetually depressed coal-producing state, "environmentalism" was for many lunch-bucket Democrats a code word for "No Jobs." When voters there were asked, "What's more important—protecting the environment or economic growth?" they chose growth by a huge 57 to 35 margin—and the pro–growth voters went for Bush by more than twenty points.

Dazed as we were from the wreck of the Florida miscall, we still knew that the Bush wins in the border states could well become the story of the night. These states—Tennessee, Kentucky, Missouri, Arkansas, and West Virginia—totaled forty-one electoral votes. Clinton had won all of them twice—and now Gore had lost them all. Taken together, the loss of these states eradicated the combined victories in Pennsylvania and Michigan. And there was more bad news for Gore: The trio of Midwest "Dukakis" states were up for grabs. In Iowa, Minnesota, and Wisconsin, Ralph Nader's votes were keeping things too close to call.

So there we were, at 10 P.M. in the East, looking at a map that was yielding no clues to the outcome except the notion that it would be a very good idea to keep the caffeine coming. The rules we had all played by for the last twenty years were out the window. Normally, we would have long since declared a winner—in fact, we would be spending a fair amount of time reassuring voters out West that their votes *did* matter, that it was *still* their chance to pick their senator, or governor, or clerk of the county courts. This time, we were in a fog of uncertainty—not in one or two states, but in more than a dozen. It was the kind of campaign you dream of reporting—were it not for the small problem of Florida.

("Could you pass the crow, Jeff?" Judy Woodruff asked me.

"Well, you know . . ." I stammered. "Listen, there's nothing more delightful—and I have to say this as a member of the press—than watching an election when you actually have to wait and see what the voters are going to do . . . all of the notions of how to look at this campaign, in which we said, 'Look, we can tell you what states it's going to come down to.' Well, it may come down to a handful of small states that really never seem to matter in the fight for the presidency.")

Others, of course, were not quite so delighted at what we had wrought, as they explained to us quite clearly. When Larry King turned to former Education Secretary and drug czar

William Bennett for his thoughts, Bennett zeroed in on the call.

"I'm not a conservative press-basher," he said. "A lot of conservatives are. But this really shouldn't happen. You should not call a state and then have to take it back. . . . This affects how people think. It takes the air out of people's enthusiasm. I'm glad that mistake is corrected, but Bill Schneider was saying, 'We're going to be very cautious.' Well, you should have been very cautious and not called them in the first place. That's really an interference in democracy."

Karl Rove, chief Bush strategist, was more specific.

"Let me tell you, Bernie, you all called Florida before Florida even closed its polls. Florida is a state which votes in two time zones. The Republican Panhandle of Florida is in the Central time zone, and you all called Florida before the polls had even closed in Panama City and Fort Walton Beach and Pensacola. We have a fabulous organization there."

In fact, the bad call in Florida had nothing to do with the relative handful of votes in the Panhandle; any election call factors in the likely size and shape of the votes from all parts of the state. What had blown up in our faces were misleading votes from sample precincts, and a badly botched estimate of absentee votes. As a matter of precise fact, Rove was wrong. As a matter of policy and politics, he was absolutely right. In days to come, Republican politicians and pollsters would make much of the idea that large numbers of Bush voters in the Florida Panhandle were discouraged from going to the polls because of the early Gore call—one pollster estimated that Bush had lost about fifteen thousand votes. Since the network calls were made about ten minutes before the polls closed, this would have taken some doing. (I suppose the idea was that thousands of voters, rushing to the polls with ten minutes left, had their car radios on, heard the call for Gore—and turned around and went home. One angry voter claimed she'd been in line to vote when she heard the call at 6:20 P.M. Central time— at least half an hour *before* any network made the call.) One GOP pollster cited as evidence the fact that the Panhandle produced a smaller percentage of the total Florida vote than it had four years earlier. That was almost surely because the percentage of the black vote in Florida surged from 10 percent of the total in '96 to 16 percent of the total. With such a huge jump, the Panhandle's share of the vote was by definition smaller—not because voters there fled the polls in the last ten minutes.

In years past, such rebuttals would have been enough, at least in my mind, to dismiss fears about early calls. I'd been hearing such fears ever since 1980, when Reagan had won in a surprise landslide, and the networks had declared him the victor two hours before the West Coast polls had closed. Back then, Democrats had charged that these calls had kept their voters home—that voters had literally walked away from voting lines in large numbers—and had thus cost them races for the U.S. House of Representatives. The argument had never made a lot of sense to me. In the first place, it was never clear *whose* voters had walked away—Democrats who knew they'd lost, or Republicans who knew they'd won. Second, an army of academics, armed with calculators, computers, and research grants, had been studying this question for two decades. Their general conclusion: *First, there is no sound basis for deciding whether any voters were discouraged. Second, we need more grants to study this further.* Moreover, when we'd looked at turnout numbers, there was simply no correlation between projections from the East and voting in the West.

There was just one small problem with taking such comfort

from the past. As with so much about the Election Night machinery, our confidence that we could call a state "where the vast majority of polls had closed" was based on history: As far as anyone could remember, no call in a state with two different poll-closing times had ever turned out wrong. So we'd built our knowledge about what *had* happened into an assumption about what *would* happen—once again demonstrating a favorite newsroom aphorism: "Assumption is the mother of all f—ups." In *this* case, we'd called it *wrong*. And in *this* case, it was clear, the vote in Florida was going to be extremely close, and could well decide the presidency. If nine people and a house cat in the Florida Panhandle had been kept from the polls because of the call, that was enough. Add to this the Bush campaign's plausible if unprovable worries about the "bandwagon effect" out West, and the consequences of the bad call seemed to grow geometrically.

So, as we sat at the anchor desk sometime past 10 P.M., there was nothing to do but smile weakly and accept our chastisement from the Bush campaign. We had screwed up; what was done was done *(hah!)*, and it was time to turn to the most compelling Election Night since we'd waited through the night in 1976 for Jimmy Carter to win Mississippi, and with it, the electoral votes needed to put him over the top. The best way to understand the feeling at that hour is to picture an incredibly sophisticated, glamorous, compelling A-list wedding, at which the brother of the bride has staggered into the hall half-naked, lurched into a corner, lost his lunch, and passed out. If you could avert your eyes from the unpleasantness, it was still one hell of an evening. Why? Because *we did not know what was going to happen—and that's exactly the kind of story journalists, and the public, love.*

If you were drawn to politics, as I was and as many of my

contemporaries were, by its tumult and drama, then come with me to a typical day at a modern political convention, and you'll understand why Election Night 2000 was shaping up to be the fulfillment of an unrequited love that went back half a lifetime. In contrast to our predecessors, who would be chasing down every political boss, every candidate's aide, in search of the latest plots and stratagems, here's what our convention days were like:

Eight-thirty in the morning: Anchors, correspondents, producers, researchers, and assistants all jam into a temporary newsroom, jury-rigged inside one of the oversized trailers that serve as the network's convention command centers. The executive producer details the night's schedule—down to the minute. Once upon a time, political parties were ashamed when they were caught programming a convention night; when ABC's Sam Donaldson got hold of the Nixon team's rundown in 1972, complete with the timing of "spontaneous demonstrations," it was a scoop of considerable proportions. These days, the campaigns distribute their schedules as if they were in charge of a beauty pageant or an awards show. In fact, it's considered something of a "gaffe" if the campaigns let the timing slip, so that their featured speakers are pushed out of prime time. ("If they can't program a prime-time convention, how can they run the country?")

Ten A.M.: Officials from the campaign meet with a small group of anchors, reporters, and producers to explain the precise political message they are planning for the night. (*"Now, last night was 'Fulfilling the Dream for All Americans.' Tonight we'll be stressing 'One Nation, One Promise, One Purpose.' That will set us up for tomorrow's 'Preserving the Future Together.' "*) As a shrewd, insightful journalist, you may have thought it would take a shrewd, insightful mind like yours to deconstruct exactly why a troop of disabled multiethnic Scouts had been chosen to lead the flag salute, or exactly why the Hispanic woman who had launched a Web site for the homeless was going to introduce the secretary of commerce. No way; the nice people from the campaign will spell it out for you in detail. (*"Ms. Fernandez, who by the way lives in the key battleground state of New Mexico, will symbolize our commitment to fulfill the dream for all Americans, while preserving our future together. She also met the candidate during the primaries, and was touched by how kind he was to her daughter when the Secret Service motorcade ran over her dog."*)

The meeting with the aides also serves as a reminder that there will be nothing approaching authentic conversation between the journalists and the operatives. One small, true-life example: During the Los Angeles Democratic Convention, CNN Correspondent John King asked Gore aide Tad Devine whether the selection of Senator Joseph Lieberman was a way of distancing Gore from the Clinton scandals.

Not at all, Devine replied. *The vice president believes Senator Lieberman's experience and insights will make him a superb vice president.* Incredulous, King asked again. It was like pulling the string on a doll. *The vice president believes . . .*

Eleven A.M. until convention session begins: Find something remotely interesting to do. If you're resourceful, you can talk with officials and operatives who will give you some sense of the political terrain. Or, you can drift from temporary newsroom to temporary newsroom, looking for old friends.

The convention: If you work for a broadcast network, you will have about an hour to cover the featured speakers, interview a familiar face or two on the convention floor, analyze the political meaning of the session (*"Sources tell us privately that the campaign intends to convey the idea that they intend to pre-*

serve America's future together . . ."), and demonstrate your perceptive capacity to spot the staging in all of this (*"In a carefully crafted effort to project an air of confidence, the campaign intends to describe the candidate as 'the next President of the United States. . . .' "*). If you work for an all-news cable network, you will have eight hours to do the same thing. If you are a print journalist, the one thing you will never do is to sit in the press gallery, conscientiously listening to all the speeches that no one else is listening to, except for the C–SPAN addicts whose remote controls have broken.

Speaking of C–SPAN, that estimable cable network has made conventions even more painful to cover, by running old kinescopes and tapes of great conventions of the past. Every morning, as you dressed for the predictable pageant that would unfold that evening, you could watch, in faded black-and-white or washed-out color images:

- The Eisenhower-Taft forces slugging it out in Chicago in '52
- The frantic second-ballot roll call for vice president in '56 between JFK and Estes Kefauver, when state delegations frantically waved their standards for recognition
- Chicago Mayor Richard Daley yelling what may or may not have been an obscenity at Connecticut Senator Abraham Ribicoff in '68, as the latter denounced "Gestapo tactics in the streets of Chicago"

Hundreds, maybe thousands, of us can recite these moments by heart. They have long since ceased to offer any hints about the way we live now. Instead, they are much like those late-night TV *Greatest Hits* compilations, packaged bits of nostalgia designed to stir memories rather than expectations. Watching them just before descending into the modern convention was something like watching one-hundred-year-old newsreels of small-town America, and then finding yourself on the faux Main Street of Walt Disney World.

For me, too much of that feeling had crept into too many Election Nights. There was something dispiriting about looking at the first wave of exit polls just after lunch and knowing with near-certainty what would unfold several hours later. Sometimes I would picture all those millions of voters, heading to the polls through the bitter cold of Illinois, the wilting humidity of Louisiana, the smog and traffic jams of California, and think to myself: *Hey—save yourself the trouble—it's over— Reagan-Bush-Clinton's got it in the bag!* Moreover, I had come to believe that all this predictability had spawned a highly unhealthy consequence: the conviction among political journalists that we had somehow developed the ability to see into the future. After all, we approached every primary night and Election Night with a battery of highly reliable exit polls; we approached every convention night knowing, down to the minute, what was going to happen and why. Why shouldn't we come to regard the entire political process as a pageant, whose future we could divine? Why wouldn't one of television's most voluble talking heads burst into a Des Moines steak house the night before the Iowa caucuses in late January, ten months before Election Day, and bellow: "It's Gore by six in November!" Why shouldn't we "know," with scientific certainty, that Gore was finished by June, that Bush was dead in the water by September? We knew the players; we had their cell phone numbers and private insights; we knew what all the polls said; we knew how to turn a two-point change in the numbers, based on three hundred interviews, with a margin for error the size of the San Andreas Fault, and explain it with blessed assurance. (*"Gore's Social Security proposal, coupled with Bush's inability to properly pronounce the name of the capital of Wyoming, helped move some undecided retired schoolteachers in the Southwest . . ."*)

Now, in the middle of Election Night itself, all bets were off. We were there as on a darkling plain, and the ignorant armies clashing by night weren't the candidates, but the armies of the press. For once, we were in no better position than reporters at a major sporting event. For years we had borrowed their imagery: *It's fourth and long and Gore has to throw a "Hail, Mary" pass. . . . There were no knockdowns. . . . It's a slam dunk for Bush tonight. . . .* Tonight, we were in their shoes, watching an event whose outcome we would not know for hours—maybe even for a whole day.

Who knew?

The campaigns were in the same boat. Inside the "Bush bubble" at the Four Seasons in Austin, close friends and family had cheered at the Florida retraction, and then begun circulating between two rooms—one filled with telephones, computers, and TV screens, the other with food and drink. (Bush's twin daughters, Barb and Jenna, were entertaining friends in a third room. "They chose to deal with all this by having a party," one Bush friend says.) As the night wore on, a computer in the war room would spit out hypothetical scenarios, based on what states were called and what states were still in doubt. As each state fell, the printouts would be crumpled and thrown away, to be replaced by new road maps to an electoral majority.

And for all the high-powered technology, for all the computers and TV screens and phone calls between campaign chair Don Evans and strategist Karl Rove, "we didn't know shit," as one intimate put it. "Everybody knew the same thing. Nobody knew anything."

At Gore headquarters, the same kind of recalculation was going full blast. Even with Florida off the boards, even with the loss of Tennessee, there was still a way for the vice president to get 270 electoral votes. Ed Rendell was looking at Nevada, a state that Clinton had taken narrowly in 1992 and 1996. Jack Quinn thought the entire election might come down to the one electoral vote in Maine's Second Congressional District that had not yet been called.

In Nashville, Senator Lieberman had been cautious even when he believed he and Gore had won Florida. In a talk he telephoned to supporters in a Nashville ballroom that evening, he was tentative in his remarks: "*If* these returns hold up . . ."

"But it wasn't in my mind that Florida could be called back," he recalled, "so when it happened, when I saw it happen on TV, I was really stunned."

On our air, even now, Karl Rove was once again embracing the theme of "inevitability," projecting high confidence that Bush would soon emerge as the clear winner.

There are, he said, "a number of states which are going to fall into the Bush column, and which already have fallen on other networks: Wisconsin, Arkansas, Iowa, Nevada, Oregon, Arizona, Alaska, Colorado. These are all states that we feel comfortable with, and there are ninety-eight electoral votes there. . . . we're going to take Wisconsin and Iowa for certain, and Arkansas as well." (In fact, *no* network had called Wisconsin or Iowa for Bush—Gore wound up winning them both, as well as Oregon.) He was even upbeat about California.

"Don't be too premature about California," said Rove, citing Republican governors who'd won once the absentee ballots were counted. "We just may surprise you on the other coast, just as we surprised you in Florida."

The possibility of that surprise was over as soon as the West Coast polls closed at 11 P.M. Eastern time. But the sense of absolute uncertainty stayed. At least eight states remained too close to call. Depending on how they broke, either Gore or Bush could win. In fact, if the states broke just the right way, Gore and Bush would wind up *tied*—with 269 electoral votes apiece, one short of a majority. And it was at this point that I began to think that before the night was over, we would wind up somewhere around the Asteroid Belt.

Remember those political fantasies I mentioned? You know: What if a presidential election winds up in the House of Representatives, and the House is deadlocked? What happens if a vice president decides to remove the president by getting a majority of the cabinet to declare the president is no longer competent, under the terms of the Twenty-fifth Amendment? And what if a president was to win in the Electoral College, but lose the popular vote?

Academics have filled the pages of legal and political-science journals mining these Constitutional veins, as have purveyors of commercial fiction. Irving Wallace's *The Man* killed off the president and Speaker (the vice presidency was vacant) leaving the president pro tempore of the Senate as president. William Safire's *Full Disclosure* used the Twenty-fifth Amendment scenario. My own effort, *The People's Choice*, killed off the newly elected president, thus triggering a revolt among the electors; and there's a kitchen in the northwest corner of Connecticut that owes its existence to Hollywood's attempt to turn that work into *One Woman's Search for Self-Fulfillment Set Against the Compelling Backdrop of a Constitutional Crisis.*

But not this time. Now it was getting near the witching hour, and some deity with a malevolent sense of humor seemed to be busily at work, shuffling the possibilities by the moment. At one point, I glanced back at the bank of monitors and saw NBC's Tim Russert frantically scribbling on a Magic Marker board. Only later did I learn he was listing the combination of states that would give Bush or Gore the White House—or give us a tie. On our air, at about 11:30 P.M., we were already asking Senate Majority Leader Trent Lott about reforming or abolishing the Electoral College.

("Our forefathers did a pretty good job," Lott said. "And while I have difficulty explaining to my own wife why you would win the popular vote but lose the Electoral College, and how that wouldn't be fair, I think the system still works pretty well.")

And everywhere, we were wondering how long it would take to learn the outcome. In Oregon, everyone had already voted by mail; surely they'd be reporting the complete results soon. Hal Bruno, longtime ABC political director, now analyzing returns for CNN, recalled an election in Washington State in which it had taken the canvassing board three days to figure out who'd won a congressional seat. And every time another state fell, no matter how tiny, we went back to our computers, calculators, or pencil stubs and scraps of paper. Nevada fell for Bush; that one remaining Maine elector fell for Gore. *So if Gore wins Florida, but Bush wins in Washington and Oregon, we've got our tie! But what if New Mexico, which we've called for Gore, winds up flipping to Bush? And if it is an electoral tie, would any of the electors be persuaded to vote for the candidate who'd won the popular vote? And if not, somebody start figuring out how the House of Representatives would go in January—when* each state *would have* one vote, *and a candidate would need an* absolute majority *of the states to prevail—but wait a second, we're not going to know how the House will line up until all of* tonight's *races are settled.*

And then, a few minutes after midnight, Arkansas was called for Bush—Al Gore had not only lost his home state of Tennessee; he had lost President Clinton's home state as well. This was another state that Democratic Chair Ed Rendell thought Clinton could have saved with a late burst of campaigning. But it was also a state where Clinton's job-approval rating was *below* his national average, and where more than 60 percent of voters disapproved of him as a person.

The loss of Arkansas was more than some symbolic rejection of the president. As John King reported almost immediately, there was "this mathematical fact: Unless he wins the state of Florida, if our projections hold up, Al Gore cannot win the White House. Now, we're told he's being told by Chairman Daley and others that they believe Florida can turn around. Governor Bush still leads right now; but they're saying the remaining precincts out are largely Democratic precincts, but that could be wishful thinking there on the Gore campaign's part."

No sooner had King finished his report than Woodruff reported that "we are calling the state of Washington for Al Gore and its eleven votes." Back we go to the numbers. Bush has 246 electoral votes; Gore has 242; and Oregon, Wisconsin, Iowa, and Florida are still out. If Bush wins Florida, he wins. If Gore wins Florida, he still needs one of the other three states to put him over. Then it begins to dawn on us in these last hours before dawn: There is simply *no way* Al Gore is going to lose *all* those three remaining "Dukakis" states. In other words, Florida is going to be the deciding state for both of these candidates. The state where both candidates had put so much time and money, the state that had been prematurely called for Gore more than four hours ago, held the White House in its hands. Thank God this time we were not relying on exit polls. Oh no; *this time,* we were relying on real live tabulated votes, county by county.

And so, having survived that first glancing blow, the *Titanic* headed straight for the iceberg again.

● It is a little after two o'clock in the morning on the East Coast. In an office in the World Trade Center, Voter News Service is gathering the numbers and entering them into its system. In other offices and newsrooms, the men and women who staff the networks' decision desks are staring at their computers—all of which display exactly the same screen. It shows the raw, tabulated vote from Florida; but it shows much more. It shows what percent of the precincts are yet to be counted; it displays estimates of how well the candidates will do in those regions; it shows what percent of the remaining vote the trailing candidate will need if he is to overcome his deficit. At some point, a "call" becomes a near certainty. Say, for instance, George W. Bush is fifty thousand votes ahead, and there are only sixty thousand votes left to be counted. Suppose those remaining votes come from a region where Gore can expect two-thirds of the vote. That would give him a net gain of twenty thousand votes—far short of what he'd need. At that point, a first-week intern could be trusted to call the state for Bush.

What could possibly go wrong?

Well, let us count the ways.

First, suppose George W. Bush isn't really fifty thousand votes ahead at all. Maybe somebody made the wrong keystroke.

Suppose a computer glitch subtracted votes instead of adding them. Suppose another computer added votes that were never cast.

Second, suppose there are a lot more votes remaining to be counted than the computer has listed. Suppose a populous county simply didn't get around to counting up its absentee ballots until very late in the evening.

Third, suppose this snafu has thrown the estimates of the vote split way off the mark; suppose Al Gore isn't going to pick up a net of twenty thousand votes, but maybe double or triple that amount.

If any one of these "supposes" turns out to be reality, then even the smartest election-data analysts will get it wrong. As it happened, *all* these "supposes" happened. And, since every member of every one of the "decision teams" at the networks was looking at exactly the same screen, every one of them made the same call. And why were they all looking at the same numbers? Because of a last-minute computer glitch that deprived the networks of a backup mechanism that might have prevented the call for Bush—and might, conceivably, have changed history. Months before Election Night, Tom Hannon recalls, the networks had asked VNS to include the raw vote totals gathered by the Associated Press in its state-by-state displays. That way, the analysts would have a separate source of information. But a late glitch in VNS's computers had developed, and there were no built-in AP tallies. Did anyone, at any network, think to punch up those totals from Florida at 1 A.M., as it became clear that Florida was going to decide the presidency? No. Why not? Good question.

So we vamped through the hour between 1 and 2 A.M., without a clue as to when we would learn the outcome, secure in the knowledge that we would be dealing with real votes. We turned to some of the other remarkable news of the night: The First Lady of the United States stood onstage at a midtown Manhattan hotel ballroom, accepting victory, managing (it seemed to us) to ignore the presence behind her of the president of the United States. A dead man appeared to be winning a Senate seat in Missouri from John Ashcroft. The Senate now had a very good chance of ending up fifty-fifty; in that case, a Gore-Lieberman victory would kick the Senate over to the Republicans, because the GOP governor of Connecticut would appoint Lieberman's successor. We scoured what numbers we had from Florida, trying to discern some pattern, any clue to the final outcome: big African-American turnout helping Gore, Bush winning the senior vote. In my own eagerness to use Larry King's last panel as a chance to inhale food and visit the rest room, I missed what may have been one of the more prescient comments of the whole night.

King asked Bob Woodward, of the Washington *Post* and Watergate fame, about the impact of the early-evening miscall of Florida.

"You can't tell," Woodward said, "but the difficulty right now is yet another misread. Clearly, there are very few votes that are the difference between victory and defeat here. Absentee ballots floating around . . . so somebody is likely to come out with the 'Dewey Beats Truman' headline and have to take that back."

Indeed.

And so it goes, past 2 A.M., as the VNS count in Florida shows Bush leading by twenty-nine thousand votes, with 96 percent of the vote in—but with some of the strongest Gore counties yet to finish. It is a picture custom-made for restraint—especially when compared with the Associated Press numbers that are showing a steady, sharp drop in Bush's lead.

Nobody looking at those numbers would have thought of making a call. But nobody is looking at those numbers. Instead, everyone is watching the VNS count—where a few minutes later, Volusia County's votes are tabulated, and Bush's lead suddenly jumps to more than fifty thousand. And *now* the experts, all of them, know that it is starting to look as if Bush has Florida just about wrapped up. With 97 percent of the precincts in, and with about one hundred eighty thousand votes left to be counted, Gore would have to win some 63 percent of the remaining votes—an almost impossible task, according to past voting patterns.

There are only two small problems with the conclusions: First, Bush does *not* have a fifty-thousand-vote lead; second, there are closer to four hundred thousand votes yet to be counted from heavily Democratic areas.

How did that fifty-thousand-vote spread suddenly appear? Thanks to a faulty computer memory card, a single precinct in Volusia County—Precinct 216—has actually *subtracted* sixteen thousand votes from Gore, and at the same time has incorrectly added votes to Bush's total. Further, a reporting error from Brevard County has added another four thousand phantom votes to Bush's total. Without those mistakes, VNS would not have estimated a final Bush plurality of thirty thousand votes statewide. But here again, simple human nature has reared its ugly head. Authorities in Volusia County had strung up yellow crime-scene tape around the election unit offices, in an effort to keep out interlopers. The local stringer for Voter News Service saw the tape, and concluded that the information lid was on. It was late; she was tired; she went home.

The local AP stringer made a different decision. He gained access to headquarters, and quickly learned that the local officials had discovered their error. He flashed the real numbers to AP, which reported the correct numbers at 2:18 A.M. By then, Fox, NBC, CBS, and CNN had all called Florida, and the presidency, for Bush. It was a scenario right out of one of those death-row dramas, where the hot line from the governor's office to the prison rings just as the warden is throwing the switch. Of course, in the movies, the call always comes just in time.

● So at 2:18 A.M., while CNN was in a commercial break, Tom Hannon alerted the four of us at the anchor desk: "We are going to call Florida, and the presidency, for Bush." And so, a moment later, Bernard Shaw announced: "George Bush, governor of Texas, will become the forty-third president of the United States."

It would be a fine thing if I could report to you that my colleagues and I feverishly objected, urged that we hold back until we were absolutely sure, or at least cautioned our viewers that this call was an estimate, that it was our best guess about the probable outcome. But it's been a long time since we've talked that way; and besides, our job was now to flesh out the story, to put it in context, to dazzle the viewers with insights about the next president and how he won this incredibly close election.

Caution? That's not the message we're sending out to the viewer. We are airing a splendid graphic, featuring a heroic picture of Bush and the words: "Bush Wins Presidency." This was no time for second-guessing; besides, we were in no position to second-guess anything. Did we have the VNS screens in front of us? Were we looking at the actual tabulated vote, as reported by AP, or the Florida secretary of state's Web site? Of course not. So we press on.

So we speak of Bush, only the second son of a president to win the White House; we speak of how close the Electoral vote is likely to be, how it is not impossible that Gore might actually overtake Bush in the popular vote. I whip out that dramatic contrast of the rivals on their respective fortieth birthdays that I'd prepared all those hours ago: Gore, the United States senator with a credible run for the presidency behind him; Bush, the failed businessman with an uncertain future and a drinking problem, whose first real success came as the owner of a baseball team. From her perch outside the state capitol in Austin, Texas, where she has been standing, barely protected, under an increasingly hard rain, Candy Crowley recalls Governor Bush's warning to his brother Jeb that if Florida goes Democratic, " 'that Thanksgiving turkey is going to be pretty cold.' So Thanksgiving dinner, apparently, is safe now for Jeb Bush."

From his perch outside Nashville's War Memorial auditorium, John King has already begun detailing the outlines of the early recriminations:

"Within the Gore campaign, already that he was hurt on the left from Ralph Nader, and on the right, if you will, among conservative Democrats, conservative elderly voters, by Bill Clinton's character problem—others already questioning the Gore campaign strategy. . . . We will hear from the vice president, we're told, in about fifteen minutes."

In the camps of the candidates, there is no reason to doubt the network calls. In the Four Seasons Hotel in Austin, the close friends and relatives of Bush explode out of every room, into the hall, embracing one another. In the Loew's Vanderbilt

Plaza Hotel in Nashville, Tennessee, Elaine Kamarck, who has fallen asleep, has somehow awakened at the precise moment CNN calls the race for Bush. A few moments later, her phone rings; one of Gore's close aides, in tears, is telling her that the vice president is calling Bush to concede, that he will soon make his way to the War Memorial, bedecked with huge hanging American flags, to congratulate the new president. It won't be long now.

In fact, at this defining moment in the majestic pageantry that is our national election process, forged in Valley Forge and Yorktown, in the miracle at Philadelphia's Constitution Hall, in these first moments of the Age of Bush the Second, and all that portends for our future, I am held by one single thought: *If Al Gore concedes by 3 A.M., and Bush claims victory by 3:30, and if my car is still waiting for me outside the CNN center, then I can get back to the hotel, pack up everything, get out to the airport, catch the 6:30 A.M. flight to New York, crash for an hour or so, and meet my friends for our traditional Wednesday lunch.*

Call it shallow, if you will, but at that very moment, there were several hundred reporters, producers, camera operators, sound technicians, and political operatives of every stripe thinking roughly the same way. It is an exciting, exhilarating way of life, the business of covering campaigns, but next to a war, there is nothing like it for ripping you away from any semblance of a normal life. Listen in on the cell-phone conversations on a press bus, and you will hear countless snatches of family ties frayed by time and distance: *I'm so sorry I missed the play, I'll bet you were great, I'll watch the video as soon as I get home. . . . What's his temperature now? Did you give him the Tylenol? Dr. Kramer's number is right there on the fridge. . . . Really, two merit badges? I'm really proud of . . . what? . . . I'm losing you, I'll call tonight, no, make it first thing in the morn-*

ing. And for everyone caught up in the life, Election Day is the finish line, the promise of shared meals, clean laundry, and the chance to exhale. Days later, I remembered a piece of newsreel footage from my childhood: a marathon runner, entering the stadium far, far ahead of his rivals, needing only to circle the track for his victory. But he is exhausted, drained of all but the last ounce of energy. He falls; the crowd rises, cheering him on; he staggers to his feet, his legs wobbly, his body slack; he hobbles a few more steps, and falls again; slowly gets upright, and half walks, half runs some more, weaving back and forth across the track, until, with one final, heroic effort, he falls across the finish line.

It is the wrong finish line.

● Shortly before 3 A.M., as we speculate on the makeup of Bush's cabinet, and the potential Democratic candidates for 2004—Gore? Lieberman? Kerry? Kerrey? Gephardt? Daschle? Edwards?—VNS finally gets the correct Volusia County totals into its calculations. Unsurprisingly, Bush's lead suddenly drops by some sixteen thousand votes. At about this time, someone in Warren Mitofsky's operation checks out the AP wire; according to the news service, Bush's margin continues to drop with gravitational force. Tom Hannon remembers hearing a disembodied voice on the open phone link say: "We better check the [Florida secretary of state's] Web site." And somewhere after 3 A.M., a conference call takes place among VNS and all the major subscribing news organizations.

"If you could have eavesdropped on Hell," Tom Hannon says, "that's what it would have sounded like: fear, anguish, everybody desperately trying to find out. People are yelling,

'Can you guys tell us what the hell is going on?' And they couldn't. It was like . . . you know the woodcut? Munch? *The Scream*. That's what it was like."

For those of us on the air, time seemed to be slowing down. John King had reported at 3 A.M. that Gore had called the governor, and was now in his motorcade on the way to acknowledge defeat. Candy Crowley had reported that Bush had told Gore: "We gave them a cliff-hanger." King went on the air before 3:30 A.M. to report that the motorcade had arrived at the auditorium. The national vote totals were now almost exactly even, and it was becoming more and more likely that Gore would become the first man in more than one hundred years to lose the White House while winning the popular vote. And it was then that Judy Woodruff called up the vote totals from the state of Florida, and noted that, with 99 percent of the votes in, Bush was ahead by 11,000 votes out of 5.6 million cast.

"John King," Bernard Shaw said, "you're standing by in Nashville. Any talk there among the Gore people about a possible recount anywhere, especially given what we've talked about, eleven thousand votes?"

"We have to assume no, Bernie," King said. ". . . if the vice president were actively planning to challenge the results, we assume he would say nothing tonight, or at least say that he was not prepared to concede defeat."

A fair assumption—except that at this moment, at least two players in the Gore campaign were desperately trying to keep the vice president from conceding. Bob Butterworth, Florida attorney general, knew that under state law, any margin of less than one-half of 1 percent automatically triggers a recount—and based on the way the votes were coming in, the final margin was likely to be somewhere around one thousand votes out of six million cast—a margin of about two-hundredths of 1 percent of the vote. Michael Whouley, a veteran Boston operative who had organized the turnout effort for Gore, watched the numbers drop and urgently paged officials, until the message worked up the chain of command to William Daley, and then the candidate: *Whatever you do, do not get on the podium and concede.*

Meanwhile, we waited . . . and waited. We picked apart the Gore campaign decisions: Should he have called on Clinton for more help? Did the debates turn it around? And then, about 3:30 A.M., came the first hints that we had another surprise waiting for us. From Nashville, John King reported that "CNN is double-checking the vote count . . . to make sure the vote is accurate . . . We've been trying to reach [Gore's] senior aides to find out the reason for the delay, but we've been unsuccessful in doing so."

A moment later, King was back—reporting that the Bush margin in Florida was now about six hundred votes, that an automatic recount was certain, and that "what the vice president is working on now is exactly what to say." At almost the same moment, Candy Crowley's producer in Austin got a call on his cell phone from Bush's communications director, Karen Hughes. He listened, handed the phone to Crowley, and said, "You'd better listen to this."

I just thought you should know, Hughes said, *that the vice president has just called the governor, and has retracted his concession.*

Say that again, Crowley said. After twelve hours of cold and rain and sleeplessness, she literally did not trust herself to have heard what she had heard.

Hughes said it again. Crowley immediately told Atlanta to put her on the air.

"Judy," Crowley said simply, "something to report to you

here on this very unusual night. The vice president has re-called the governor, and has retracted his concession, saying Florida is too close right now."

And Judy said: "Whoaa."

And I thought: *I don't think I'll be catching that 6:30 A.M. flight to New York.*

We didn't leave the air until almost two hours later, after Gore chairman Daley had told the revived crowd in Nashville, "Our campaign continues," and until after Bush chairman Don Evans told the stunned crowd in Austin, "They're still count-ing. And I'm confident that when it's all said and done, we will prevail." At CNN, we were privileged to air the single most bizarre moment of the night—at 4:30 A.M., actually—when actor-director Rob Reiner, a hard-core Gore backer, joined John King at his perch.

"Why are you here?" King asked. "You have a comfortable life, you could be home watching this on television."

"Well, you know," Reiner said, "I'm quite attracted to you, John, and that's why I'm here . . . we've had two close moments tonight, so anything can happen. Even an important relation-ship between you and me could happen."

"Hate to disappoint you," King deadpanned, "but I'm going to rule that out."

It was a badly needed moment of levity. What we faced was a lot less humorous: We were now in the middle of the weird-est political story of our lifetimes, when the machinery of our political system was about to be put to a test it had not faced in nearly 125 years. Moreover, we already knew that the media's machinery for reporting this race had been tested and had failed . . . not once, but twice in the same evening. I'd been at this for twenty years. And over those twenty years, I'd felt absolute exhilaration, absolute embarrassment, and absolute exhaustion. I'd just never felt all of it at exactly the same time.

And so, shortly before six o'clock in the morning, thirteen hours after we began, we left the anchor desk. My parting remarks were a product of that exhilaration, embarrassment, and exhaustion.

"Folks," I said, "in the year 2004, please could you make up your minds a little more conclusively, because I think we can't take another election like this one." Had I known we'd still be at it more than a month later, I'm not sure that my words would have been fit for public consumption—even on cable.

CHAPTER 4

"And You May Ask

Yourself—Well . . .

How Did We Get

Here?"

● **NOBODY KNEW THE**

color of the sky—in fact, at
least one of the players didn't
even know where he was.

When Jack Quinn awoke
after two and a half hours of
sleep on Wednesday morn-
ing, he turned on the TV in
his Nashville hotel room to
find out if anything had been
resolved, and heard a news
report that he was on his way

to Florida along with Gore aide Ron Klain and former Secretary of State Warren Christopher. He was so groggy, so rocked by what had happened Tuesday night, that he walked over to the window and pushed back the curtains—just to make sure he hadn't gotten himself down to Florida in the predawn hours. Then he looked back at the TV to see a picture of Jack Quinn on the screen: not Jack Quinn, onetime chief of staff to Vice President Gore, but Jack Quinn, the Republican Congressman from upstate New York. Quinn the Democrat flew back to Washington.

When Ed Gillespie, the longtime Republican operative and lobbying partner of Quinn's, awoke, he began to pack his bags for his trip to Washington; he'd been away from his home and his three small children for three months, working at Bush campaign headquarters in Austin. He'd planned to spend Wednesday cleaning out his stuff from the office he'd borrowed from Communications Chief Karen Hughes, then head home on Thursday. By the end of the day, Gillespie was heading down to Palm Beach.

For operatives like Quinn and Gillespie, the question was where they should be going. For hundreds, thousands of others, the question was more cosmic: What were they going to be doing with the next four years of their lives?

- Colin Powell, arguably the most admired public figure in the United States, woke up on Election Day wondering whether he would be the next secretary of state or a prominent private citizen still bearing the mantle of "presidential possibility." He woke up the next day with the same question.
- Jack Desmond, a lawyer in his late fifties, was what people meant when they spoke of "the best and the

brightest," without the irony inherent in David Hal-
berstam's title. Desmond was first in his class at a
top-ranked law school; clerked for a Supreme Court
justice; served in the Carter White House; enjoyed
a stellar (if involuntary) career as a lawyer during the
Reagan and Bush years; then served in the higher
councils of the Clinton administration. When he
woke up on Election Day, Desmond did not know
whether he would be heading back to the private
sector, or beginning his own campaign for a "flag
rank" subcabinet position under President Gore. He
still didn't know.

- Drew Crocket was a twenty-four-year-old assistant in
  the Chairman's Office of the Republican National
  Committee. Politics had been in his blood all his
  young life. He worked in two congressional races, a
  lieutenant governor's race, and then for the RNC for
  free, until becoming gainfully employed earlier in
  the year. When he went to bed in the early hours of
  Wednesday morning, Bush had been declared the
  winner; and somewhere in the second Bush administration, Drew knew, there was a job waiting for him
  beyond answering the phones and fielding comments from Republicans around the country. Then
  he awoke a few hours later, wondering if he had
  dreamed the accounts that Bush had won.

- Samuel Lane was a recent college graduate who
  worked for a Democratic congressman. He was another one of the legion of the politically obsessed:
  Lacking cable, he spent every Sunday listening to
  four hours of the Washington talk shows on C-SPAN
  radio. He spent Election Night at the Mayflower

Hotel at a party sponsored by the Democratic Senatorial and Congressional Campaign Committees. He remembered the cheers and shouts of "we win!" when the networks called Florida for Gore; the tears and anger and smashed glasses when the networks took it back. He was at home when Bush was declared the winner, and when that call was taken back. He had his résumé ready to send to the transition office. On Wednesday, he went back to work; it was, he says, almost as if he and every staff member he ran into, Republican and Democrat, were moving around in a trance. ("Do you believe it? Do you believe it?" was the phrase of the moment.)

• And one network talking head woke up around noon in an Atlanta hotel room, turned on the news, heard about planeloads of lawyers flying down to Florida, and saw the next glorious days of his life disappear: that speech in Palm Springs, that week in Santa Barbara, that beach in the Caribbean, all on hold—it could be, I thought, a whole week before we had a final conclusion to this race. Only when I called home to say I'd be another day in Atlanta did my Highly Significant Other remind me of something I'd said to her just before I left New York for CNN headquarters.

"I almost hate to mention this," I'd said, "but there's this tiny, remote chance that we might actually not know who's won by Tuesday night."

Remembering this in the light of what happened sounds improbable at best, like a line from one of those British period dramas of long ago:

"Anything in the news, Lord Faversham?"

"No, no . . . just some obscure archduke in Sarajevo shot by some malcontent. Tennis, anyone?"

Nevertheless, that still small voice inside me must have picked up something in the air, to raise ever so tentatively the possibility of a postelection train wreck. What was it? It was a sense that this was unlike any election I'd ever seen, an election that conformed to *none* of the rhythms of any other race. For anyone covering elections for a living, this was maddening beyond belief, for if there's one thing we know, it's that presidential elections are a twist on that familiar *Sesame Street* ditty—one of these things is just like the others. Call it an occupational twitch, but operatives and journalists alike spend an unhealthy amount of our time trying to see what template defines every election.

For instance, Bush strategist Karl Rove spent the better part of two years arguing that this election year would resemble 1896. Back then, the nation was in the midst of transforming itself from an agricultural to an industrial economy; while William Jennings Bryan was championing the glories of the sacred family farm, William McKinley was proclaiming the virtues of the new industrial era, and he prevailed in a landslide. (Rove usually did not point out that, under the tutelage of political boss Mark Hanna, McKinley's campaign outraised Bryan's by a margin of about forty to one. The Bush campaign's record fund-raising demonstrated that this particular lesson of McKinley was not lost on them.)

If 1896 was too obscure, Republicans would cite 1992 as a reference point. That's when a fresh voice from outside Washington, unfettered by the vulnerabilities of the congressional wing of his party, unseated the far more experienced Washington hand who was simply unable to connect with the body politic. Thus, Al Gore as George H. W. Bush (1992 model), and George W. Bush as . . . Bill Clinton.

For their part, Gore partisans liked the model of 1988. A charismatically challenged vice president, serving eight years in the giant shadow of the incumbent president, defeats the outsider by portraying himself as a serious, qualified leader, while portraying his opponent as unqualified to hold the reins of the presidency, views that placed him outside the mainstream of American thought. Thus, Al Gore as George H. W. Bush (1988 model), and George W. Bush as . . . Michael Dukakis.

Neutral observers pointed to 1960, when a charismatically challenged vice president, serving eight years in the giant shadow of the incumbent president, battled a less experienced, more personally appealing challenger in a contest that ended in a virtual tie. Thus, Al Gore as Richard Nixon, and George W. Bush as . . . John F. Kennedy.

For me, the problem was that, depending on what day of the week it was, the campaign kept changing shape. Sometimes, it looked like all those campaigns smushed together; at other times, it looked like none of the above. It was Winston Churchill's pudding that had no theme; it was Gertrude Stein's Oakland—there was no "there" there. It was Bill Schneider's months-old mantra: The country believed, at one and the same time, that they'd never had it so good *and* it was time for a change. And no single event in the campaign ever brought a decisive plurality of the voters to one side or the other. If you believed the polls, they told a different story—Bush with a huge lead from March through August; Gore surging to the front in the wake of the Democratic convention; Bush taking the lead after the fall debates; Gore keeping it close until the end. But if you believed that the polls were actually measuring the real intentions of the voters, I've got a Votomatic machine I'd like to sell you. Here's a different take: The voters were so disconnected from national politics that the poll numbers might as well have been written on sand, for all that they reflected any strong set of convictions about the electorate. Even the tumult of the primary campaigns was a case of surface excitement concealing pedestrian reality. So, with "history on hold," as the brilliant headline in the Austin *American-Statesman* put it the day after the election, pause while this talking head tries to answer the question posed by the original Talking Heads: Ask yourself—well . . . how did we get here?

● Consider first the Democrats. By the fall of 1999, former Senator Bill Bradley seemed perfectly positioned to offer a serious challenge to Vice President Gore. He had raised more money than the vice president—a shocking break with the traditional insider-outsider pattern. He'd forced Gore to abandon his pricey headquarters on Washington's K Street, where lobbyists dwell, and relocate to Nashville, Tennessee—jettisoning some of his most loyal supporters in the process. Polls showed Bradley leading in New Hampshire and New York, and competitive in California. And then the campaign began, and it was over before it had begun. The money raising and the preprimary polling—slightly less reliable than the horoscopes in your favorite monthly magazine—gave surface credibility to the premises of the campaign.

Bradley was blunt and concise that fall when he met with senior executives of Time-Warner for a lengthy question-and-answer session. He also displayed a playful sense of humor. When asked how he would deal with criticism that he was insufficiently exciting, he stood up, took off his jacket, and feigned an intent to disrobe. Later, when he joined a small group for dinner, someone asked him to put aside the noble substance for a moment and explain how he intended to win the nomination from Gore.

Stay competitive in Iowa, he began. Come close in New Hampshire. Five weeks later, on Super Tuesday, win in New York and California, and maybe another state or two. Then hunker down for a protracted campaign that will go on all spring, ending in his adopted home state of New Jersey. And what about Gore's huge advantage in endorsements, all those senators and representatives and governors? *We understand that,* his campaign chairman said. *But once we demonstrate Gore's vulnerability, they'll fall away—just as they did with Ed Muskie in '72 when he failed to clinch early.*

It was a reasonably plausible strategy, undercut by three implacable facts:

•First, incumbent vice presidents who want their party's nomination get it, barring some highly unusual conditions: for instance, Spiro Agnew's nolo contendere plea to a charge of criminal bribe taking and tax evasion, which was a bad career move. They do so because they have built up enormous chits among the party's base, and because (in almost every case) they inherit the loyalty the party feels for the incumbent president. Bradley's fate may well have been sealed on October 13, 1999, when the AFL-CIO, at the personal behest of its president, John Sweeney, formally endorsed Gore for the Democratic nomination. At the least, this early endorsement by the one Democratic constituency with massive amounts of money and manpower tilted the playing field sharply;

•*Second,* Bradley could never figure out how to present his most powerful selling point to Democratic voters: that he represented a clean break with the liabilities of Bill Clinton. One reason why intraparty insurgency campaigns almost never work is that they so often demand that primary voters turn away from the most prominent member of their party in order to save it. Insurgencies can work when there is no leading figure in the party; that's why Goldwater won the nomination in '64. They can flourish when a party is divided by a great cause, and new voters suddenly show up at the polls (Goldwater in '64; McCarthy and Robert Kennedy in '68.) Under most circumstances, though, even a weak incumbent or semi-incumbent has enough claim on the party's heart to turn away an insurgent; that's why Ronald Reagan just failed to unseat the unelected President Ford in '76, and why Gary Hart ultimately failed against ex–vice president Walter Mondale in '84.

This time, the Bradley campaign believed that it could not attack President Clinton frontally for his personal misbehavior—not with his astronomical approval ratings among Democrats, particularly core Democratic voters. (In January of 2000, Clinton had an 89-percent approval rating among Democrats.) Bradley was thus reduced to making a different case: first, that he was the candidate of "reform," committed to cleaning up a corrupt political process symbolized by Al "No Controlling Legal Authority" Gore and his fund-raising excesses from the 1996 campaign; second, that he would meet the needs of the dispossessed whom the present Democratic administration had failed. The reform message, as we shall see in a few moments, was severely undercut by the emergence of John McCain in New Hampshire. The substantive message meant that Bradley had to run at Gore from the Left: exactly the position that Clinton had led Democrats away from eight years earlier. It's hard to summarize just how wrongheaded this decision was. It forced Bradley into offering a massive health-care plan that left him wide-open to the charge from Gore that Bradley would simultaneously bankrupt the budget *and* fail to cover adequately the uninsured *and* destroy the Medicaid system. At the same time, it won Bradley no support from Democrats who might seem most likely to respond to such appeals. Labor was with Gore from the start; black Democrats overwhelmingly transferred their affection for Clinton to his designated heir; environmentalists were split at best. Finally, a Bradley campaign defined by a "no-enemies-to-the-Left" strategy was completely alien to Bradley's eighteen-year career in the Senate, when he had won unusual respect across the political spectrum for his independent streak.

His tax-reform package in 1986 combined lower marginal rates with significant closing of tax loopholes, making the system simpler and fairer, and winning the enmity of Donald Trump—both achievements of which any politician might be proud. He'd been one of the first Democrats, along with Massachusetts' Paul Tsongas, to urge the party to stop its ritual business-bashing and try to find common ground with the financial community on matters such as the environment. His speeches on race reflected his years as a pro basketball player, where it was said of him (as it was of Jack Kemp) "He's showered with more blacks than most white folks know." Perhaps because of that familiarity, he was able to speak some hard truths about race: acknowledging not just black distrust of white institutions, but white fears of black lawlessness. He had on one occasion even voted for aid to the Nicaraguan "Contras"—the only nonsouthern Democrat to do so—because he believed, under the circumstances, it would help bring the

Sandinista government to the peace table. It was a vote clearly based on conviction, given that it could not conceivably do Bradley any good in a future presidential run. Yet now, he was running as much against his own record as against Vice President Gore.

•*Third,* Bradley never really answered the bell. He believed he could run and wage a successful presidential campaign without genuinely engaging his opponent. It was a belief powered by his deep conviction that the political process had become ignoble, trivial, dominated by an attack-dog sensibility that repulsed him. It was what he meant when he announced he was retiring from the Senate in 1996, proclaiming that "politics is broken," and entertaining speculation that he might be thinking about an independent run for the presidency that year. Shortly after he left the Senate, we sat down for coffee at a sidewalk café on Manhattan's Upper West Side, and we had a conversation that was close to an interior monologue. *Could you run a presidential campaign that was different, really different? Did you have to run a campaign based on sound bites and thirty-second commercials and all the trappings of politics as usual? Couldn't the campaign itself demonstrate the kind of president you intended to be?* So committed was Bradley to changing the rules of the game that he proposed a Constitutional amendment to the First Amendment itself that would nullify a Supreme Court decision permitting wealthy candidates to spend unlimited amounts of money on their own campaigns.

When the primary campaign began in earnest, however, Bradley's determination to run a different kind of campaign turned into something else: a decision not to answer the attacks from the Gore campaign, but to deplore them—hoping an electorate repelled by such politics would turn against the aggressor. For the Bradley campaign, an unwarranted attack by Gore would underscore the idea that Gore had a tendency to bend the facts, as when he seemed to claim credit for creating the Internet. Alas, for Bradley, when it comes to negative campaigning, the public is as maddeningly misleading about its true desires as it is about its alleged taste for high-quality television and nutritious foods. It *says* it has no use at all for attack politics; it votes on a very different basis. And maybe it's not just a matter of hypocrisy, but of an intuitive question that a turn-the-other-cheek politician raises in a voter's mind: *If he won't fight for himself, how can I be sure he'll fight for me?*

Hobbled by this Gandhi-like strategy, the Bradley campaign was either unwilling or unable to use some powerful weapons—weapons that had the potential to raise serious character questions about Gore without confronting directly the looming figure of President Clinton. Early in 2000, two *Boston Globe* reporters, Walter Robinson and Ann Scales, unearthed memos from staff members of Gore's 1988 campaign. One warned him that "your main pitfall is exaggeration." Another said that "[your] image may continue to suffer if you continue to go out on a limb with remarks that may be impossible to back up."

Even for a candidate determined not to throw the first punch, such material would be ideal for a counterpunch. In addition, there was no candidate in recent American politics who would offer an opponent more chances for a counterpunch. Behind the policy-wonk demeanor, Gore was a "take-no-prisoners" campaigner, with a special penchant for springing surprises on an opponent during political debates. In the 1988 primaries, it was Gore who raised the prison furlough issue against Governor Michael Dukakis that appeared that fall as the "Willie Horton" issue (Gore never mentioned Horton's name, nor displayed a picture of the menacing, very black murderer who had raped and terrorized a woman while out on a furlough.) In his 1993 *Larry King Live* debate against Ross Perot on free trade, he'd presented the short-tempered billionaire with a framed photograph of Senator Reed Smoot, co-author of the infamous Smoot-Hawley tariff of 1930. There was every reason to believe Gore would try a similar tactic against Bradley, and those 1988 staff memos were the perfect tool with which to paint the vice president as an attack-dog politician who'd do anything to win. All Bradley needed was the right moment, the instinct for the counterpunch, and the preparation to do it right. On January 8, 2000, that moment came—and went—and with it, any chance that the Bradley campaign might pose a protracted threat to Gore.

It was during a debate sponsored by the Des Moines *Register,* one that focused heavily on Iowa issues, just sixteen days before the Iowa caucuses. Bradley's presence in those caucuses was itself testimony to the questionable strategy of his campaign. Because they take place one week before the first-in-the-nation New Hampshire primary, they attract an enormous amount of media attention, despite the fact that they are, in a fundamental sense, a massive fraud on the body politic. They emerged as a full-blown event in 1976 when long-shot candidate Jimmy Carter used a second-place finish (well behind "uncommitted") to vault into a primary victory in New Hampshire. Four years later, George Bush shocked front-runner Reagan with a narrow victory. Ever since, candidates have felt compelled to contest these caucuses, which require participants to bundle up on a freezing Iowa winter's night and spend hours inside firehouses, school cafeterias, pubic libraries, and living rooms. About 3 percent of eligible Iowa voters attend; and thus presidential candidacies are launched, weakened, or killed by margins that represent the graduating class of a midsize Chicago high school. On the Republican side, Arizona Senator John McCain had chosen to skip the caucuses, aiming his insurgent campaign squarely at New Hampshire. Perhaps because he was a native of neighboring Missouri, Bradley felt he could not do it; and so here he was, standing face-to-face with Gore, when the vice president sprang his trap: he produced a "Skutnick."

A Skutnick is a human prop, used by a speaker to make a political point. The name comes from Lenny Skutnick, a young man who heroically saved lives after the Air Florida plane crash in Washington in 1982, and who was introduced by President Reagan during his State of the Union speech the following year. Presidents have featured Skutnicks at State of the Union speeches ever since; under President Clinton, they have become *tableaux vivants*, living symbols of his anticrime bills, or his crusade for family-leave programs. Now, during this debate, Gore invited Chris Peterson to stand up. Mr. Peterson, Gore explained, was a hardworking Iowa farmer who had been devastated by the great floods that had swept the state in 1993. As a senator, Gore noted with a mixture of shock, sadness, and incredulity, Bradley had *opposed* the administration's flood-relief program.

"Why," Gore asked Bradley, "did you vote against the disaster relief for Chris Peterson when he and thousands of other farmers here in Iowa needed it after those floods?"

Now: As a matter of fact, Bradley, along with a number of Democratic senators, had opposed that particular bill because as originally drafted, it would have threatened the delicate budget negotiations between the two parties. Even a farm-state senator like Nebraska's Bob Kerrey opposed it. A few days later, a new version of the bill was offered, and it passed by a voice vote. So, armed with those facts, and with the warning given to Gore by his prior presidential staff, here is what Bradley *might* have said.

"Mr. Peterson, I am going to answer that question—and when I am finished, I hope the vice president will have the decency to apologize to you for using you in so appalling a manner. The fact is, every one of us in the Senate was determined to get relief to you and your neighbors as quickly as humanly possible. Unfortunately, the administration's first bill would have been a nightmare—it would have endangered the entire budget process. That's why Senator Bob Kerrey of Nebraska—whose own state was in need of immediate relief—couldn't support it. A day later, the bill was rewritten, and it passed unanimously. Now, Mr. Peterson, you're not a politician—you couldn't possibly know these details. But the vice president surely does—and yet, he persuaded you to stand up here, so he could use you for his political purposes. I hold you blameless, sir—but Mr. Gore, you I hold morally responsible.*

"You know, Al* [switch to the familiar here], *I know people will discount what I say about your tactics—after all, you're my opponent. So let's see what your paid staff members said about your tactics the last time you ran for president. Your press aide told you in writing that 'your biggest danger is exaggeration.' Your communications director warned you to stop making statements 'for which there was no factual basis.' Now, in the first stage of this campaign, you're at it again—and apparently you are so hungry for office you are prepared to subject this good and decent Iowa farmer to the public spotlight to lend credence to your false charge. I can't believe you are this desperate to win,* *and I strongly suggest you abandon these tactics—so that your staff this year doesn't have to start writing a whole new set of memos about your instinct to play fast and loose with the facts."*

In the days when I worked in politics, we used to call this the "Full Welch." We named the tactic in honor of Joseph Welch, the crusty New England lawyer who effectively ended the career of Wisconsin Senator Joseph McCarthy by quietly excoriating him for blackening the reputation of a young Boston lawyer and asking, "Have you no sense of decency, sir?" It is the perfect device for answering an untrue or misleading charge; its power lies in the swift pivot by which a defensive maneuver becomes a deadly riposte aimed right at an opponent's character. Seldom has a participant in a debate been handed so tempting an opportunity for a Full Welch.

Now: Here is what Bill Bradley *actually* said in answer to the charge that he had callously ignored the needs of this desperate Iowa farmer.

"This is not about the past. This is about the future."

Ummm . . . not quite as effective, is it?

With that, any chance Bradley had of making a decent showing in the Iowa caucuses was gone; and the time and money spent in Iowa may well have been the difference when he narrowly lost the New Hampshire primary a week later. On January 26, Bradley put aside the pacifist tendencies long enough to come up with his single best debate line: "Why should we believe that you will tell the truth as president if you don't tell the truth as a candidate?"

Unfortunately for Bradley, he had his own problem with candor: Less than a week before the primary, he was forced to leave the campaign trail and check into a hospital for treatment of an irregular heartbeat. It was hardly a life-threatening condition, but it was one that Bradley had neglected to reveal when he began his run for the presidency. As a campaign issue, it was three problems in one: 1) voters don't like the idea of a candidate with any kind of "heart" problem; 2) public figures who first gain fame as star athletes aren't supposed to wind up in a hospital in the middle of the biggest fight of their lives; 3) a candidate who runs on issues like "trust" shouldn't leave this part of his medical history blank—even if, as Bradley claimed later, it was all a matter of excessive caffeine, too much cream soda.

There are those who worked for Bradley who believe this was the turning point of their entire campaign. Absent the hospitalization, campaign chair Doug Berman would later argue, Bradley would have won the New Hampshire primary; he would then have had five weeks before the next critical Democratic tests, those sixteen Super Tuesday primaries and caucuses, to ride that victory into New York and California, and force a weakened Gore into that protracted months-long battle that had been the Bradley strategy all along.

Maybe that would have happened; maybe the massive manpower advantage that the Gore campaign had in states like California, Ohio, and New York would have made New Hampshire a distant memory by Super Tuesday. In any event, Bradley's loss, combined with John McCain's landslide win in New Hampshire, took all the air out of the Democratic fight. Thanks to the vagaries of the primary calendar, the Republicans would have a half-dozen battles or more before the Democrats clashed again. Those battles were where all the energy, all the action, was. In the theater that is presidential politics, the Democrats had suddenly become the lounge act, the sideshow, the street band outside the arena where the rock concert of the year was going on.

The most poignant moment of the entire campaign was

captured in a photograph that appeared in late February; in a desperate effort to attract some attention, Bradley had declared the Washington State caucuses a major battleground. On the morning of February 28, he took the Seattle Bainbridge Island commuter ferry across Puget Sound. He stood, hunched over, clad in a raincoat, holding a cup of coffee, hair askew, looking remarkably like a panhandler hustling for small change. What was so telling was that so many newspapers and TV newscasts chose to use that picture; it was the perfect symbol of a campaign nearing the end of its rope. Had Bradley been leading in the polls, had he in fact won New Hampshire and been breathing down Al Gore's neck, there is no way on God's green earth that such a picture would have gotten such widespread attention.

It was also another demonstration of one of the crueler aspects of presidential politics: how thoroughly dismissal comes, after a lifetime during which success and adulation have seemed as much a part of life as air and water. Bill Bradley was the subject of a full-blown biography while he was still in college; he was being touted as a future president before he was old enough to vote. He led his Princeton basketball team to an improbable appearance in the NCAA Final Four, where his 29-point performance against Michigan remains one of the signature moments in college basketball. He won a Rhodes Scholarship, an Olympic gold medal, became a key player on the only New York Knicks championship teams. He was a United States senator, being touted as a future president—this time for real—before he was old enough to be eligible for the job. Now he was the subject of scorn and condescension, because he had committed the one unforgivable sin in American political life: He had lost, badly.

And what if he had run a different campaign? What if everything had broken his way, if he had been honed for a fight, sharper with his message, consistent with the Bill Bradley of his Senate days? Could he have prevailed in an insurgency against the heir to the most popular incumbent Democratic President since FDR? There is a clue in what happened to the other insurgent, who provided the most compelling story of the entire campaign—and a story that ultimately rested on illusion.

● Look now at the Republican battle. It is Wednesday morning, January 26, six days before the New Hampshire primary, and outside the Crowne Plaza hotel in Nashua, New Hampshire, the converted van is packed with reporters and campaign aides, and if there is a particular gleam in our eyes, there is good reason: This is the E-Ride of the Year, the hottest ticket in town, the laminate with "ALL ACCESS" in big, bold letters across it. This is the Straight Talk Express, John McCain's Wild Ride, and he is the man in The Zone.

Every so often in the course of a New Hampshire primary campaign, a candidate hits The Zone. It's not a matter of polls or fund-raising, but some kind of much more elemental connection between a candidate, his audiences, and the times; something you can sense the way people who live close to the land know when a storm is brewing in the middle of a sunny day. The candidate's words are just right; the crowds come alive in a way that never happens with the crowds that have been assembled by teams of advance men, whose cheers always have a tinny, mechanical sound. The word goes through the political hive as if by drum—*this is where it's happening, he's the real deal, they were expecting two hundred in Concord last night, eight hundred showed up, they had to open up another whole room at the Sheraton.* The camera crews emerge out of the ether, and the press aides who a week ago were begging for coverage from a low-wattage radio station are now trying to squeeze a network anchor in between two syndicated columnists.

I've seen this phenomenon for the better part of twenty years. I saw Gary Hart come to New Hampshire in 1984 on the heels of a distant second-place finish in the Iowa caucuses, and within forty-eight hours emerge as the fresh, young alternative to a Walter Mondale already beginning to show signs of political sclerosis. I saw Bill Clinton rise from the dead in 1992, and regain life by sheer force of will. I saw Pat Buchanan, for one brief moment in 1996, sailing through New Hampshire with a glint in his eye, with a sense of absolute freedom from the hesitancy that entraps so many candidates in a capsule of fear and self-doubt.

(A few days before the primary, I went to his hotel for an interview. He was tapping away at his computer. *Be with you in a minute—I'm just rewriting an ad. No, it's okay, you can leave the camera on.* There are candidates whose security personnel would bludgeon you unto unconsciousness if you tried to shoot such a scene. Buchanan, in The Zone, was the candidate romantic liberals had dreamed of for years, free from focus groups, speechwriters, and consultants, crafting his own words by his own hand, Lincoln with a laptop, bashing powerful corporations and global financial giants with gleeful irreverence.)

Never, never had I seen a candidate more in The Zone than John McCain was in New Hampshire early in 2000. Once his aides had finished assembling the press inside the Straight

Talk Express—reporters doubling up on the chairs, sharing armrests and patches of the floor—McCain came bursting into the van, eyes flashing, arms tight at his sides, fists pumping together in a truncated motion, almost like a mechanical doll— a legacy from his North Vietnamese captors, who had inflicted permanent damage on his arms. The one-liners came bursting out of him, like a *tummler* in the Catskills, casting insults all about him, every one of them a coveted token of affection—a reporter greeted with the cry of "Trotskyite" would treasure the label much as a patron of Toots Shor's restaurant half a century earlier would have thrilled to be called a "bum."

"How much of an issue are you going to make out of being kept off the New York ballot?"

"Not at all. Surely you must understand that my presence in front of the Russian Embassy last week was just a matter of random chance."

It was a permanent floating interior monologue on wheels, every word of it on the record, every question answered, as McCain's eyes darted from one reporter to another: *Okay, who's next? Who's got one they think is too hot for me to handle— bring it on.* Among those less enamored of McCain, the conviction grew that he was little more than the darling of the media, the flavor of the month. And in fact, there was a heavy infatuation born of McCain's gift for flattery-by-insult, and the heady sense of all-access-all-the-time. By the last week of the campaign, presidents of network news divisions, managing editors of major magazines, folks who rarely packed New Hampshire gyms and church basements to follow a candidate on his winter's rounds were wedging their way into the Straight Talk Express for a taste of the action.

And yet, this notion of McCain as media darling missed the point. McCain was connecting not because of the press, but because of who he was, and what he represented. If you traveled to one of his town meetings, you would see almost exactly the same event: same jokes ("I would never use this campaign to plug my book, *Faith of My Fathers*, Random House, twenty-four ninety-five"), the same rhetoric ("The Clinton Administration has conducted a feckless photo-opportunity foreign policy"), and then a question-and-answer session remarkable for its bluntness. *No*, he would say to a Portsmouth crowd, where shipbuilding was an engine of the local economy, *we need a base-closing commission. Well,* he would answer a question on abortion, *I am pro-life, but both sides have politicized the issue for their own narrow benefit.*

And then you would notice something else: At almost every town meeting, the men would be there, some middle-aged, some elderly, clad in their service uniforms or service caps, or in jackets bearing the names of their military units, some of them with ribbons and medals, some of them with wives or sons or daughters in tow. As often as not, they would simply listen, but every once in a while one of them would stand and say, *No, I don't really have a question, Senator. I just want you to know that you've made me feel proud again.*

In that statement lay the heart of McCain's campaign, and not just for men in uniform.

McCain was the real anti-Clinton: After eight years of the first baby-boom president, with all his energy and sloppiness, his policy successes and personal disgraces, his striking cognitive and political gifts and his striking emotional infantilism, after his self-absorption and dog-ate-my-homework mendacity, here was someone who was a grown-up. It wasn't just his age, although that helped. While McCain was only a decade older than Gore and Bush, that was enough to lift him well out of the baby-boom generation, into an earlier, presumably more serious age category. It was also where he had spent his younger days: Clinton was the symbol of baby-boom meritocracy, who had struggled up from modest beginnings to earn his way into the most elite of institutions—Oxford University, Yale Law School—and who was damned if he was going to risk all that he was headed for in some mindless, stupid war. Bush, for all his Texas good-old-boy demeanor, was from Yale and Harvard Business School, and it was his bloodline and connections that got him into the Texas Air National Guard. McCain's military life stretched back generations, to the founding of the country; his father and grandfather had risen to the highest of ranks in the United States Navy. This was not some privileged politician out of Greenwich Country Day School or Yale Law mouthing platitudes about "responsibility" or "a thousand points of light." This was the real deal.

McCain almost died for our sins, and he wasn't pissed off about it: By the year 2000, the men who were young during the Vietnam era were well into middle age; they were running the country, at or near the top of the corporation and the academy, and holding the reins of media power as well. And if they were well situated enough—if they were in a university, for instance—they had quite probably avoided military service. There was a moral dimension to this, of course; the war had been wrong, pointless, immoral, wasteful. But there was no getting around the fact that if you were black, brown, a poor white kid who was working in a foundry or a warehouse or a construction gang, you were going into the army; if you were a graduate student, a young aide to a governor or mayor, or if you had a doctor in your family, you were not. This was an uncomfortable fact that few of us cared to face dead-on. (One of the few who did was writer James Fallows, in a memorable piece in the *Washington Monthly* called "What Did You Do in the Class War, Daddy?")

This sense of unease was heightened with the fiftieth anniversary of World War II; a spate of books and movies reminded us that the older generation, before it had become the symbol of barbecues, tail fins, gray flannel suits, and crushing conformism, had put its collective life on the line. Somewhere between thumbing through *The Greatest Generation* and eyeballing *Saving Private Ryan*, we began to understand that what they had gone through was a pretty big deal. It might even have occurred to some of us that the reflexive antimilitary attitude so prevalent during the Vietnam era may have been a little . . . shallow.

John McCain, of course, was not of the World War II generation. But he looked as if he might have been; more to the point, he had borne burdens for his country as had no other major politician of his generation. While many of his contemporaries were home reaping the harvest of sex, drugs, and rock and roll, he was in a Hanoi prison being tortured almost to death. What made McCain so striking was that he seemed to bear these contemporaries no ill will. He became very close to at least one antiwar leader, and comforted him as he died young. He stood with President Clinton, providing him badly needed cover to normalize relations with Vietnam. He repeatedly (almost too deliberately) denied that he was a hero, speaking instead of his (nonexistent) weakness under torture. There was in him, despite a sometimes fearsome temper, a sense of grace, of a link to something more substantial than baby-boomer self-indulgence. In this sense, he was not only the anti–Clinton— he was the anti–Bush *and* the anti–Gore.

McCain the Man was *The McCain Campaign:* Every insurgent campaign carries with it a cause; it can be an antiwar protest, or a rage against an intrusive federal government. It can be a demand that the government put its fiscal house in order, or that it stop the surrender of our sovereignty to international power brokers. In John McCain's case, the issue was campaign-finance reform. But it wasn't, not really. Every survey showed that the public was profoundly indifferent to the issue. It even sounded boring. But by running on the promise to combat the undue influence of money in politics, McCain's campaign was saying something else: *This guy is not afraid of anything. Once you've had the living crap pounded out of you in a Hanoi hellhole, you're not about to let the Washington big shots roll over you, or cave in and play by their corrupt rules.*

It was the most engaging and compelling campaign I had seen since my days as a very junior aide to Senator Robert Kennedy in 1968. And underneath it all, even as it was celebrating its great triumph in New Hampshire, the McCain campaign knew that winning the Republican nomination was an almost impossible task.

On December 5, 1999, McCain had come to the Ninety-second Street YMHA—a New York City cultural landmark where I had been staging conversations with notables for the better part of two decades. I'd hosted talks with powerful politicians and media mega-heavies, before audiences that were overwhelmingly Jews of the classically liberal persuasion. No one—*no one*—had ever received the kind of greeting John McCain got that night. More than a thousand people brought him onstage to cheers worthy of a rock star, or—this being one of NYC's cultural landmarks—an Isaac Stern, a Rubenstein.

My questions were blunt, his answers more so: Yes, he was pro-life; yes, he had voted against gun control; yes, he had voted to confirm Clarence Thomas. The audience groaned audibly; they *wanted* to be with this Arizona conservative Republican—if only he wasn't so . . . Republican, so . . . conservative. But still they had listened raptly to the sound of a politician speaking utterly without guile, and when we had come off the stage (McCain's eyes lighting up as he greeted two comely young women backstage, a touch of the dashing young aviator and swordsman he had been), I asked one of his senior advisors whether they could overtake George W. Bush on Super Tuesday.

He shook his head. No, what they had to do was knock Bush out of the race not *on* Super Tuesday, but *before* it. Before Super Tuesday, seven states held Republican primaries; almost all of them were open to independents, some even to Democrats, where McCain's reform message would be most potent. On Super Tuesday, by contrast, almost every key primary was closed, including California. The 162 California delegates added up to almost 20 percent of what a Republican needed to win the nomination, and under the rules it was winner-take-all. No, there was no way for McCain to win that contest, or any of the other major Super Tuesday primaries, against the designated candidate of the entire Republican establishment.

"If Bush is still standing on Super Tuesday," the aide said, "it's over."

Yes, McCain had to win New Hampshire, had to knock Bush back on his heels, had to strip the cloak of invincibility from the crown prince. That would bring McCain what it always brought the upset winner of the New Hampshire primary: massive television exposure; the covers of *Time* and *Newsweek*; a flood of money; instant, admiring reappraisals of his political strengths. It would also put Bush under real scrutiny for the first time; stories would report "private grumbling rolling through Republican ranks," "questions raised about the long-term-survival prospects for the now-shaken front-runner, armed with limitless amounts of money and support, clobbered in the first round."

It was all absolutely necessary in order for McCain to win. It was not, however, enough; not nearly enough.

Why? For one thing, the Republican Party had a history, at least twenty years long, of subjecting the front-runner to a kind of trial by ordeal—something between a fraternity initiation rite and a tribal survival test. If it wasn't written into the Republican Party's Official Rules, it might as well have been. For no matter how popular a figure might be, somewhere early in the nomination process, he'd be tested mightily. George Bush the first had done it to Ronald Reagan in Iowa in 1980; that victory had prompted a prominent NBC political correspondent to announce that "Ronald Reagan was politically dead." Bob Dole and Pat Robertson had done it to Bush eight years later, sending him to a third-place finish and, according to one report, "placing the vice president's political viability in doubt." Pat Buchanan had done it to Bob Dole in 1996, beating him in New Hampshire. In each case, the shaken front-runner had found his footing and survived. Beyond history, there was a special dimension this year: Never had the Republican Party put more of its chips on a front-runner than it had on George W. Bush.

When Bob Dole had gone down in flames in 1996, it had left the GOP without a logical heir for the first time since Nixon had lost in 1960. There was no national voice of the party in Washington; in fact, the Republican leadership in Washington was badly battered by its (mostly losing) fights with Bill Clinton. The government shutdown of 1995 and the budget fights of 1996 had all gone the president's way. During the '96 campaign, tens of millions of dollars in Democratic soft-money ads had gone to portraying "Dole-Gingrich" as something close to an infectious disease. Nor did the party do itself much good during the Lewinsky scandal–impeachment saga of 1998. In a negative sense, it was an impressive achievement to go into a congressional election against a president who had been caught dead to rights in a tawdry sex scandal and lied about it for months—and wind up being the first opposition party in sixty-four years to *lose* seats in the House to the incumbent party.

If the congressional Republicans were striking out with the public, the Republican governors were a very different story. By the time the 1990's were ending, they had control of every big state in the Union with the exception of California. More impressive was their track record once in power: In state after state, they had engineered major changes in everything from taxes to education to welfare—winning landslide reelections in the process. When they thought about the next presidential election, Republicans looked at their statehouse successes, and then looked at what the Democrats had done eight years earlier. In choosing Clinton, they had picked a candidate outside Washington, unencumbered by the public's disaffection with the 1980s model of Democrats. Now, Republicans thought, it was time for us to do the same. We need to find us a governor. But who?

It couldn't be a pro-choice governor. The Republican base would no more accept an advocate of abortion rights than the Democratic base would accept a pro-life candidate. (Republicans, unlike Democrats, did permit the opposing voices—pro-choice, in their case—to be heard at their conventions, but they didn't permit them to be nominated.) That eliminated New

York's Pataki, New Jersey's Whitman, Pennsylvania's Ridge. The candidate had to be personally compelling; that eliminated Michigan's John Engler and Wisconsin's Tommy Thompson. Even though both had demonstrated powerful political appeal in their respective industrial midwestern states, they both violated what has become an Iron Law of Presidential Politics: No Portly Men Need Apply.

Had 1994 turned out the way the pros thought it would, the obvious choice would have been Bush—Jeb Bush, who was widely favored to become the governor of Florida that year. (His brother George W. was a clear underdog against Texas Governor Ann Richards.) Jeb was the natural politician in the family: bright, immersed in public policy, while George W.'s only claims to fame were as principal owner of the Texas Rangers baseball team and a reputation as a party animal. Jeb lost, George won—and turned out to be prime political goods. When he was reelected by a two-to-one margin in 1998, the Republicans had found their man. From the time of Bush's reelection through the New Hampshire primary, it was less a campaign than a courtship—delegations of House and Senate members and state legislators regularly journeying to Austin to beseech Bush to run. By the time the first half-frozen Iowan stumbled into a caucus in January of 2000, the Bush campaign had already raised sixty-seven million dollars in increments of a thousand dollars—more than Bob Dole spent in his entire 1996 campaign. He had the backing of thirty-three Republican senators, 166 members of the House, twenty-five governors.

So John McCain was not about to persuade the Republicans to desert Bush, even after he had beaten the Texas governor by nineteen points in New Hampshire—one of the larger margins ever in a contested presidential primary. Indeed, McCain's win proved to be a pearl of great price for Bush. It brought the conservative movement to his side without forcing Bush to give up a single component of his "compassionate conservative" message.

The reason? To those who make up the Republican and conservative establishments, John McCain as presidential nominee was not an opportunity, but a mortal threat. The Arizona senator had long been a thorn in the side of orthodox Republicans. Within the Senate, as he liked to put it, he was unlikely to win the "Miss Congeniality" award from his fellow Republicans. As with many conservative legislators, he delighted in attacking "pork barrel" government spending; unlike many of them, he meant it. He would denounce wasteful spending even when it involved pet projects of Republican senators. Further, McCain had a fuse shorter than the attention span of a thirteen-year-old with a remote control. In the close-in battles with fellow senators, he would at times turn a legislative disagreement into a personal matter. It was the same story back home. At one time or another, he had feuded with just about every Republican in the state of Arizona, including the attorney general, once one of his closest allies, and the governor. And his battles with the *Arizona Republic,* the state's biggest newspaper, were legion. On October 31, 1999, the paper, which had repeatedly backed his House and Senate campaigns, ran an editorial explicitly raising the issue. "McCain's temper is a legitimate issue," it said, questioning whether McCain had "the temperament and the political approach and skills" to be president.

What really raised the blood pressure of his fellow Republicans was not McCain's temper but his views about money. On two fronts—campaign funding and tax policy—McCain was at war with the heart and soul of the modern Republican

Party. Yes, the public was relentlessly indifferent to the issue of campaign-finance reform; to conservatives, it was nothing less than a threat to their survival. In its view, the power to raise and spend limitless sums of money was not only a First Amendment right; it was also the Right's only protection against an army of interest groups on the Left, principally organized labor. Drive interest groups from the playing field, they believe, and labor will be left with its phone banks and Election Day "Get Out the Vote Operations," all paid for by compulsory union dues. Bush crystallized this view admirably during a debate in Durham, New Hampshire, on January 6.

"My objection," he said, "is, he is proposing a campaign-funding reform that will hurt Republicans and the conservative cause. He's asking us to unilaterally disarm, which I will refuse to do." McCain's triumph in New Hampshire left Bush as the only credible candidate left who could protect Republicans from an enemy within, determined to strip them of their political clout.

An even bigger heresy was McCain's opposition to sweeping tax cuts—a centerpiece of the Republican canon ever since Ronald Reagan rode the issue to victory in 1980. By 2000, this had become less an economic issue than a moral, ideological one. Taxes were involuntary dollars, conscripted out of the pockets of hardworking Americans by force. These dollars were used to fatten up an inefficient, arrogant, hostile federal government. The way to keep government from growing larger was to deprive it of its fuel. Let the economists and think-tank wonks argue the economic merits of the issue: *Resolved: a cut in marginal tax rates is the surest way to a robust economy*. As a political matter, a Republican candidate for president had to call for lower taxes—especially if that candidate was the son of the last GOP president, who had stirred his party's hearts with his ringing "read my lips: no new taxes" declaration, then broken those hearts as president.

Yet here was McCain, labeling himself a "proud Reagan conservative," asking every town-hall audience, "Don't you think it's a good idea to pay down the national debt?" He might as well have been popping in and out of churches, asking parishioners, "Come on—do you *really* think Mary was a virgin?" The flinty voters of New Hampshire might admire that approach to fiscal discipline. It might play well with political independents, who had flocked to Ross Perot's "fight-the-deficit" campaign of 1992. For the men and women who had enlisted as foot soldiers in the Reagan Revolution, it was close to treason.

Seen through the eyes of his supporters, John McCain was exactly what the Republican Party needed: a candidate whose life, demeanor, and message would draw millions of independents and Democrats to his side, who would stand in stark contrast to the Al Gore of shady campaign fund-raising and Clintonian language. Seen through the eyes of conservatives and Republicans, he was The Enemy. And it was at his moment of greatest vulnerability that George W. Bush saved his campaign by redefining it as a fight against heresy.

I was part of a *Larry King Live* panel on primary night when the Texas governor appeared for an interview. When King asked him what had happened, Bush gave a simple answer— one he repeated on every other interview that night.

"He came at me from the Left," Bush said. When I heard those words, I sat bolt upright in my chair. It's not often that a politician's words affect me that viscerally. But here, I thought, Bush was laying out his whole future strategy. *John McCain is not a real conservative. No real conservative would stand against tax cuts, fight to take away the power of conservative interest groups to speak their minds.* In one stroke, Bush had answered one of the key questions of his campaign: Could he win over the conservative base? That base had never warmed to his father. It was uneasy with the "compassionate conservatism" theme of Bush's campaign, with its implication that there was something "uncompassionate" about regular conservatism. It did not like Bush's warning to congressional Republicans not to "balance the budget on the backs of the poor." That sounded an awful lot like the way Democrats talked. But now, with McCain coming at the nomination "from the Left," Bush suddenly emerged as the conservative savior.

In a weird sense, McCain had become for Bush what Speaker Newt Gingrich had been for Bill Clinton. In 1995, the Gingrich specter so spooked the Democratic base that they said to Clinton, in effect, "Do whatever you have to do to beat this guy. You want to end welfare entitlements, stiff the unions with your free-trade policies, bend the campaign finance laws like a pretzel, you go, Bill." In 2000, the Republican base looked up on the day after New Hampshire and saw Bush—and no one else—standing in John McCain's way. They had the same message for him that the liberal Democrats had had for Clinton five years earlier: "Do whatever you have to do to beat this guy. You've got to save the Republican Party from this usurper."

Now Bush had more than money, organization, and endorsements. He now had an ideological advantage as well. In the past, insurgents have done well by appealing to their party's base, arguing that the front-runner is in fact betraying the cause. Barry Goldwater, Eugene McCarthy and Robert

Kennedy, Ronald Reagan, George McGovern all spoke to the passions of their parties. The intensity of their campaigns helped defuse the logistical advantages an insider always maintains. Now, Bush was running both as a front-runner *and* as the true Republican. And as the McCain campaign looked down the road—at all those closed primaries just five weeks away, where only enrolled Republicans could vote—they knew that only an early knockout could save them. Their campaign had to mount an absolutely perfect effort in South Carolina to have any hope of that knockout.

Now, there's a problem with such a task. Nobody runs a perfect campaign. Winning campaigns are always treated as masterpieces; losing campaigns are always scorned as inept. The truth is, every campaign is a mix; you just have to hope that good decisions, timing, luck, and the other guy's mistakes wind up giving you the victory. (Early in his administration, President Kennedy was reading a magazine article describing his aides as "coruscatingly brilliant." "All I know," he said, "is that eight thousand votes the other way in Illinois, and we'd all be coruscatingly stupid.") McCain's campaign hit the wall with a single campaign commercial, when John McCain looked into the camera, and said of Bush, "He twists the truth like Clinton."

Understand the provocation: In South Carolina, the attacks on McCain had turned incendiary. On talk radio, in direct mail, in telemarketing phone calls, McCain and his family were attacked for everything from his wife's addiction to prescription drugs to his adoption of a multiracial child. The Bush campaign denied any link to these tactics. But Bush himself had stood next to a spokesman for a fringe veterans' group, while the spokesman charged that McCain had "abandoned" veterans. Whatever the provocation, comparing a fellow Republican to Clinton was a tactical error of the first magnitude. By 2000, Clinton was not simply the Republicans' adversary; he was their enemy, the enemy of all things good and decent. What's more, he had beaten them at every turn, survived investigations, even impeachment, and remained president and unrepentant. Compare a fellow Republican to *Bill Clinton? The horror, the horror.* In political terms, this was a huge gift. It permitted Bush to assume the mantle of wounded warrior. In an ad worthy of the Full Welch, he spoke more in sorrow than in anger that McCain had questioned his trustworthiness. Four days before the primary, in a *Larry King Live* debate, Bush was ready when McCain said he had pulled all his negative advertising off the air. Brandishing a flyer, Bush said:

"You didn't pull this ad."

"Yes, I did," McCain said.

"This ended up on a man's windshield yesterday—this is an attack piece."

"That is not by my campaign," said McCain.

"Well," said Bush, "it says, 'Paid for by John McCain.' "

The laughter of the audience was like a death knell for the Arizona Senator in South Carolina. His mistake—a political misdemeanor—robbed him of his most essential campaign attribute: that here was someone above the mud wrestling that politics had become. His eleven-point loss in South Carolina four days later meant that Bush was no longer damaged goods, no longer a paper tiger. McCain would remain in the ring with victories in his home state of Arizona and in Michigan. But even that Michigan victory revealed a fatal weakness in his campaign: He won with the votes of independents and crossover Democrats. Among Republicans, he received barely 30 percent of the vote. And when Super Tuesday arrived, McCain won only a handful of New England contests. In New

York, in Ohio, and in winner-take-all California, Bush won—and with it, the nomination. John McCain had brought something remarkable into the contest. He had shown again that there is a perennial hunger for a candidate who is not cut from the mold of traditional politics. He had, however, inadvertently shown something else that is a hardy perennial of American politics: If you want to be nominated by a major political party, you have to be able to persuade the members of that party. No matter how powerfully you appeal to those outside the party's ranks, no matter how strong a general-election candidate you may be, that won't persuade party loyalists.

● On the evening of March 7, I was in Atlanta as part of the CNN anchor team covering Super Tuesday. Unlike the night we were to live through eight months later, there was no suspense at all about the outcomes. In this case, the early exit polls were blessedly free from all doubt. Bill Bradley was losing every Democratic primary, and losing by wide margins. John McCain was losing big among Republicans in Ohio, Georgia, and California, and losing narrowly in New York. Nonetheless, I was impatiently waiting for the evening to unfold. I wanted to hear what the candidates and their surrogates would say, and how they would say it.

Journalists often scorn the stagecraft of politics, regarding it as nothing more than packaged fluff. But victory nights and campaign talking points are valuable clues precisely because they represent a campaign's conscious effort to shape a message for the public. For me, these words and images often provided a sharp, clear picture of a campaign's major premise. This may have been a legacy of my years as a political operative. As a one-time speechwriter and media consultant, I remember working on this stagecraft with special care. Everything counted. Who would stand just behind the candidate— Wife? Kids? Politically diverse group of supporters? Jowly, corrupt-looking, yet politically invaluable ally? What would the candidate say? (Put the message first; there's time to thank every county chairman *after* the cameras have been turned off.) This was our chance to speak directly to voters, without some smart-ass journalist processing the message, and by God, we would take advantage of it.

On this Super Tuesday night, the competing messages could not have been clearer. Consider the Democrats who fanned out across the TV networks. California Governor Gray Davis, for example, appeared on CNN, with the same message others were carrying to other networks. There were, he said, three issues that would hurt Bush badly in November: gun control, abortion, and the environment. What was Davis really saying? (I had long since become one of the smart-assed journalists I had scorned in an earlier life.) What he—what the Gore campaign—was saying was that they would try to paint Bush as the Republican version of Michael Dukakis: as a figure outside the mainstream.

Dukakis furloughed murderers; Bush signed a law that permitted concealed weapons to be carried in Texas. Dukakis presided over the pollution of Boston Harbor; Bush had presided over the pollution of Houston's air. Dukakis supported teachers who refused to lead their pupils in saluting the flag; Bush was running on a party platform that would ban all abortions, even to save the life of the mother. Welcome to 1988.

And Bush? He was introduced on Super Tuesday not by a congressional Republican, or by a stalwart conservative activist. No, he was introduced on national television by an

African-American woman educator from Texas. His victory speech was written as if the primaries had been a small blip in the uninterrupted message he'd been delivering for more than a year:

"Republicans must expand our prosperity, and extend it to those who still struggle. We must be a strong nation that also cares for the weak and forgotten." He again drew a clear line between himself and other Republicans, particularly in California, who had made political capital with attacks on immigration—alienating countless Hispanic voters in the process. "We must welcome the new Americans—Americans by choice—because legal immigration is not a source of national weakness; it is a sign of national success."

Once again, George W. Bush was the outsider with a view in striking contrast to the congressional Republicans who had overplayed their hand—a "different kind of Republican," who would break with that part of his party's message voters had found wanting.

Welcome to 1992.

● When I left the anchor desk late on the night of March 7, I found myself in the grip of a mild but unmistakable depression. Once again, the American voters, in a fit of spite, had deprived the political community of a protracted nomination struggle. Only a few days earlier, we had dared to dream of a Republican primary fight that would last all through the spring; maybe even fights over rules and credentials and platform planks on the floor of the convention itself. Maybe we would not be left once again looking at those C-SPAN reruns, or listening to the old war stories (*I remember when the Taft forces thought they had Chicago wired, but then came the pro-Ike telegrams from all the folks watching back home on TV, and . . .*). It wasn't just regret that had me blue. It wasn't even the political equivalent of postcoital depression: a sudden end to what had been an exhilarating ride. It was also the sense of what lay ahead these next eight months.

I can best convey my approach to the general election season by recalling one more incident from the primaries. On the night he lost the South Carolina primary, Senator John McCain delivered a "concession" speech almost unparalleled in its take-no-prisoners defiance:

"As this campaign moves forward, a clear choice will be offered," McCain said, reading verbatim from a speech, in contrast to his usual practice of ad-libbing. "A choice between my optimistic and welcoming conservatism and the negative message of fear . . . A choice between a record of reform and an empty slogan of reform. A choice between experience and pretense . . . I will never dishonor the nation I love or myself by letting ambition overcome principle, never."

Startled by the intensity of the language, I pushed McCain hard when he appeared for an interview later that night, asking him repeatedly why he was using language he had never before used in his entire campaign.

Finally, McCain had had enough of me.

"Why don't you come to some of my town-hall meetings?" he asked. "It's the same message that I've been saying throughout this entire campaign in South Carolina. And I'm sorry you haven't had the time or the energy to come down and join us. You'd enjoy it, Jeff."

As a matter of fact, McCain was wrong. Correspondent

John King, who had traveled with the candidate throughout the primary, confirmed as much. (For his part, the Senator was underwhelmed by my rhetorical analysis, and later that week refused to be interviewed by me on the air. He has since forgiven me—I think.) But, as a travel analyst, he was dead right. It's become my practice over the years to all but abandon the campaign trail once the Iowa and New Hampshire contests are over.

Why? Part of the reason, I confess, is that it is an exhausting, demeaning way to spend your time. One example: So draconian has security become that it is sometimes difficult to remember that you are part of a profession protected by a Constitutional amendment. On one of the few days when I did venture out last year, Vice President Gore traveled to Des Moines, Iowa, to hold a citizens' forum meeting on . . . something. When we arrived at the downtown Civic Center, dozens of reporters, producers, camera operators, and audio technicians poured out of the press buses. As a cluster of Secret Service officials and local police looked on, we surrendered purses, backpacks, laptops, and cameras, which were all thrown together in an enormous pile on the sidewalk. It looked as if an antipress terrorist group was preparing to make a bonfire of all things that smacked of late-twentieth-century journalism. Instead, a team of security agents then began going through the pile, one object at a time. A moment later, they were joined by trained dogs, who burrowed through the pile in search of bombs, weapons, and food—trampling on a fair number of computers, cell phones, and pagers in the process. When you go through this on an almost daily basis, the song of the open road begins to sound tinny.

But that's not the real reason I stay away from the trail. For my money, once the retail campaign season ends, the candidates become utter slaves to the imperious demands of television news. As a consequence, *nothing of any importance happens on the trail, except by accident.* Everyone remotely familiar with American politics has known this truth for nearly a quarter of a century: If you are watching a presidential campaign in person, with your own eyes, you are *not* watching the campaign at all. The election is not happening at the airport rally, the town-hall meeting, the heartwarming conversation between candidate and single mom. It is happening on tens of millions of television screens that evening and into the next morning. It is on these screens where a candidate's fifteen-hour day will be distilled into snippets of images on the news. It is on these screens where a campaign's paid messages will play in between the night's entertainment.

Don't misunderstand me. Some of the most important political information in any campaign comes from the systematic exercise of shoe leather. Reporters who go door-to-door with canvassers, who work the shopping malls and diners and bowling alleys, often get an early whiff of the political wind. They begin to sense that blue-collar Democrats are fleeing the party of their parents, or that suburban Republican women are not with their candidate this time. Back in January of 1992, I went up to New Hampshire for a few days, to get a feel for the state that had saved George Bush four years earlier. In 1988, their votes were a "thank you" to the Reagan-Bush administration for a thriving economy. By 1992, the state was flat on its back. I went to a huge shopping center in Manchester, where every single storefront was boarded up, with just two exceptions: the welfare office and the unemployment office. I went to a mall in Concord, where a store that had survived the Depression had just gone under. I picked up the Manchester *Union-Leader,* thick with classified ads—for bankruptcy auctions. I came back convinced that the Republicans of New Hampshire were going to stick it to President Bush with a barrelful of votes for challenger Pat Buchanan. The key was that *I was not traveling with the candidate.* I was not inside the bubble; I was not wearing the credentials; I was not shuffling from plane to bus to filing center to bus to plane. I was on my own. When it comes to watching the candidates themselves, give me the TV screen any day.

I thought I had learned this reality more than thirty years ago, as a political operative. I had written hundreds of campaign commercials, briefed God knows how many candidates. But it wasn't until I started covering politics that I learned, from painful experience, that the ringside seat so prized by reporters is the worst possible place from which to judge a presidential campaign.

In 1988, my first year as a convention-floor reporter, I watched Michael Dukakis accept the Democratic presidential nomination on the floor of the Omni in Atlanta. The cheers, the music, the lights, the sheer force of energy generated by thousands of acolytes transformed the speech from a more-or-less conventional oration into something close to the "Cross of Gold" speech. I have never watched a convention speech "face-to-face" since. Even when I am on the floor of a convention, I walk until I can watch the speech on a television monitor. That same year, I was in the auditorium in Omaha, Nebraska, for the October 5 vice-presidential debate between Senator Lloyd Bentsen and Senator Dan Quayle. Each TV network had a platform in the back of the hall, and I had the perch for ABC News. We had a TV monitor, but the picture was so ghostly and snowy it was impossible to view. So I watched the debate "live"—and completely missed Dan Quayle's memorable "deer-in-the-headlights" visage that was so apparent to tens of millions of TV viewers.

I tell you this because I watched the 2000 general election the same way you did: in front of a television screen. Yes, I spent hours at the conventions talking with officials, campaign workers, and delegates. I worked the phones some, though with much less enthusiasm than many of my colleagues, who work valiantly to fight the dreadfully low signal-to-noise ratio that emanates from every campaign. But at the risk of demystifying the business of political journalism, most of the authentically important moments in a campaign take place—literally—right in front of our eyes. Those speeches and public tableaux I spoke of a few pages ago are even more important once the primary season ends. Now, the candidates are speaking not to the base of their party, but to a much larger, much less involved audience. The words they choose, the settings in which they appear, the people who surround them are embodiments of the campaign's central assumptions. I value these "outside" events far more than the "inside" information doled out by campaign operatives.

On the day after November 7, with the country in a state of suspended political animation, demonstrators were already filling the streets of Palm Beach. Battalions of lawyers were already beginning to choke the Florida legal system with lawsuits. Catchphrases were already beginning to harden into clichés; the talk of "uncharted territory" and "uncharted waters" made the newscasts sound like a cross between *Survivor* and *Gilligan's Island.* Overshadowed by this astonishing spectacle were the tallies of the national exit polls. God knows the previous night had offered eloquent testimony to their flawed reliability. But as a portrait of how and why Americans voted, it was as clear a look as we were likely to get about why the election had ended in a dead heat. Look back at the general-election campaign through the prism of these numbers through the memorable moments of last spring, summer, and fall, and you can see exactly where and how the candidates succeeded, and failed, in defining themselves. Look at what the votes and the voters said, and you can see why we woke up Wednesday morning with no real clue about the identity of the next president.

● What had the voters said? On just about every question you might think of, they had said, clearly and decisively, "Uh, we're not sure."

Take the gender gap. As I mentioned in the first chapter, ever since it emerged some twenty years ago, the gender gap has worked the same way: Men lean Republican; women lean Democratic. In 1988, George Bush the Elder ran close to even among women, and won a landslide among men. In 1992 and 1996, Clinton essentially ran no better than even against Bush and Dole among men, but his landslide win among women gave him the White House.

This time? Bush ran eleven points ahead among men. Gore ran eleven points ahead among women. Since there are very few who fit the category of "other" (except in a few select neighborhoods), those numbers are likely to produce an overall tie.

Look at another key number: party identification. The road to the White House is simple: Hold your base, make inroads with members of the other party, and get a plurality of Independent voters. This time, *both* candidates held their base:

Gore got 86 percent of the Democratic vote, Bush got 91 percent of the Republican vote, and Independents split just about down the middle. That's another good recipe for a tie. What helped turn the Clinton romp over Dole in 1996 into a dead heat in 2000 was a buyer's remorse among Independents. The vice president lost 15 percent of Clinton's voters to Bush, while Governor Bush lost only 7 percent of Dole's voters to Gore.

Those are the broad strokes of what voters said. To appreciate the voters' other messages, we need to look back at the signal events of the campaign—all played out in full, open view—and see how those events helped shape what the voters did. These numbers reveal something else: that the political figure who played the most decisive role in the election results was neither Al Gore, nor George W. Bush—but William Jefferson Clinton.

● When the primary season effectively ended in March, the Gore campaign believed it had come out well ahead. After New Hampshire, Bradley had faded from the field, leaving Gore to position himself for the fall. Bush, by contrast, had retreated from the center, into the comforting arms of the conservative Republican base. Now (to borrow a phrase from Bush's youth), he was looking to scramble to get back to where he once belonged: the center. The polls showed Gore and Bush more or less even just after Super Tuesday; good news for the vice president, considering he'd lagged behind Bush by twenty points or more when the primary season began. Moreover, his campaign believed it had caught the prevailing wind that usually decides who wins.

"We were the candidate of the future," Ed Rendell reflected, "and he was the candidate who had gone to Bob Jones University."

The campaign also found strength in history: No candidate of an incumbent party had ever run for president under sunnier economic skies. In typical elections, the economic mood of the voter drives the vote. Indeed, for those political scientists who labor under the delusion that there is anything "scientific" about politics, the heady mixture of full employment, no inflation, consistent economic growth, and the increase in real incomes meant that Vice President Gore was a certain winner. Using these facts, and blending them with public-opinion polls and indices of voter satisfaction, these academics had concocted a series of competing formulas to predict presidential elections. They had applied these formulas—retrospectively—to elections going back to 1948. The formulas, they argued, worked without fail. No need to wait for the campaign, no need to listen to the candidates debate. Just apply the formula, and the identity of the next president would be clear. This time? Every formula pointed to a clear win by Gore—perhaps by a landslide.

"It's not even going to be close," Michael Lewis-Beck of the University of Iowa wrote in May. His model showed Gore winning 56.2 percent of the two-party vote. Other forecasters gave Gore anywhere from 52.8 to 60.3 percent of the two-party vote.

If these numbers made the Gore campaign take heart, they did not stir fear in the Bush camp. It was not exactly a secret to them that the good economic numbers added up to a powerful argument for staying the course. Their mantra was the same one they had been chanting since their campaign began: "This election will not be decided on the issues; it will be decided on the basis of character and leadership." The Clinton scandals, they believed, had created an appetite for someone new—not a change of *course,* but a change of *tone.* And from the beginning, they believed Al Gore would be an unwitting but crucial ally in their argument. In his public personality lay the seeds of his own defeat.

What exactly was it? You could find a dozen different assessments, each of them grappling with the same idea:

"He's the kid in the back of the class who reminded the teacher she'd forgotten to give out homework the day before Christmas break."

"He's the hall patrol monitor, turning in a kid for smoking in the bathroom so he could get extra credit."

"He's the kind of guy who seems like he's lying even when he's telling the truth."

His partisans argued that this was a case of mistaken identity, or of a public persona sharply at odds with the easygoing, self-deprecating, private Gore, with an irreverent sense of humor and a gift for mimicry. This may have been true—although journalist Joe Klein argued that *this* was the artificial persona, and that the stiff, unctuous, public Gore was in fact the real deal—but it didn't matter. There is an infallible rule in politics: When a candidate's supporters tell you "he's great in small groups," it's just like being told your blind date "has a wonderful personality, and all the girls in the dorm love her." The real meaning of such faint praise is: *Our guy just doesn't light it up; he just doesn't know how to behave in public.*

Gore at times seemed to invite the idea that he was, in a much-repeated notion, a cyborg candidate, programmed to say whatever he needed to say to win over whomever he was talking to. Indeed, there were times when his tactics approached self-parody. Had he really hired Naomi Wolf, a famous feminist author, to advise him on how to become an alpha male, and how to dress for political success with the proper choices of color and fabric? This was the stuff on which late-night comedians feast. More fundamental was how Gore's public demeanor opened him up to a line of attack that Bush pursued through-out the fall: Gore is the candidate of Big Government.

At one level, this attack is utterly predictable. Republicans always accuse Democrats of being the party of Big Govern-ment, just as Democrats always accuse Republicans of being the party of the Rich. Indeed, there is enough truth in both charges to make them attractive weapons of choice. In 2000, however, there was reason to think the Republicans might have trouble making this one stick. Hadn't Bill Clinton declared in his 1995 State of the Union Address, "The era of Big Govern-ment is over"? Hadn't Al Gore run the "Re-Inventing Govern-ment" operation, ferreting out waste and duplication in the massive federal bureaucracy? Hadn't he gone on David Let-terman, and broken an ashtray to show the absurdity of gov-ernment procurement policy? Yes, yes, and yes. Moreover, why would the public see government as a malevolent force in their lives, given that almost every economic and social indicator had improved on the Clinton-Gore watch? Clinton had even taken welfare—the perennial poster child of antigovernment sentiment—and ended it as a federal entitlement. Here, you might think, was a ready rebuttal to the "Big Government" charge.

And yet, it worked. When voters were asked who shared their view of government, Bush prevailed over Gore by a 51 percent to 46 percent margin. Intriguingly, *no other question* was a more certain predictor of a vote than this one—not abortion, not gun control, nothing. Fully 95 percent of the voters who shared a candidate's view of government voted for that candidate. In an election this close, that distinction was critical. So why did it stick? Why did voters see Gore as a Big Government guy? Well, it didn't help that he'd spent virtually his entire adult life in Washington. When you're elected to Congress at the age of twenty-nine, that's going to happen. There is, I'm convinced, another reason, rooted in Gore's public personality.

When people think of "Big Government," what do they mean? They don't necessarily mean a particular program, or even a particular branch of government. Instead, I think, it's an image, maybe part of a stereotype, maybe part of memory. It's a guy in a blue suit and wing-tip shoes, carrying a briefcase or clipboard, knocking on a homeowner's door in the middle of the day.

"That tree house in your backyard?"

"Yes, my son and I built it with our own hands; took us most of the summer, but it's his pride and . . ."

"Yes, well, unfortunately that structure is in violation of Section 136.67c(iii) of the zoning code, which expressly forbids freestanding structures of that size. It is . . . let me see . . . three and a quarter inches over the limit. You will please remove it within forty-eight hours, or face a fine, and possible imprisonment."

It's the clerk at the Department of Motor Vehicles who takes your registration application after you've been waiting in line for forty-five minutes, stares at it for a moment, and hands it back to you with a look of barely suppressed triumph.

"Your make and model number are in the wrong boxes. Get another form, and go to Line Seven."

"But my lunch hour's over in—"

"Sir, *it is your responsibility to fill these forms out according to the proper procedure."*

It's the Department of Labor bureaucrat who tells a fifteen-year-old high school student he can't work as a batboy for the minor-league baseball team in his town; the planning official whose highway off-ramp will demolish a neighborhood park. It's anyone with an official title who acts if he is ever so much smarter than you are, who is prepared to place an abstract set of rules above any pain and suffering he is likely to inflict on you—and who deals with you as if you are simply too dumb to understand his unquestionable wisdom.

Has there ever been a candidate who more perfectly fit this stereotype than Al Gore?

Voters did not see Gore as Mr. Big Government because of his views on Social Security, or Medicare, or prescription drugs, or education. In fact, on every one of these issues that define what Big Government is, voters preferred Gore's views to Bush's by huge majorities. Only on education did Bush come close to Gore, and on that one issue, Bush favored a big increase both in federal spending *and* oversight (see below). They saw Gore as a Big Government guy because of how he looked and talked and moved. Why didn't they see Clinton in the same light? He was too disorganized, too sloppy, too much a creature of appetites ever to be mistaken for an uptight government bureaucrat. Bureaucratic types do not gobble down fast food. They don't show up an hour late for meetings. They don't play the tenor sax. They don't make phone calls while being sexually serviced by a woman half their age. Whatever else people saw in Clinton, they did not see the soul of a bureaucrat. They saw it in spades with Gore. As we'll see, they saw it most dramatically in the very forum Gore most welcomed and Bush (supposedly) most feared: the presidential debate.

● The effort to move Bush back to the political center that began on the night of Super Tuesday was a dominant theme of the spring and summer, but this notion, in my view, misses the key to what the campaign was doing. Yes, Bush appeared in venues most Republicans avoided like the plague. He went to day-care centers, senior citizens' homes, and community centers in inner-city neighborhoods. Every day, you could see Bush standing among black and brown faces. The coverage of the Republican convention in Philadelphia was dominated by talk—ranging from respectful to skeptical to cynical—about the heavy presence of minorities on the convention stage. ("More blacks on stage than in the whole audience—it's like the Utah Jazz," went one refrain.) Colin Powell and Condoleezza Rice were the featured speakers of the first two nights; Hispanics from California and Florida and Texas talked about local and private programs in jobs and housing. As for the congressional Republicans, they were so invisible that you half-expected to see their pictures start showing up on milk cartons. (The only exception was House Speaker Dennis Hastert, whose appearance featured one of the few glitches of the entire convention. Someone thought it would be a fine idea to have Hastert, a former wrestling coach, introduced by the Rock, champion of the World Wrestling Federation. Whoever came up with the idea had neglected to note that the "Rock" persona featured a heavy dose not only of gratuitous violence, but also of remarkably crude sexual hijinks.)

In his acceptance speech, Bush struck the same note of inclusion; as crafted by chief speechwriter Michael Gerson, the compassionate conservative was back in full force.

"We will extend the promise of prosperity to every forgotten corner of this country," he said. More strikingly, he spoke of visiting a juvenile jail in Marlin, Texas, and hearing from a fifteen-year-old inmate: "What do you think of me?"

"He seemed to be asking, like many Americans who struggle, 'Is there hope for me? Do I have a chance?' And frankly . . . 'Do you, a white man in a suit, really care what happens to me?' "

Flash forward now to Election Day. Judged simply by the exit-poll numbers, all of that effort to reach beyond the Republican base failed. Bush got just 9 percent of the African-American vote—the smallest percentage for any Republican since Barry Goldwater ran in 1964 as an avowed opponent of the Civil Rights Act. The problem with this analysis is that it assumes Bush was aiming his appearances and his remarks solely, even principally, at blacks. What Bush was doing was the same thing Bill Clinton had done, only in reverse. He may have been speaking to and about blacks, but he was also—maybe even principally—talking to *whites,* easing their minds about his approach to race.

When Bill Clinton in 1992 attacked provocative comments by rap singer Sister Souljah at a Rainbow Coalition convention, the message could not have been clearer: *I am not going to pander even to this most loyal of Democratic constituencies. As a white southerner, I am not afraid to criticize African-Americans to their faces and even on Jesse Jackson's home turf.* Depending on your politics, this was an act either of courage, or of contrivance. Either way, it reflected an uncomfortable truth about politics. By the end of the 1980s, a lot of white voters saw Democrats as a party working less for equal opportunity than for special treatment. Clinton's "Sister Souljah" number was aimed squarely at these voters. *"I am tough enough,"* he was saying, *"to stand up to anybody."*

Bush's campaign reflected a different political truth: The white majority may not want special treatment for black Americans, but they want fair treatment. As far back as the summer of 1967, when cities from Newark to Detroit were exploding into flames, when backlash sentiment was running highest, Senator Robert Kennedy was pointing out to his staff the remarkable poll numbers. Yes, people wanted the violence stopped, they wanted rioters punished, but they wanted a lot more money spent on jobs and education in black neighborhoods. By 2000, it was part of a president's job description to acknowledge that black Americans were still getting the short end of the stick. Consciously or not, there were messages here for white voters as well: *If I'm fair-minded enough to pay attention to those who have the least, I'll be able to hear your calls for help as well.* And, *if you want to know how I'm a "different kind of Republican," here's one big piece of evidence. When was the last time you saw Trent Lott or Tom DeLay talking sympathetically about fifteen-year-old black inmates?*

It would miss the point, though, to look just at *where* the Bush campaign was going. Even more central was *what* it was saying. The spring and summer were aimed not simply at making Bush a figure of compassion, but at making him a figure of stature as well. People seemed to like him, but that wasn't going to be enough to put him in the White House. In a political sense, George W. Bush needed to put on some weight.

Watching Bush in person (as I did in the early days of the primary), you saw a man who could work a room as well as anyone, as well as Clinton. The eye contact, the pat on the shoulder, the exchange of a word or two, all spoke of a man at ease with himself. Television was not always as kind to the governor; it captured the furrowed brow, the squint, and—famously—The Smirk, an expression that seemed to say, *I've put it over on these bozos again.* Just as Al Gore's demeanor seemed to speak volumes about his sense of the voters, so Bush's demeanor seemed to speak volumes about his sense of himself. Back in 1988, Democrats loved to describe Bush the Elder as "a man who was born on third base, and thinks he hit a triple." Even Bush the Elder, however, had a father who was only a senator—not a president. George W. was clearly vulnerable to an attack that painted him as the ultimate affirmative-action candidate of privilege:

Got into Yale as a legacy . . . a party animal whose past might not bear up under scrutiny . . . got into Harvard Business School through connections . . . a complete flop as a small businessman, bailed out by his daddy's rich friends . . . a genial front man for the Texas Rangers who got rich because his daddy's big-shot friends got the public to pay for a new baseball stadium that turned his tiny investment into fifteen million dollars. Now his daddy's friends are pouring all that money and sending all his old government hands to surround this lightweight and make him the president.

How do you deal with this line of attack? In part, you can turn it around through the art of Political Judo: a term I coined in 1980, in a book called *Playing to Win,* to widespread indifference. (The book is now available at fine church rummage sales everywhere.) Political Judo consists in using the strength of an opponent's attack against itself—by acknowledging the truth, but challenging its meaning. The classic example: When Ross Perot was challenged in 1992 about his lack of Washington experience during the first presidential debate, he answered, "That's right—I have no experience in running up a four-trillion-dollar debt." For Bush, Political Judo meant pointing to the well-known, experienced people around him and saying, *"Am I enlisting experienced Washington heavyweights? Of course I am. That shows you I'm serious enough about what I'm doing to seek out the best minds I can find. In fact, I'm going to pick a running mate who brings absolutely no political advantage to the ticket. He's not charismatic; he's not movie-star handsome; he comes from a state with three electoral votes that always goes Republican. I'm picking Dick Cheney because I'm serious about governing.*

Political Judo, however, only goes so far. The more telling answer from the campaign was to have George Bush spend four months talking about serious public-policy proposals—one of which no candidate for national office had dared touch. If you didn't see Bush surrounded by photogenic children of diverse pigmentation, then you saw him offering detailed policy messages, sometimes surrounded by reassuring figures with powerful political credentials.

On April 11, for example, Bush was on Cleveland's West Side, before some three hundred fifty church and community leaders, talking about "New Prosperity" initiatives: tax cuts, incentives to turn renters into homeowners, a program for prescription drugs for the uninsured—all wrapped up in another assertion that Bush was not some blindly antigovernment reactionary.

"It is true that government can undermine upward mobility, as welfare once did," Bush said. "It is equally true that government—active but limited government—can promote the rewards of work. It can take the side of individual opportunity."

On May 23, Bush went to Capitol Hill to talk about national security. Flanked by Colin Powell, former Secretaries of State Henry Kissinger and George Schultz, and former National Security staffer Condoleezza Rice, he once again broke with the spend-every-dime-you-can-find school of Republican thinkers:

"We should not keep weapons that our military planners do not need," he said.

And on an almost daily basis, Bush talked about his ideas on education—the one area where he seemed immersed in the details of reform, accountability, the need for standardized testing. Again and again, he would talk about the injustice of a system that assumed the poor—especially the black and Hispanic poor—would fail, and he would attack "the soft bigotry of lowered expectations." It's hardly unusual for candidates to make public-policy pronouncements. If nothing else, it forces political journalists into writing something about what the candidate may actually be thinking, rather than more stories about staff disputes, bad poll numbers, or youthful indiscretions. What Bush did on May 15, however, *was* unusual. More than that, it was a campaign moment of real political significance.

In a speech in Ontario, California, at the Rancho Cucamonga Senior Center, Bush outlined his approach to Social Security. While promising to leave the current system intact for the elderly and near-elderly, he proposed "personal retirement accounts" for younger workers—permitting them to "take some portion of [the] payroll tax, and put it in a fund that invests in stocks and bonds."

With this notion, Bush had done something no candidate is ever supposed to do: He had "touched the third rail" of American politics. For decades, Democrats had profited from the notion that Republicans were just waiting for the chance to end Social Security. Barry Goldwater had proposed making the system voluntary in 1964—he went down to a landslide defeat. The mere whiff of a thought that the Reagan administration might want to change the system helped cost it twenty-six seats in the House in 1982. And here was this weak-on-the-details Texas governor proposing to alter the system to its roots. For Vice President Gore, it seemed like a target of maximum opportunity. Gore seemed to have a special taste for the "risky scheme" description of his opponent's plans. He used the phrase to attack Bob Dole's tax plan in 1996; he used it to blast Bradley's health-care plan in the primaries. There was something about the sibilance—"ris-s-s-s-s-s-ss-ky sche-e-e-eme"—that suggested a snakelike quality to the idea. Or maybe it was the image of some mad-scientist-turned-policy-wonk, Lex Luthor with a Heritage Foundation research grant, plotting to undermine the well-being of the citizenry.

Yet here, as it turned out, Bush had caught a prevailing political wind. By century's end, about *half* of all Americans were invested in the market, either though their own investments or through pension funds. For a decade, the financial markets had been rising as if the law of gravity no longer applied. Even those with modest paychecks watched the unbroken rise every day on their televisions and in the papers with fascination and envy. The great majority of Americans had never lived through the Depression; for many, the very idea of an economic downturn was something out of the distant past. In this sense, at least, Karl Rove's "1896" template seemed fitting. It was Bush who was looking toward the new economy; it was Gore and the Democrats who seemed frightened to change, seeing only "risk." (Would Bush's plan have seemed more frightening had the bear market of early 2001 arrived by Election Day 2000? Maybe.)

Moreover, Bush used his acceptance speech in Philadelphia to neutralize Gore's attacks with what may be the single most effective tool in politics: humor.

"Every one of the proposals I've talked about tonight," Bush said, "[Gore] has called a 'risky scheme,' over and over again.

"If my opponent had been there at the moon launch, he would have called it a 'risky rocket scheme.'

"If he'd been there when Edison was testing the lightbulb, it would have been a 'risky anticandle scheme.'

"And if he'd been there when the Internet was invented, well . . . I understand he actually was there for that."

Coincidence or not, Gore abandoned his beloved "risky scheme" mantra almost immediately.

Did all this spadework pay off? Look at the exit polls. There was no way that Bush was going to beat Al Gore on the question of experience and detailed knowledge of government. When asked, "Who has the knowledge to be president?" 37 percent said, "Only Gore," and 24 percent said, "Only Bush." But 30 percent of the voters said, "Both," and they cast their votes overwhelmingly for Bush—71 to 27 percent. It was as if some of these voters were saying, "I don't want to vote for Gore—I'd like to vote for Bush—but you have to show me that he's got the weight, the substance for the job." That question often comes up in campaigns when a vulnerable "insider" runs against a relatively unknown "outsider." When the outsider convinces voters he can be trusted with presidential power, he wins (Reagan in '80, Clinton in '92). When he can't, he loses (Dukakis in '88). In 2000, plenty of voters had plenty of doubts about the Texas governor—enough doubts to deprive him of a popular-vote victory. But without that months-long recitation of detailed policies, those doubts might well have been enough to sink him. The voters on Election Day *favored* Bush's Social Security investment plan (57 to 39 percent), and favored his across-the-board tax cut plan over Gore's proposals for targeted cuts (51 to 44 percent). There was one more notable number. Traditionally, voters who cite education as the most important campaign issue vote overwhelmingly for Democrats. In 1992, Clinton won the "education" voters by twenty-five points; he won them by thirty-six points in 1996. In 2000, Gore won among these voters by only eight points—a strong indication that Bush's countless visits to classrooms had not been in vain.

● It was the spring and the summer of Al Gore's discontent.

It almost seemed as if the vice president's campaign had made a conscious decision: Go into political hibernation, and wait for George W. Bush to step on a political land mine. Maybe something in the governor's past would emerge, something far more damaging than an occasional youthful toot. Surely, there was enough in the Texas record to give the lie to the "compassionate conservatism" mask. That did not happen.

"The media bought Bush's spin that he's talking about education, social security," says Ed Rendell. "He was able to slip back into compassionate conservatism. The media never looked at Bush's record in Texas on the minimum wage, health care."

More significant, Gore was clobbered in midspring by a grievous political wound. The event was beyond his control, but the political damage was, in substantial measure, a self-inflicted wound that struck at the heart of his greatest vulnerability. Ever since Thanksgiving Day, 1999, the U.S. Justice Department, Florida's Cuban-American community, and much of the political world had been transfixed by the case of Elián González. The six-year-old boy had been fished from the waters off the Florida coast after a small boat had capsized, drowning his mother and several other Cubans fleeing the Castro regime. Elián's father wanted him back. The Clinton administration agreed. The Cuban-American community saw Elián's mother as a martyr, his rescue as divine intervention; the unemployed Floridian who plucked him from the waters became the "Fisherman," endowed with the saintly qualities of Peter the Apostle. As for sending the boy back to Cuba, well, would you have sent a six-year-old Jewish boy back to Hitler's Germany in 1939 after his mother had sacrificed her life for his freedom?

After months of silence, Gore distanced himself from his own administration in April, suggesting that the case be resolved in Florida family court. It was the same position Elián's American relatives were staking out, and the same position most Republicans embraced. But when Gore came out on the side of the Cuban-American community, he did it under a cloud. It was not a question of intelligence or experience, but of character. Wasn't Gore the consummate politician, the man who seemed to conduct an internal poll before expressing an opinion about everything from tax policy to the designated-hitter rule? There was grumbling within the Clinton administration: *Gore is breaking with us not because he believes it, but because he's petrified of losing the Cuban-American vote.* There was skepticism among Cuban-Americans: *He wants our votes now, but isn't this the man who loyally served Clinton for eight years, who needs his money and support to win?*

Whatever slack Gore had on this issue disappeared in the

early-morning hours of April 22. Federal agents raided the home of Elián's relatives, and plucked the boy from the arms of Donato Dalrymple, the "Fisherman," who was hiding in the closet holding the boy in his arms. There was one more person in the room: a news photographer named Alan Diaz, who snapped a photograph that instantly assumed iconic significance. The picture showed a combat-ready federal officer, clad in full battle gear, apparently leveling a massive automatic weapon at the boy, whose mouth was open in sheer terror. Later, Attorney General Reno would argue that *no, the weapon wasn't pointed at the boy; that impression was left by the angle of the photograph; and just moments later, the boy was in the arms of a female agent, who was comforting him with the promise that he would soon be reunited with his father.* To borrow a phrase from the late Senator Dirksen, the explanation had all the impact of a snowflake on the bosom of the Potomac River. There are times when an image is impervious to analysis. Was that photo of the Marines raising the U.S. flag on Iwo Jima posed? Was the victim of that Saigon street-corner execution after the 1968 Tet Offensive an enemy agent? No matter. That first photo will always stand as a symbol of American resolve and triumph. That second photo will always stand as a symbol of a cruel, futile war. And that photograph of a terrified little Cuban boy was—especially in Florida's politically potent Cuban-American community—a symbol of a brutally uncaring government. On Election Day, the Cuban vote in Florida broke for Bush by four to one. Had Gore come close to Clinton's 1996 showing in that community—he wound up with a little more than half of it—all the chads and butterfly ballots in Florida wouldn't have kept him from carrying the state. Nationally, it confirmed that sense of Gore that hung around him like a toxic cloud: *This guy will say anything to win.*

Mix the González case with the somnolent pace of the campaign—"everybody was sitting around measuring the drapes for the White House," Gore aide Carter Eskew said later—and the numbers for Gore began looking like those of a dot-com stock. Taken together, the poll numbers had Gore even with Bush just after Super Tuesday. By June he was trailing Bush by six or seven points. A month later, as the Republican convention opened, the margin was hitting double digits. When it closed, the traditional convention "bounce" pushed Bush's lead to fifteen, sixteen, eighteen points.

It was at that point that Vice President Gore turned a rout into a race. Faced with the two biggest decisions of his campaign, he made exactly the right choices. The choices were essentially his—a striking departure from a campaign encrusted with focus groups, polls, consultants, and caution bordering on paralysis. And in both cases, the choices pointed to the possibility that the stereotypes about the vice president were overdrawn: that he could be his own man; that he could find a way to separate himself from the shadow of Clinton; that he could find a fit between who he was and what he said and did as a politician. In that month framed by the Lieberman pick and the acceptance speech, the Gore campaign found itself—for a while.

In days gone by, speculation about running mates usually began a few days before the national nominating conventions began. There were good reasons for this. First, it didn't make a lot of sense to guess about the running mate if nobody knew who would win the presidential nomination. Second, the vice president was an insignificant political figure, forever immortalized by the character of Alexander Throttlebottom in the classic musical *Of Thee I Sing*. (His only glimpse of the White House came when he took the official tour.) Even the fact that vice presidents became presidents every twenty years or so did not enhance the office's status. But beginning with Jimmy Carter, presidents began delegating substantial responsibility to the vice president. Over that same quarter century, the nominating contests became more and more truncated, giving the vice-presidential choice a lot more attention. Notwithstanding Dan Quayle, the second slot on the ticket had real weight and visibility.

Despite this, I have never developed a real taste for vice-presidential speculation. I always figure that the nominee will let us all know when he's made a choice. More to the point, no candidate has ever tipped me off in advance. I tend to treat the whole speculation game with my tongue firmly in cheek. One example: A piece I wrote for the *New York Times* op-ed page predicted a monosyllabic-named running mate. The victories of George Bush and Al Gore, I reasoned, proved the public was so impatient with politics that it would no longer tolerate any nominee with a lengthy name—no more Eisenhowers, no more Stevensons. This year, we had chosen two candidates with a combined syllable count of four—the absolute minimum. In that same spirit, I forecast a running mates whose names were brief. For the Republicans: Ridge (governor of Pennsylvania); Dole (Liddy, not Bob). For the Democrats, Hunt (governor of North Carolina); Graham (senator from Florida). And Lieberman?

"Don't hold your breath," I advised.

A more serious glimpse of my myopia came on the opening night of the Republican convention, when *Larry King Live* turned to the question of Gore's running mate.

"Al Gore and Bob Shrum are sitting there saying—they're racking their brains for something that's—that will be an . . . interesting choice. . . . But I think they're looking through that deck saying, there's got to be somebody who changes the equation."

Who, I asked my fellow panelists, could Gore pick who would change our perception of the vice president?

A deadly silence fell upon us all.

The vice president, however, did have an idea—and not the one that his high-priced consulting talent was promoting.

"All the campaign aides were against Lieberman," one campaign aide remembers gleefully. "They all wanted John Edwards," a young, attractive first-term senator from North Carolina. "Some of them had worked for him in his Senate campaign, and they were pumping Edwards. In fact, they'd prepared B-roll for the networks on Edwards, and they were leaking all over town that it was John Edwards. Some of us were appalled at their behavior, because we wondered what on earth the attraction of Edwards would be. We couldn't see what the rationale would be."

The Lieberman rationale, by contrast, was apparent. After Clinton's confession of August 17, he was the first Democrat to denounce not just the president's lies, but his behavior as well. On September 3, 1998, Lieberman went to the Senate floor and took the president to task. It was not, he said, a private and personal matter.

"My immediate reaction . . . was deep disappointment and personal anger . . . The president is a role model who, because of his prominence and the moral authority that emanates from his office, sets standards of behavior for the people he serves . . . So no matter how much the president or others may wish to compartmentalize the different spheres of his life, the inescapable truth is that the president's private conduct can and often does have profound public consequences."

In choosing Lieberman, Gore would be sending an unmistakable sign. He was embracing the president's toughest critic in his own party.

There was, of course, another matter. Lieberman was Jewish, an observant, orthodox Jew, who kept the Sabbath and who spoke often and openly about the meaning of faith in his life. If this election was going to turn in significant measure on questions of values and character, Lieberman was a public figure who walked the talk.

No one save Al Gore knows precisely how these factors weighed in his choice. What his most loyal supporters saw, however, was something that went beyond the political benefit of the choice.

"When Gore picked Lieberman," says Elaine Kamarck, "I knew it was really his choice, and that he was really now operating on a level of authenticity that he hadn't been able to reach in the campaign."

That decision, she believes, propelled Gore into shaping his own convention acceptance speech.

"I only wrote him one e-mail during this time," Kamarck says. "I said that authenticity was all that mattered in this election. That was what McCain had tapped into. And that, whatever he did in his campaign speech, he had to be authentic. He wasn't a poet—he was a substantive issues person." On the Thursday night of the Democratic convention, it was a "substantive issues person" who stood at the Staples Center arena and accepted the Democratic nomination.

One of my favorite challenges in the work I do is trying to analyze major political speeches on the fly. I spent a decade writing speeches for politicians, and it has given me a fair amount of confidence that I can read between the lines. I'm always looking for parallels, for "lifts" from other major speeches, for arguments that strike the primary chords of a campaign message. When I read Gore's speech, two elements jumped out at me. First, he had clearly taken to heart George H. W. Bush's classic 1988 acceptance speech in New Orleans. In that speech, Bush acknowledged that he had labored in the shadow of Ronald Reagan. Now, he implored the country to "see me for what I am." In his speech, Gore acknowledged that he had labored in the shadow of Bill Clinton. Now, he declared, "I stand here tonight as my own man, and I want you to know me for who I truly am." In 1988, Bush acknowledged his lack of charisma and—in a graceful act of Political Judo—said, "I am a quiet man, but I hear the quiet people others don't." In 2000, Gore unveiled his own judo move:

"I know I won't always be the most exciting politician, but I pledge to you tonight I will work for you every day and [take *that,* Mr. President] I will never let you down."

The second striking feature of the speech was that at its core it looked much more like one of Clinton's State of the Union speeches than an acceptance speech at a political convention. In our time, the acceptance speech has evolved—or devolved—from a political statement to a far more personal one. Richard Nixon spoke in 1968 of the little boy in a small town listening to train whistles in the night. George Bush in 1988 spoke of a move from New England to Texas to start a new life. Bill Clinton told us, "I never knew my father." In his previous convention speeches, Gore had gone perilously close to the edge with his personal tales. In 1992, he spoke at length about the near-death of his son in a traffic accident; he then compared the state of the American economy to his unconscious son, waiting for help. In 1996, he went into harrowing detail about the death of his sister Nancy from lung cancer; this experience, he argued, had made him a staunch foe of Big Tobacco. (It was left to churlish journalists to note that in 1988, four years after his sister died, Gore was running for president in southern primaries boasting of his lifelong ties to tobacco.) He did not stint on family this time, showering love and praise on his parents, his wife, and his children. And the kiss he planted on Tipper before the speech began was clearly the visual highlight of the entire evening. (In a rare act of restraint, I did *not* point out on the air that the picture of the Democratic nominee for president passionately kissing his own wife was another clear symbol of his break with Clinton.)

The heart of the speech, however, showed that Gore had learned well from the president. Every year, Clinton would ride down to the Capitol and deliver a speech, salting the audience with Skutniks—not just heroes, but ordinary individuals symbolizing a Clinton policy proposal. Every year, commentators would deride the speech: It was too long, it was a laundry list, there was no theme. Every year, in the wake of such comments, Clinton's approval ratings would jump dramatically. So Gore did the same. In a speech largely of his own crafting, Gore offered himself to the country as . . . Al Gore. *Yes,* he said in effect, *I am a man of government, but I know how to put the government on* your *side.*

"I've learned the issues before us all have names," he said. "And I don't mean the big fancy names we put on programs and legislation. I'm talking about family names like Nystel, Johnson, Gutierrez and Malone—people and families I've met in the last year, all across this country."

And sure enough, there they were, in the hall: each of them introduced to put a human touch on policies:

- Mildred Nystel, a welfare-to-work success story, who will send her daughter to college with a targeted tax cut

- Jacqueline Johnson, a seventy-two-year-old woman nearly pauperized by her medicine bills, who will be protected by Gore's prescription drug program
- The Gutierrez family of San Antonio, Texas [are you listening, Governor Bush?], whose daughter is forced to attend "a crumbling and overcrowded" school
- Ian Malone, an eight-year-old boy deprived of needed care by a heartless HMO, who will be protected by a patients' bill of rights.

In later days, Gore's need to humanize himself by drawing on "real people" would do him serious harm. On this night, in this setting, it worked like a charm. What worked even better, and what the text of the speech could not hint at, was how he delivered it. The Al Gore of the campaign trail seemed to have two different voices, each of them remarkably unappealing: Al Gore the policy wonk, patiently instructing his cognitively challenged audience; or Al Gore the faux southern preacher, voice suddenly ragged and hoarse, accent suddenly displaying a thick coat of sorghum and molasses. On this night, Al Gore spoke calmly, quietly, deliberately talking over the applause, clearly understanding that his audience was at home, not in the hall. On this night, the populist themes he had embraced during the campaign—"I'll fight for *yew!*" "*I'm for the people, not the powerful!*"—found a more graceful turn of phrase.

"So often," he said, "powerful forces and powerful interests stand in your way, and the odds seem stacked against you, even as you do what's right for you and your family. How and what we do for all of you—the people who pay the taxes, bear the burdens, and live the American dream—that is the standard by which we should be judged."

The Lieberman pick and the acceptance speech turned the fortunes of the Democrats around. When the convention opened in Los Angeles, uneasiness was the prevailing mood; when it ended, you could almost hear the new thought: *Hey! We could actually win this thing!* The traditional postconvention "bounce" was more like the liftoff of an Atlas rocket. Gore and Lieberman were suddenly running ahead of Bush and Cheney in the polls. The first days after the convention brought to mind the Clinton-Gore bus tour of Middle America. This time, it was Gore and Lieberman cruising down the Mississippi River, the literal middle of America, with big crowds and buoyant polls, and a Republican campaign suddenly afflicted with glitches. An offhanded Bush comment to Cheney, caught by an open microphone, calling a *New York Times* reporter "a major league asshole"; a Bush campaign ad that seemingly contained a sub-liminal message; a Bush remark that twisted that word into "subliminable." Those of us afflicted with that *Sesame Street* impulse—"this campaign is just like the others"—began to see the first discernible signs of 1988. The weak incumbent vice president was looking like a winner. The challenging governor was looking wobbly on his feet.

Measured by the exit polls, Gore was helped all the way to the end of the campaign by the way he framed the issues. Even without his convention speech, Gore would have done better among voters who thought the most important quality in a president was an "understanding of the issues." But would he have won among "issues" voters by a more-than-three-to-one majority without that convention speech? That success, however, was fatally undercut by another finding from the exit poll: Only 13 percent of voters thought that "understanding issues" was the key to their votes. By contrast, nearly a quarter of the voters thought that being "honest" or "trustworthy" was the most important quality in a president. Among *those* voters, Bush beat Gore eighty to fifteen. Why that enormous margin? There are two reasons, I believe, that taken together, formed Al Gore's political Kryptonite: one, Al Gore's public persona; the other, the lengthened shadow of Bill Clinton. Nowhere did the two come together with greater damage to Gore than in the presidential debates.

● Let me take you to the site of a modern presidential debate. It's usually held in an auditorium on a college campus, or maybe a civic center somewhere downtown. A seat inside the auditorium itself is the toughest ticket in town, as hot as a Super Bowl seat on the fifty-yard line, or fifth-row-center at a reunion of a legendary rock band. High-voltage politicians, civic leaders, deep-pocket contributors, and other worthies crowd the aisles. Anybody with an interest in the debate's political implications is hunched somewhere in front of a TV set. Somewhere near the auditorium, a cavernous room—as often as not the school gym—has been converted into a press room. Hundreds of tables are lined up along the room's width. Television sets appear every thirty or forty feet. A network of telephone and computer lines snake under the tables, so that the press corps can file their stories instantly. At different corners of the press room, television cameras from the broadcast and cable networks face jury-rigged platforms. It is here that campaign surrogates will appear immediately after the debate, to proclaim the event a total victory for their candidate's side. They know that even the sharpest anchor cannot resist the question: "How did your man do?" (Someday, a campaign spokesman will say, "My guy got his butt whipped." That will occur a moment before the Messiah arrives.)

In other rooms, or in trailers that serve as campaign command centers, operatives from the campaigns wait, briefing books and computers at the ready. As the debate is taking place, these operatives are listening for any inaccuracy, contradiction, or other words damaging to the opposition.

"Aha!" one will shout. "That five-year revenue projection is *flatly* wrong!"

"We got him! He's completely misunderstood the FBI victimization statistics!" These instant responses will be printed out and rushed to the waiting press corps while the debate itself is still going on. The proclamations of total annihilation will be on every reporter's desk before the candidates' final statements have been delivered. Meanwhile, back at the networks' polling centers, "callbacks" are going out to a few hundred voters who said they'd be watching the debates. Within an hour, the networks will be reporting these numbers as if they were an indication of the debate's political impact. Every once in a blue moon, they are. Usually, they are meaningless, if not misleading.

What's really going on is happening in tens of millions of homes, where political passion does not run high, where the campaign has not been a matter of obsessive interest for the last year and a half. Most of them have made up their minds long ago (in the sense that every major-party candidate starts out with 40 percent of the party's vote at worst). The indecision of the coveted "undecided" voter is as likely to result from indifference as from a judicious examination of the candidates. What these voters are looking for is an impression, a sense of the candidate. That impression doesn't form as a snap judgment. It can take a few days to crystallize, as people talk it over at work, at the market, at the PTA. Sometimes, if a candidate makes a big enough mistake, these voters might even turn to the press for guidance; when President Ford pronounced Poland free of Soviet domination in 1976, it took a barrage of press reports before the public realized he had put his foot in his mouth.

Every candidate, every media consultant, every journalist understands this—at least in theory. That's why any television or newspaper account of a presidential debate goes something like this:

Nixon's lousy makeup job in '60 cost him the White House; Ford prematurely liberated Eastern Europe; Reagan said, "There you go again" and asked voters if they were better off than they were four years ago in '80; Reagan looked befuddled in the first '84 debate but made a joke about Walter Mondale's "youth and inexperience" to recover; Dukakis was insufficiently emotional about the prospect of his wife's rape and murder in '88; Bush looked at his watch in '92 and seemed bored.

(Nobody talks about the Clinton-Dole '96 debates, because the election was effectively over long before they were held.)

That's also why it is all but impossible for predebate analysts to avoid uttering the single most witless observation known to modern political man:

"What Bush has to do tonight is to appear *presidential.*"

I confess here to a long-held fantasy: One day, I hope to see a candidate walk onto a debate stage wearing a stovepipe hat, a shawl, and a beard and read his opening remarks off the back of an envelope. But I digress.

For Bush, the debates had been politically costly before the first one even began. His campaign had rejected the plan of the Commission on Presidential Debates for three ninety-minute meetings on all the networks. They proposed instead one "official" debate; one joint appearance on *Larry King Live;* and one with Tim Russert on *Meet the Press.* Since Gore had said he'd debate Bush "anytime, anywhere," they hoped to force the vice president's hand. Nobody bought the ploy. Since there was no chance that other networks would carry NBC's Russert program or CNN's Larry King, the obvious implication of Bush's plan is that the debates would be seen by a far smaller audience than the commission's plan would allow. Ultimately, Bush caved. The image of the less experienced Texas governor ducking the vice president was too costly a political price to bear.

And that's what made what happened at the debates so remarkable. The vice president, a veteran of forty debates during his political career, the man who had demolished Ross Perot on a free-trade debate on *Larry King Live,* the man with a sharp instinct for the political kill, *lost all three debates.* He lost them not because George W. Bush was especially impressive, but because Gore managed—*in every one of the debates*—to ram home the impression that he was precisely the smug, condescending politician of the stereotype who would in fact say anything to be president. This is a harsh conclusion. What makes it especially sad is that some of Gore's most devoted supporters share it, even if they would use different words to describe it.

Political legend has it that voters who listened to the very first Kennedy-Nixon debate in 1960 thought Nixon had won; those who saw it on television thought Kennedy had won. Read the bloodless transcript of the first Gore-Bush debate from 2000, and you might well judge Gore the winner on points. He hammered the governor repeatedly on the inequity of his tax cut, peeled away the shortcomings of Bush's prescription-drug plan, and in general showed a much better grasp of federal policy. Watch a tape of the debate, and a very different picture emerges. Gore repeatedly interrupts, demands more time to explain himself, behaves like the smartest kid in class impatiently insisting on correcting everyone else's mistakes. He rolls his eyes, shakes his head, and sighs audibly if not theatrically.

At one point, moderator Jim Lehrer attempted to wrap up an argument on prescription drugs. Gore was like a terrier who could not let go of the bone.

"Jim, if I could respond."

"Just quick, and then we need to move on."

A moment later, Lehrer tries again:

"Excuse me, gentlemen."

"Jim, can I—can I make one other point?"

A moment later, as he and Bush continue, Bush tries to defend his plan:

"All seniors are covered under prescription drugs in my plan."

"In the first year? In the first year?"

"If we can get it done in the first year, you bet. Yours is phased in in eight years."

"No. No. No. No. It's a two-phase plan, Jim."

Forget the fact that Gore's makeup looked like it had been the work of a student of mortuary science. Any undecided voter who was wary of electing a big-government know-it-all to the White House had his worst fears confirmed in that first debate. Yes, the instant polls showed a narrow Gore victory. But it was the kind of victory the villainous wrestler scores with a questionable chokehold. A lot of voters were saying, "Yeah, he won—but *I don't like that guy.*"

Inside the Gore camp's trailers, the rapid-response team

was banging out its rebuttals, cheering every time their man went after Bush on the weaknesses of his plan. Other staff members watched in horror. While the network polls were suggesting a Gore victory, the vice president's own results from focus groups were dismaying.

"They were saying, 'We don't like him,' recalls one campaign aide, "Or they would say, 'Al Gore won, but we don't like him,' There were still people that night who thought he'd done fine, but by the time we got to Nashville two or three days later, it started to sink in."

One reason why it had sunk in was that the press had once again discovered Al Gore stretching things a bit. As he had in his acceptance speech, Gore drew on the personal experiences of "real Americans" to make his policies more vivid. He spoke of Winifred Skinner, a seventy-nine-year-old woman forced to collect deposit bottles to help pay for her medicine. He spoke of Kaylie Ellis, forced into a classroom so overcrowded she had no desk. When Governor Bush recalled fires and floods that had devastated parts of Texas, Gore noted that he'd traveled down to Texas with James Lee Witt, director of the Federal Emergency Management Agency. Well, Winifred Skinner had an affluent son who was more than willing to pay for her medicine, but she had a stubborn streak in her. And Kaylie Ellis only had to stand for a day or so; there were plenty of desks in her school. And Gore hadn't actually traveled to Texas with Witt to inspect the damage. He'd been down there with Witt's deputy.

Under other circumstances, this would have been no big deal. Even Ronald Reagan's most loyal supporters will acknowledge that he frequently blurred the line between fact and fiction, cited movie scenes as historical events, quoted facts that were sometimes fancy. The political fallout from such whoppers? Zero. Nobody doubted that Reagan held a clear, consistent set of political beliefs, and had held them for decades. Not even his critics thought Reagan would adjust his ideas to fit the current political currents. This was, after all, a man who'd begun his national political life in 1964, speaking for Barry Goldwater—a candidate clearly headed for a historic defeat.

Not so with Al Gore. These exaggerations and missteps peeled the scab off an old wound. The man who had invented the Internet, the man who turned "no controlling legal authority" into a symbol of oleaginous speech was at it again. Worse, the combination of Gore's exaggerations and personality served to strip him of the goal that was at the heart of his debate strategy.

"Everybody knew that the underbelly of the Bush campaign was competence, just like our underbelly was likeability, trust," says a campaign insider. "And yet, because of the likeability issue, we couldn't make competence as strong as he wanted to—because Gore going on the attack on Bush not being ready to be president was clearly something that was going to come back and bite him in the ass. So we were in this terrible Catch-22 situation."

That became evident in the second debate a week later, in Winston-Salem, North Carolina. Stung by the criticism of his demeanor, captured by a brilliant *Saturday Night Live* parody, Gore appeared sedated, even contrite during that debate. At one point, he even apologized for his exaggerations and misstatements in the first debate. In the process, neither he nor the campaign nor the press was able to home in on some king-size whoppers by Governor Bush. The governor, for example, claimed that the state of Texas spent $4.7 billion a year on the poor, but he was counting public *and* private money. He took credit for a patients' bill of rights law he had opposed. He bent if not broke the truth when he denied that a president had the power to ban RU-486, the abortion pill. There was little if any press pickup on these errors. The Gore story was much more potent; the ground for Gore-as-serial-exaggerator had been laid for years.

There is one more incident from the debates that speaks volumes about what happened to Gore—and why. Before the last debate, the Gore camp gathered for its final "prep" at a resort just outside St. Louis. Once again, Gore participated in a practice debate, on a set designed to resemble the real thing as much as possible. This last debate was designed as a "town hall" format, with undecided voters, rather than Jim Lehrer, asking the candidates questions. In 1992, Clinton seized the format to engage his audience physically, leaving his stool to walk over, make eye contact, ask a question or two of the panel member. The rules this time prohibited this kind of interaction, but Gore had a different idea. In the middle of the practice debate, as the Bush stand-in was asking a question, Gore walked over and stood behind Bush.

What do you think about this? He asked. There was a near-unanimous reaction: *Don't do it. It will look staged, phony, planned.* The press corps assumes nothing in these debates happens by accident anyway, and at this point, Gore is the last person on earth who would be credited with spontaneity. Beyond this, all the talk in political circles was of the New York Senate debate. There, Representative Rick Lazio had walked over to Hillary Clinton's podium, demanding she sign a campaign finance reform pledge. It was widely seen as a clumsy flop of a ploy. Gore had a different notion.

I'm taller, bigger than Bush. I've forgotten more than he'll ever know. If I move close enough to him, I can rattle him; I can show people I'm literally the bigger man for the job, and in tele-vision that matters.

Faced with the vice president's determination, the team literally mapped out the parameters of this strategy:

Here's your chair, and here's your table. And there's his stand, and there's his stool. Okay. Don't go farther than right here.

His team even drew lines on the stage, to set the limits of where Gore should stand.

That third debate was Bush's least effective performance. He was so fixated on describing Gore as a big-government in-sider that at one point he said, "One thing about insurance, that's a Washington word." That answer left an impression that the governor was indeed uncomfortable with words of more than two syllables. He was less sure of himself on what his proposals would do than in either of the first two debates.

It didn't matter. About ten minutes into the debate as Bush was answering a question, Al Gore left his stool and walked slowly, stiffly toward his opponent, arms at his sides, palms pointing behind him, looking oddly like Gort—the robot in *The Day the Earth Stood Still.* Bush glanced back over his shoulder, took a beat—and nodded once, as if to say: *Hi, there—be with you in a moment.* The audience laughed, and Al Gore was finished for the night.

Within days of the debate, Gore had again fallen behind in the polls. The numbers varied—he was two down in the CBS/*New York Times* poll, four down in the ABC News/*Wash-ington Post* poll, six down in the CNN/*Time* poll—but the movement was clear. Al Gore had been weighed in the balance, and had been found wanting.

What did all this mean on Election Day? The "honest and trustworthy" gap became a chasm. As noted earlier, nearly a quarter of the voters named that as their most important consideration. Because those voters were by definition responding to the Clinton factor, Gore never had a chance to capture this group. Their eighty-to-fifteen-percent preference for Bush, however, was at least in part a measure of how badly Gore had failed at closing the gap. Two other questions framed the consequence of Gore's public personality even more dramatically.

"Who would say anything to win?" one exit-poll question asked. Given the traditional American skepticism about politicians, it's not surprising that 41 percent answered: "Both." But while 17 percent said "only Bush" would say anything, *33 percent—almost twice as many*—said that "only Gore" would say anything.

"That was the one question I paid the most attention to throughout the campaign," says a Gore aide. "And we were never able to close that gap except for a brief moment after the convention—the one time in the whole campaign when Gore was most himself."

"Who attacked unfairly?" the poll asked. "Both," answered more than a third of the voters. "Only Gore," said a quarter. "Only Bush," said 14 percent. The "soft underbelly" of the vice president's image—Gore as slippery pol, Gore as bully—suffered a devastating hit on Election Day.

● For all that Gore did to harm himself, there was one issue over which he had little control: How did people feel about his boss? More specifically, would they use their votes on Election Day to ratify the record under Clinton, or to punish Clinton by rejecting his designated successor? Ever since the Lewinsky scandal, the numbers all told the same story: Most Americans thought he was doing a good job, most voters certainly did not want him removed from office, and most voters had no use for him personally at all. It was a delicate balance for everyone.

George W. Bush, for example, had no desire at all to revisit the issue. Part of his "change the tone" message was aimed squarely at the fire-breathing Republicans who had rammed impeachment through the House of Representatives in the face of clear public disapproval. They may well have genuinely believed that the president was a perjurious adulterer who had disgraced the White House, but it did not matter. Between the GOP majority and Ken Starr, the politically tone-deaf independent counsel, the whole enterprise left a bad taste in the public's mouth. Even the more general anti–Clinton emotion among conservatives was a potential liability for Bush. At the Republican convention in Philadelphia, for example, the entire arena was sanitized for Bush's protection: no signs about Hillary or Gennifer or Monica—and Bush's acceptance speech itself contained an effective "more-in-sorrow-than-in-anger" look back at Clinton.

"Our current president embodied the potential of a generation. So many talents. So much charm. Such great skill. But in the end, to what end? So much promise, to no great purpose."

Only Dick Cheney, in his acceptance speech, laid out a line of attack. Speaking of Gore and Clinton, he noted dryly, "Somehow, we will never see one without thinking of the other."

Gore's job was much tougher, politically and psychologically. The public's low opinion of Clinton the person made the "time for a change" argument much stronger than it would have been if Clinton had simply thanked Ms. Lewinsky for the pizza and showed her the door. There was also an element of personal betrayal as well; Clinton had lied to Gore, just as he had lied to his staff and to the country. How, then, could Gore embrace the Clinton record, take credit for the astonishing good times, yet push himself away from the mess? In the end, despite the Lieberman pick and the effective acceptance speech, he couldn't.

The dilemma was evident even in the campaign's first days. In Hanover, New Hampshire, on October 27, 1999, Gore participated in a town-hall debate. The very first question concerned campaign finance reform, and the public's cynicism about government. Here is what Gore said:

"I understand the disappointment and anger that you feel toward President Clinton, and I felt it myself."

If there was any doubt that the Clinton issue was in the forefront of Gore's concerns, that answer dispelled it. The heavier consequence, though, lay in what Gore could *not* say—or do. He could not get past the Clinton issue to get to the administration's record. And, for reasons more political than psychological, he could not wheel out the president to rally the base in the last days of the campaign.

As for Clinton himself, his opening-night speech at the Democratic convention in Los Angeles was classic fare: powerful, self-indulgent, effective, exasperating. His entrance itself was right out of Hollywood (literally: It was staged by Harry Thomason, longtime friend and TV producer). Clinton strode through the subterranean halls of the Staples Center in an endless walk—a blend of Travolta in *Saturday Night Fever,* Russell Crowe in *Gladiator,* and the boys of *Spinal Tap.* (Watching the giant screens from the anchor booth, I almost shouted out, "Hello, Cleveland!") As he walked, graphics popped onto the screen, one after the other, extolling the record: *twenty-two million new jobs, longest economic expansion in history, one hundred thousand new police on the street, crime down 27 percent.*

In his speech, the president celebrated the record, and prodded the Republican opposition with a scalpel, not a bludgeon.

"We sent our [economic] plan to Congress," he recalled. "It passed by a single vote in both houses. In a deadlocked Senate, Al Gore cast the tie-breaking vote. Now, not a single Republican supported it. Here's what their leaders said. Their leaders said our plan would increase the deficit, kill jobs, and give us a one-way ticket to a recession. *Time has not been kind to their predictions* [emphasis added]. Now, remember, our Republican friends said then they would absolutely not be held responsible for our economic policies. I hope the American people take them at their word. . . . You know, Harry Truman's old saying has never been more true—'If you want to live like a Republican, you better vote for the Democrats.' "

Then came the clincher: a restatement of Ronald Reagan's classic closing statement from the 1980 Cleveland debate, reworked with a Democratic twist.

"Let's remember the standard our Republican friends used to have for whether a party should continue in office. My fellow Americans, are we better off than we were eight years ago?

"You bet we are!

"Yes, we are. But we're not just better off; we're also a better country. We are today more tolerant, more decent, more humane, and more united. Now," he added, using Bush's own campaign line, "that's the purpose of prosperity."

It was a blueprint for a Gore argument; one that required no defense at all of Clinton's personal misbehavior. The president himself apparently understood. According to one source at the highest level of the Gore campaign, Clinton's advice went something like this: *Sixty percent of folks think I'm a really good president, and 60 percent of folks think I'm a son of a bitch. So don't defend what I did, just go with the record.* From Gore's own staff came the same guidance. During debate preparations, someone suggested Gore turn to Bush and ask simply, "Just what is it about eight years of peace and prosperity you don't like?"

Yes, good idea, Gore would say. But it never became a dominant theme.

As for bringing Clinton out in the last days, yes, that was the advice coming from Chairman Ed Rendell, and from a raft of local politicians. The campaign had a different view: *You can't bring him into black neighborhoods in Cleveland without the picture showing up on TV screens in the suburbs of Cuyahoga County; you can't put him in Detroit without them seeing the picture in Oakland and McComb and Wayne.*

So what did the voters say about Bill Clinton? Asked directly, they said what they had been saying for the better part of two years: *bad guy, good president.* Fifty-seven percent approved of Clinton's job performance; 41 percent didn't. Only 36 percent looked at him favorably as a person; 60 percent did not. How would he be remembered? For his leadership, said 29 percent; for the scandals, said 68 percent.

But that's not all they said. Because of who Bill Clinton was, where he came from, the generational issues he seemed to embody, he put the battle over culture squarely into Campaign 2000. In the words of *Time* magazine's Eric Pooley, "This election reflected a culture war. There are two sides here, and they break down as follows: Was Bill Clinton good or bad for America? Were the 60's good or bad for America? Were the 'loosenings' that followed in the 1970's good or bad for America?"

No exit-poll numbers were more striking than the cultural divide painted by the numbers—a divide that went far, far beyond "the gender gap." There was a "marriage gap"—married voters went for Bush by nine points; single people went for Gore by nineteen points. There was a "parent gap"—voters with kids went for Bush by fifteen points; the rest of the voters went for Gore by seven points. Regular churchgoers went for Bush by twenty-seven points; those who never went to church went for Gore by twenty-nine points. Gun owners went for Bush by twenty-five points; non–gun owners went for Gore by nineteen points.

The most dramatic display of this culture gap came two days after the election, in the form of a map published in *USA Today*. It displayed a county-by-county vote: Bush counties in red, Gore counties in blue. There were blue patches along the East and West Coasts, throughout the industrial Midwest, in metropolitan areas in the South and West. And all through the empty corners of America, through the South, the Midwest, and all through the mountain West, huge globs of red. A driver starting out on the Carolina coast could drive clear into Orange County, California, without passing through a single county that Gore had carried.

Bill Clinton did not create this culture war. In fact, his own campaign for president had tried to heal that gap, by demonstrating that Democrats cared about crime and individual responsibility. By his own conduct, however, he had helped reopen that war, and he had laid a heavy burden on Al Gore's shoulders. He almost carried that burden across the finish line. The Bush campaign stumbled at the end. A long-hidden arrest for drunk driving surfaced in the last week of the campaign: "It cost us Maine, and maybe half a million to a million votes nationally," one top Bush aide says. Bush took a day off nine days before the election: "That might have cost us Iowa or Wisconsin." And Democrats were coming home, persuaded that Bush might not be up to the job after all: Had he really said it was wrongheaded to think that "Social Security is some kind of federal program"?

With ads challenging Bush's readiness for the job, with a twenty-four-hours-a-day finishing kick, with unprecedented money and manpower from labor, the NAACP, and local Democrats in cities from Philadelphia to Detroit to Miami, Gore closed fast. By Election Day, for the first time since the debates, he was actually even with Bush in at least one last-minute poll.

In the end, from all these streams of tactics and counter-tactics, strategic triumphs and flops, one hundred million Americans had gone to the polls and produced—a tie. Not just an ordinary, run-of-the-mill tie, but a tie that meant the election would be decided in a single state, where the margin stood at roughly five one-thousandths of 1 percent of the votes cast.

The voters had produced one of the strangest Election Nights in history.

It was going to get a lot stranger.

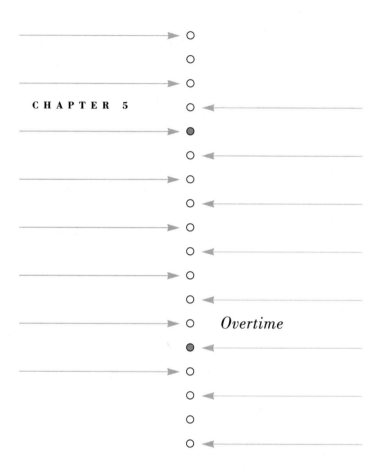

CHAPTER 5

Overtime

THE BEST MOVIE
about the modern media was
made more than half a century ago: *Ace in the Hole,* by
writer-director Billy Wilder.
(You can rent it these days
under its current title, *The
Big Carnival.* It was also the
inspiration for a third-rate
knockoff a few years ago
called *Mad City.*) In the film,
Kirk Douglas, a once-famous

reporter, now a washed-up, embittered alcoholic, lands a job on a tiny paper in the Southwest. On his first day on the job, he wanders into the desert, where he chances on a miner who is trapped in a cave-in. Within a day or two, his exclusive story has become a national sensation. Papers across America are clamoring for his accounts, and the world descends on this small southwestern town. Special trains and tour buses convey the curious to the site of the cave-in; vendors set up shop to sell food, drink, and souvenirs; radio and the then-new medium of television arrive to report, hour-by-hour, on the rescue operation.

On Wednesday morning, November 8, the big carnival was on its way to Palm Beach. Staggering under the weight of an election that had ended in a tie, the election machinery had buckled, just as the predictive machinery had collapsed the night before, in full view of horrified millions. Trapped inside was the identity of the next president. The excavation tools, designed in the eighteenth and nineteenth centuries, had sat idle for well over a hundred years. For decades, those of us in that small band of Constitutional Catastrophists had been warning about this rusted contraption. Like the wise old hands in the first scenes of all those disaster movies, we'd been shaking our heads, muttering, "Don't like the looks of this. You put too much pressure on her, an' one of these days, she's gonna blow." Now, we were about to find out.

In one sense, this was familiar territory. Every once in a while, a story emerges that sweeps aside everything in its path. Millions gain intimate knowledge of people and places they had barely heard of before; once-obscure players become household names, invested with the cloak of hero, villain, comic foil—sometimes all at once.

Sometimes these stories have no greater meaning; they

take the spotlight because they involve wealth, power, sex, death, sometimes all at once. Ninety years before a famous football player stood accused of murdering his wife, a New York millionaire named Harry K. Thaw stood trial for murdering famed architect Stanford White, the one-time lover of showgirl Evelyn Nesbitt, later Thaw's wife. The case made headlines around the world; the *New York Times* called it "the trial of the century." Nearly seventy years ago, the kidnap-murder of the infant son of aviator Charles Lindbergh seized the world stage. When Bruno Hauptmann went on trial for the crime, the New Jersey courtroom became a required stop for celebrities, and the telephone company installed enough lines for the press to meet the needs of a fair-sized city

In our own time, God knows, we have no shortage of compelling stories whose claim to significance is highly dubious. In fact, one of the ways the "higher" media get to frolic in such stories is to invest them with Deeper Meaning. In 1994, when millions of us were watching O. J. Simpson lead the police on a low-speed chase down Southern California's freeways, one network anchor asked, "What does this say about our society?" The correct answer: nothing, except that wealth and fame are no guarantee against evil. Some Greek dramatists may have had something to say about this a long time ago. Anyone who needed the Simpson case to learn that race was still a matter of great moment in America must have been living in a cave since birth.

When Woody Allen and Mia Farrow took their child-custody fight into court, the tabloid press played it for what it was: two famous people with highly unusual private lives. The "high class" press explained how the case threw intriguing light on child-custody issues. When Donald Trump and Marla Maples divorced, the tabloid press treated it as a peek into

Lifestyles of the Rich and Narcissistic. The *New York Times* explained that the divorce threw intriguing light on the use of public-relations professionals.

I tell you this because it supplies the backdrop for one element in the story of the Florida vote. If the atmosphere seemed familiar, there was something gloriously unfamiliar about its import. *This was a really big deal; it was about the presidency; it was about the Constitution.* For the press, it was as if scientists had discovered that a diet of double-bacon cheeseburgers, fries, and hot-fudge sundaes cut cholesterol, extended the life span, and dramatically increased sexual potency. As with other stories, the election deadlock sent news ratings through the roof. But it also made the arcane intricacies of the Constitution come alive; it made history teachers and political-science professors purveyors of quality goods; people even dragged their eyes from the financial markets long enough to watch an ongoing political and legal battle. Best of all, when the day's news was over, nobody felt as if it was time to go home and take a long, hot shower.

This is, of course, an unseemly perspective, reducing the most contentious presidential election in a century and a quarter to its impact on my self-interest. I take some comfort in the fact that it was no different for the combatants—at least in its first stage. The early days in the fight for Florida featured a political battle unlike any I can recall: a battle in which each side was utterly convinced that the other side was out to steal an election, in which each side cheerfully advanced propositions that were either flatly false or utterly ridiculous. In a more fundamental sense, it was never an even fight. At root, the Gore campaign was on the defensive from beginning to end. Why?

•*First,* all the critical political machinery was in Republican hands.

•*Second,* in the end, the Republicans wanted Bush to win more than the Democrats wanted Gore to win. At the national level, the GOP was fully prepared to go nuclear; most Democrats were not. The reasons for that emotional imbalance were rooted in the same elements that had proven so costly to Gore during the campaign: his own political character, and the legacy of Bill Clinton.

•*Third,* whatever the potential consequences of a protracted fight for the White House—and they were serious—the public never had more than a spectator's interest in the outcome. In an exquisite irony, the very sense of well-being that characterized the campaign led the broad American middle to conclude that it really did not matter all that much which one of these contestants won the presidency. So could they please get on with it?

● Two days after Election Day, I got off a plane at La Guardia Airport in New York, to find an urgent message from Sid Bedingfield, the executive in charge of CNN's news coverage.

"How soon can you get down to Palm Beach?"

"What do you mean, 'how soon'?"

"I mean, 'now.' I want you to host a town meeting tonight."

"Not today. I'm begging you. Laundry emergency. I'll be on a plane first thing in the morning."

It was less than two days after the polls in Florida had closed, and already, protesters were crowding the streets in front of the Palm Beach County Governmental Center; already, Reverend Jesse Jackson was in town, drawing parallels with the struggle for voting rights in Selma a generation ago. Already, the TV networks had set up camera stands so that their reporters were standing directly in front of the protesters. It made for good television, I suppose, although I have always had doubts about the merits of a solemn piece of reportage taking place in front of screaming, chanting sign-wavers. (My doubts deepened in these first days when I saw a huge sign being borne aloft behind the demonstrators. It was a placard condemning infant circumcision. I believe this was a completely different "dangling chad" issue. But I digress.)

The facts seemed clear enough:

•More than nineteen thousand voters in Palm Beach County spoiled their ballots by punching more than one hole. Was this anything like the usual total? No. In neighboring Broward County, the so-called "overvote" was 1.7 percent. In Palm Beach, it was 4.1 percent. And in the 1996 presidential election, the "overvote" total was only about three thousand. Something had confused a whole lot of Palm Beach voters this time. Almost certainly, it was the "butterfly ballot," with the names of candidates aligned to the left and the right of the holes.

•Reform Party candidate Pat Buchanan received 3,411 votes in Palm Beach County, a community heavily Democratic and heavily Jewish. It was an impossibly high number, fully *six times* the total for Buchanan in Duval County, Buchanan's northern-Florida stronghold. The candidate's sister, Bay, said on the morning after Election Day, "There's clearly been a problem. This vote is much larger than one would expect for us." Since the hole for Buchanan on the ballot was right over the hole for Gore, this startlingly high vote total was without question the result of ballot confusion. Why the certainty? Consider what the Palm Beach *Post* discovered in its exhaustive examination of the vote: Lakes of Delray is a retirement community where nearly all the residents are Jewish. It cast forty-seven votes for Buchanan—the highest total of any in Palm Beach. Was it possible that a community of elderly Jews had suddenly embraced the candidate who had repeatedly condemned U.S. policy toward Israel as too supportive? Were they attracted to his recently published notion that the United States had been too hasty in opposing Hitler in the run-up to World War II?

What had happened in Palm Beach County was obvious. A new, confusing ballot design had befuddled thousands of voters, causing some of them to vote for the wrong candidate, and causing many thousands more to spoil their ballots by punching two holes. Faced with this fact, Republicans simply denied the reality of what had happened, while Democrats demanded an impossible solution.

In a television appearance on *Talk Back Live* two days after the election, Republican Congresswoman Tillie Fowler asked rhetorically, "Where were these protesters in 1996, when fifteen thousand ballots were thrown out for the very same reason, for double-punching on the presidential ballot? Where were they then? This is a ballot that has been used in the past in Palm Beach County. It's a ballot that was approved by both parties, by both campaigns, by their Democrat supervisor of elections."

Her first "talking point" was the same one virtually every Republican spokesman used in the first postelection days. It found its way into a column by George Will. It was a constant refrain among Bush supporters. And it was flatly wrong. In 1996, a *total* of about fifteen thousand ballots was thrown out in Palm Beach County for "overvoting" *and* undervoting. The comparable total number for this election was some twenty-nine thousand—a huge increase. Nor had the "butterfly ballot" ever been used in a Palm Beach County election among rival candidates for office.

It was then the turn of Democratic Congressman Peter Deutsch, who turned immediately to a possible remedy for this "illegal ballot."

"Florida law," Deutsch said, "requires that a judge, if presented with this type of case, determine the intention of the voters and in fact exercise that. So, whether through a statistical adjustment which has occurred in the state of Florida, Al Gore won this election. If it does not occur, Florida law will require that there be an adjustment of the number in Palm Beach County." Though his argument was a bit tangled, this is what Deutsch was saying.

A judge should look at Pat Buchanan's vote in surrounding counties. He should then conclude that the Buchanan vote in Palm Beach County was the product of an obvious mistake, and allocate a substantial portion of the Buchanan votes to Gore and to Bush, depending on how neighboring counties voted.

Under that proposal, Al Gore would have gained some two thousand votes—enough to give him the state of Florida, and therefore the presidency. It would have happened because a judge in Florida decided that a clear vote on a punch card for Pat Buchanan didn't mean what it said. It was an argument that made for terrific conversation in the classrooms of our finest law schools. As a real-life solution, it was a surefire recipe for absolute chaos.

Thus the conflict: a Bush supporter who denied the obvious fact of *what* had happened; a Gore supporter who proposed a clearly impossible remedy for what to *do* about it. And there was more to come.

A few minutes later, Representative Deutsch—his pitch

and volume rising by the minute—demanded that Fowler explain why "four percent of the people [made] a mistake in that election?"

"I think you've got some uninformed people, maybe voting down in Palm Beach County. I don't know why they keep making the same mistakes, four years in a row." She was repeating here that inaccurate GOP talking point that there had been no increase in spoiled ballots from one presidential election to the next. Barely ten minutes later, Fowler was arguing that the Buchanan vote in Palm Beach County might not have been a mistake after all.

"There has been a one hundred and ten percent increase in the registration of registered voters in the Independent, Reform, and American Reform Party. They got about seventeen thousand people in that county now registered in these parties. This is not an anomaly for that county."

Thus the Republican position in a nutshell: The Buchanan votes represented the actual choice of the voters, and if they didn't, it was simply one of the normal sort of mistakes that happen in every election, and if it wasn't, then it was the voters' own fault.

Now turn to the Democratic partisans. If a judge could not "adjust" the vote and allocate ballots based on some mathematical formula, then at least the courts should order a "revote" in Palm Beach County. A few hardy souls suggested that only the voters who had mistakenly cast Buchanan ballots, or who had voted twice, be permitted to vote. Of course, given the secret ballot, it would be tricky to determine *which* voters had cast *what* particular ballots. Beyond that, even if a "revote" was confined to those voters who had cast ballots on Election Day, some pretty daunting problems remained. The voters in Palm Beach would be armed with information available to no other voters in the country. Nader voters, for example, would know with absolute certainty that their votes would make the difference between a Gore and a Bush presidency. (Nader got 97,000 votes in Florida, 5,565 of them in Palm Beach County.) Wouldn't a large number of them switch to Gore in a revote? Was it fair, even Constitutional, to stage what was in effect a runoff in one overwhelmingly Democratic county while the rest of the state—and the nation, for that matter—stood idly by?

These were some of the questions I intended to raise at CNN's "town meeting" Friday night, as we gathered in the gymnasium of Palm Beach's Atlantic Junior College, far from the crowds outside the county's Governmental Center. I was determined to cut like a laser beam through the spin and the talking points. And I succeeded brilliantly—for a total of about a minute and a half. I asked Mayor Joel Daves of West Palm Beach, a nominal Democrat of impressive bearing and few excess words, whether he had any qualms when he saw the sample butterfly ballot.

"No," he said. "I'm sure that some people did. But I voted and I voted for Al Gore and did not have any problem with the ballot."

Even more impressive, one Republican woman in our audience acknowledged that the ballot was indeed confusing.

"I am a Republican," she said, "and I knew that George Bush was at the very top of the ballot, and he was the first one. But I've had a problem with my right eye, and as soon as I looked at it, I noticed that the holes were extremely close together, that the staggered method of having one candidate on one side and the other candidate on the other side was confusing. And I breathed a sigh of relief that I was a Republican, and just had to punch the top button."

With that, our supply of unpredictability was exhausted.

Mary McCarty, a Republican Palm Beach County commissioner, said the high vote for Pat Buchanan in the county was not at all surprising. GOP Party Chairman Frank DeMario noted that "If you go back to the ninety-six [primary] election, Pat Buchanan got nine thousand votes in an election with only a fifty-five-percent turnout." Republican State Senator Ken Pruitt said, "I was on the ballot and not one person contacted my office to tell me or contacted me to tell me that they were having problems with the ballot."

By contrast, William Washington, of the Palm Beach County NAACP, told of an elderly woman who repeatedly sought out workers at her precinct to explain the ballot to her. Rabbi Jerold Levy of Temple Beth-El in Boca Raton said, "I walked out of the voting booth thinking that I had voted for Al Gore, and when I began to hear people talking about the confusion that they had with the ballot, I began to scratch my head . . . and say to myself, 'Well, maybe I didn't really vote for Vice President Gore."

One woman in the audience put her argument for a revote this way:

"There are many people in Palm Beach County that are elderly. We have many senior citizens. We have people that are dyslexic and handicapped. We have black people who were denied their education until 1954 because of segregation. They have difficulty reading and writing. They were confused by this ballot. I think we should have a revote."

It was somewhere at this point that I began to have one of those fantasies again, about the kind of observation I am so often tempted to make when a live television camera is on. I have come to think of these as my "Froggy the Gremlin" moments. For those of you who have not reached my advanced age—in other words, most of you—Froggy the Gremlin was a character on an old, old kiddie TV show, *Smilin' Ed McConnell and His Gang*. Every week, a straitlaced, pompous grown-up would show up—a teacher of elocution, say, or of good manners.

"Now, children" he would say, "the one thing we must always say to our host when bidding farewell is—"

—and Froggy would mutter, "I can't believe how fat you are."

—and the pompous grown-up would unwittingly repeat: "I can't believe how fat you are—Oh! Oh! No, no, no! I am *so* embarrassed!"

My Froggy the Gremlin moments, no doubt a product of my years writing for the *National Lampoon,* come when the rhetorical fog grows so thick you can barely make out the TelePrompTer copy to lead into the next commercial break. It's the kind of moment Peter Finch experienced in *Network,* when he told the audience that the prospect of losing his job was so horrifying that he intended to kill himself. In this town-meeting setting, I experienced a passing but powerful temptation to stand up and (with apologies to Dennis Miller) rant:

"Wait a minute, here. Listen up, Republicans. There's not a person in this room who doesn't know—I mean know, *deep down in your hearts—that the ballot design screwed up thousands of voters, right? You just heard an editor of your local paper tell you the calls started coming in barely an hour after the polls opened, and they just didn't stop. Of course it wasn't deliberate, of course it was an accident, but that's the* only *reason Pat Buchanan got thirty-four hundred votes in this county. That's the* only *reason nineteen thousand voters punched out two holes. It never would have happened without that butterfly ballot, okay?*

"But you know what, Democrats? You can't do anything

about it! *Maybe if half the ballots in the county had been screwed up, you could try to make a case. But ninety-six percent of the voters got it right. And anyway—this is a* presidential *ballot. There's never been a court anywhere in the country that's ordered a revote in a presidential election, much less in a case where one county could wind up picking the president for the whole nation. It isn't going to happen. You lost your vote because you got confused, and either you were too embarrassed to admit it, or the local officials were too incompetent or indifferent to help you out, okay? Nobody gets to vote a second time for president!"*

Such words never left my lips. Chalk up another triumph of Zenlike self-restraint.

Besides . . . if these local officials and citizens were set in their arguments, no one could blame them. The campaigns themselves came into the Florida overtime battle with their own premises locked firmly into place. Because they were so central to the battle that followed, these premises deserve a closer look. In the dramatic differences between the two camps lies a major reason why Al Gore never had a chance to win the battle for the White House. In chronicling these premises, I know that few partisans are prepared to credit the other side with an ounce of sincerity. These premises will seem nothing more than cynical rationalizations for an attempt to steal an election. So call it hypocrisy or self-delusion; for my money, both sides believed completely in what they were saying.

FROM THE BUSH CAMPAIGN:

● *George W. Bush won the Florida vote. He was ahead when they stopped counting Tuesday night. He was ahead when they ran the ballots through the machines again. It's over; the only reason the Gore campaign wants to prolong the process is to "find" votes that aren't there. That's something Democrats know how to do.*

The Bush campaign's case was totally free of ambiguity. There was no call to "make sure the will of the voters prevail." There was no appeal to compromise or negotiation. *We won, you lost. Get over it.* The appeal, instead, was to every Republican of every stripe: *We are all in this fight together. You've got to stay with us until victory is assured.*

That was the signal sent out to Republicans when James Baker, one of Bush the Elder's oldest friends, emerged in Florida as the campaign's chief spokesman. Everyone knew that Bush the Younger had "issues" with Baker, believed he hadn't gone the last mile when he ran the president's reelection campaign in 1992.

"So," explains one prominent Republican, "if there was any tension in the Bush–Baker relationship, this indicated that the Republicans were coming together for one reason; and that was for George W. to win the presidency. So much had been written about their relationship, and all of a sudden, Jim is front and center. People knew that Jim prided himself on now becoming a world statesman. And nobody thought the political wars in Florida were part of that world. So he sacrificed a bit of himself—and that was a symbol, too. There's nobody better than Jim Baker at sending out symbols."

Speaking of symbols, recall the photo sent out to the country two days after the vote: Governor Bush seated with some of his top advisors—Condoleezza Rice, Larry Lindsey, running mate Dick Cheney, Chief of Staff designate Andrew Card—in what looked a good deal like the chairs that are grouped around the fireplace in the Oval Office. No hubris here, but the prudent planning of the next president. Or, as Governor Bush put it, "I understand there's still votes to be counted, but I'm in the process of planning in a responsible way a potential administration."

What about the uncomfortable fact that Al Gore now had a commanding lead in the popular vote? Not only was it Constitutionally irrelevant, said the Bush people, but you could blame that glitch on the news networks. That early call for Al Gore at 7:50 P.M. Eastern time, they argued, had kept countless Republicans from the polls in the midwestern and western states.

"There's no doubt in my mind," lead Bush strategist Karl Rove said much later. "The early calls by the networks *did* have an effect on the turnout. Look at what happened to us in California. Ten minutes after that call, Gerry Parsky, our California chairman, called and said, 'People are getting up and walking out of their phone banks.' He called back ten minutes later. He said, 'We're getting reports all over the state. In our areas—Orange County, the Inland Empire—people are walking away from polls. I'm not saying we would have won California, but could that call have cost us enough votes around the nation to cost us the popular vote? Sure."

There may be after-the-fact justification in that notion. After all, by Election Day, everyone in the higher reaches of the Bush campaign knew it had been a mistake to let the governor sit out a Sunday nine days before the election, and knew that the late revelation about the old drunk-driving arrest had shaved several hundred thousand votes off the Bush total in the last four days. There was, however, no ambiguity about another conviction that was rock-solid throughout the Republican ranks: Given half a chance, the Democrats would steal this election right out from under George W. Bush.

Where did that conviction come from? For a surprising number of congressional Republicans, it was rooted in a fifteen-year-old battle over "Indiana's bloody eighth." In 1984, a House election in Indiana's Eighth Congressional District had ended in a dead heat. The fight had gone to the Democratic-controlled House of Representatives where—after months of wrangling and on a straight party-line vote—the House seated the Democratic candidate. Republicans stormed out, and for many of them, the conflict demonstrated that Democrats were not to be trusted with the counting of any votes, anywhere, anytime.

"The Republican House members from that era had a visceral reminder of 'stealing elections,' " says Connie Mack, who was in the House that year and who went on to serve two terms in the U.S. Senate. "When the recount talk started in Florida, it seemed like an instant replay, a sense that the Democrats would go to any extent to win. You could feel it when Bill Daley [chair of the Gore campaign] attacked the butterfly ballot: That was so orchestrated to incite a 'tainted' feeling about the election. There was just a sense that they'd do anything to win. And so you begin to lose faith in the other guy's perspective. You start raising questions about their motives, you get a sense that there's no limit."

Even those without memories of the "bloody eighth" had their own reasons to think the Democrats would resort to underhanded methods in order to win. There was, for example, the sheer presence of Bill Daley, the Gore chairman. Wasn't he the son of the late mayor of Chicago Richard Daley? Doesn't everyone remember what had happened to Richard Nixon in the back rooms of Chicago in 1960? It is an absolute article of faith among core Republicans that the Daley machine in Chicago cooked the books until John F. Kennedy was able to claim Illinois by an eight-thousand-vote margin. Now, here was his son, down in Florida, where the canvassing boards in three populous counties—Miami-Dade, Broward, and Palm Beach—were solidly in Democratic hands. Case closed.

"We were careful never to accuse anybody of stealing the election," Bush campaign operative Ed Gillespie says. "We were confident the outcome was going to result in our favor, and in any case, we didn't want to burn down the village in order to save it. But clearly there were people in the conservative Republican base who expressed that viewpoint. You know, 'Here they go again.' "

Democrats see the figure of Bill Clinton behind much of the Republican outrage. Jack Quinn—who is Ed Gillespie's partner in a Washington lobbying firm, and who was Al Gore's onetime chief of staff:

"It reflected their belief that for the last eight years [the Democrats] have been an illegitimate force. It started as far back as '92, right through all the investigations, the impeachment. Al Gore got the full force of their anger, the fury over Clinton."

"It was eight years welling up over thirty-seven days," says Ed Rendell. "The Republicans believe Bill Clinton got away with something; they were gonna make damn sure it didn't happen to them this time."

There was at least one more factor driving the Republican intensity: The networks had *told* them Governor Bush had won—at 2:18 in the morning, to be precise. We'd shown the celebrations, flashed the graphic proclaiming: "Bush Wins Presidency." We'd talked about Cabinet nominations and the White House staff, tried to game out his legislative strategy, started speculating—God forgive us—about the leading Democrats for 2004. It was theirs—and then it had been taken away.

And they were not going to let it happen again. They were not about to turn the fate of the White House over to a bunch of partisan Democratic vote counters, under the likely supervision of a campaign operative whose ability to manipulate votes was a genetic gift.

Finally, there was simply the nature of what it means to be in the biggest political fight of the century.

"I grew up in Brooklyn," Ken Duberstein says. "When we played stickball, you could occasionally have a 'do-over.' You know, the ball bounced under a car, or the chalk line was erased. Here, there wasn't a 'do-over.' This one was for keeps. There was going to be a winner, and a loser. So it should come as no surprise that no one on our side's going to say, 'Oh, of course we should do this over. Of course, there is merit on Gore's side.' No. This is called 'switchblade time.' You're going to fight this out. This is a gun battle. This is for keeps."

It was the way a lifetime political professional would see it.

And it raises one of the more intriguing questions of the whole postcampaign seasons: How come so many lifelong Democrats didn't see it that way?

FROM THE GORE CAMPAIGN:

● *We really don't know who got the most votes in Florida. There was a lot of confusion at the polls, a lot of ballots the machines missed. We want all the votes to be counted, as thoroughly as possible, so that we can really know what the Florida voters wanted.*

As a political and legal matter, it was probably the best argument the Gore folks had. As a rallying cry, it lacked a certain emotional punch, especially when contrasted with the

Republican mantra *We won, and they're going to steal it if they get half a chance!* Nonetheless, it was the dominant Democratic theme.

Several days into Overtime, I met for breakfast in Washington with a man who had spent years in the service of Al Gore's political fortunes. I fully expected him to reflect the same high-voltage intensity that was radiating from the other side.

The *Wall Street Journal* editorial page was calling the vice president's strategy a "coup d'état," a phrase quickly echoed by the vigorously conservative *New York Post*. Columnists who'd gnashed their teeth for years over the Clinton escapades now turned their full fury on Gore, lambasting his "serial mendacity" and "corrupting hunger for power" (George Will), his "revolting" campaign crowded with "hacks and political thugs" (Michael Kelly). House Majority Whip Tom DeLay had proclaimed flatly, "What we are witnessing is the theft of an election." He and fellow House Republican John Shadegg were already circulating material noting pointedly that the Congress had the power to reject a slate of electors submitted by the states.

So what did this longtime laborer in the Gore vineyards say?

He compared the struggle to a recent Washington Redskins' football game, where the outcome turned on a last-minute judgment call: Was there a fumble?

"The two campaigns are looking at the same facts, and seeing two different things," he said. "Gore believes he fell on the ball, and it's his. Bush sees it the other way. So the question is, when is the play called dead—and who's blowing the whistle?"

That was it. He was talking like a referee. Every Republican I talked to, with one exception, was talking like a combat platoon sergeant, waving his arms and shouting at his men, "Take the hill, dammit! Take the hill!"

The one exception is intriguing. I don't live in Washington, because I believe I stay more in touch with typical, hardworking Americans by living amongst them in the heartland of the nation—the Upper West Side of Manhattan. (A typical political view in my neighborhood: Exhume the Rosenbergs and give them a federal pension.) When things heat up in the capital, though, I head for the capital—specifically, the Green Room of CNN's Washington bureau. When a political crisis is brewing, everyone you could possibly want to speak with winds up waiting for a turn in Skip Smith's makeup chair, drinking astonishingly bad coffee, and exchanging pleasantries. Sometimes, the groupings look like something out of a Theater of the Absurd production, in which a playwright imagines a meeting between, say, Eleanor Roosevelt, Leon Trotsky, and Fats Waller. On this evening, Senator Joe Lieberman and former House Minority Leader Robert Michel were chatting cordially, when in walked . . . former Independent Counsel Ken Starr, looking about fifteen years younger than he had when he was at the center of the impeachment scandal. The three chatted with easy amiability.

A short time later, the atmosphere turned from warmth to heat. One of the best-known figures in the conservative movement was on a talk show, animatedly arguing the Bush view of the postelection battle. The conversation grew steadily angrier, until it was time for a commercial break. Out of curiosity, I switched the channel to pick up the closed-circuit feed from the set. Normally during a commercial break, the conversation among political adversaries quickly turns collegial; there is talk of kids, sports, gossip. This time, you could feel the tension on the set through the screen.

"He's trying to steal it," the conservative said. *"They're just gonna keep counting 'til they get the lead, and then they'll shut it down. That's what you can do with a hand count."*

"There's only one reason you want to shut it down," his adversary said. *"You're afraid you'll lose. You just can't stand all those black votes making Gore the president. For God's sake, they hand-count in* Texas. *Bush signed the bill!"*

When he returned to the Green Room, the conservative motioned me over.

"So," he said very quietly, "who do you think really won Florida?"

That was the only hint of doubt I heard from the Right through the entire postelection period. From Gore supporters, it was very different. Within two days of the election, for instance, the *New York Times* editorial page, a resolute voice of politically correct liberalism that had strongly endorsed Gore, was warning that remedies such as a revote in Palm Beach County "seem politically unsound, legally questionable. It will poison the political atmosphere if presidential elections are seen as a starting point for litigation." The *Washington Post* made the same point. Two Democratic senators, Louisiana's John Breaux and New Jersey's Robert Torricelli, were cautioning against a legal war of attrition. A long, drawn-out battle, they said, would not be in the national interest. No one on the Republican side was offering any sentiments like that. Instead, moderates like Montana Governor Marc Racicot, New Jersey's Christine Whitman, and New York's George Pataki were flying down to Florida to rally the troops and pour scorn on the very idea of a hand recount.

"The ballots have been counted, recounted, and counted again," Pataki said four times in eight minutes on one CNN interview, thus setting a modern record for remaining on message.

While Democrats did make their way down to Florida, there was nothing like the certainty or the passion that ignited Republicans. The only exception: African-Americans. For all the furor over Palm Beach, it was black precincts where voters had been turned away, denied a ballot because some had been mislabeled as felons, blocked from voting because of bureaucratic bungles, or because the huge increase in black turnout had overwhelmed local officials. For those with memories going back four decades, all this was no accident. It was instead a painful reminder of the days when the battle for a ballot was, literally, a life-and-death matter. At an NAACP-sponsored hearing in Miami four days after the election, prospective voters told of police cars blocking the way to the polls, of voters harassed by election workers. It was anecdotal evidence at best, and local authorities argued persuasively that the police presence near a polling place was pure coincidence. Such explanations did little to lessen the sense of anger among black Democrats. That is one reason why the only members of Congress to object to the counting of Florida's electoral votes during the mandated joint session of Congress were a handful of black House Democrats. Their objections died because they could not find one Democrat in the all-white Senate to join their protests.

So why was that? Why, with the presidency itself on the line, was there such a passionless response from so many Democrats? Here's what some of them told me.

"For one thing, they expected to win. We didn't," Senator

Bob Kerrey said. "They heard Gore concede. But there's something else. Their base—the economic, religious, and cultural conservatives, the right-to-lifers, the NRA—they *get* the executive branch, the regulatory authority. Our base? Some get it, but on the whole, Democrats think more about legislation. If you asked people to choose between controlling the White House or the Congress, most Democrats would rather have the Congress. Republicans would rather have the presidency, because they get it. Democrats don't—even though Clinton used the executive authority like mad. I know in eighty-eight, when I first got here, I didn't understand this."

"I hate to say this to you," said another Democratic official, "but I feel the campaign itself was so superficial, disappointing, mundane, that in a funny way, given the way the debates went, and the personalities, I almost thought it was the perfect scripted ending. It fit. It was a perfect reflection of a race that left people unexcited, wishing 'a pox on both their camps,' unable to decide. So it was the ultimate ratifier.

"On our side, nobody could get particularly excited about a lockbox. The other guys? They were ready to kill—because they'd been out of the White House for eight years, because they hated Clinton, and because they care more about power than about a specific issue. They're a White House party. They're more invested in that. We're inured to being out. And besides," the officeholder said, "they convinced themselves that people were changing the rules after the fact. But they never looked at the kinds of outrage being expressed by the black community. When was the last time Republicans cared about disenfranchisement? 'Too bad there were some dumb Democrats.' That's their Darwinian sense of politics."

Even within the highest councils of the Gore campaign,

there was a fear of pushing too hard, of being seen as "sore losers." *Look,* the argument went, *there's only so far we can push this. Don't make it look like we're sore losers. It will hurt the Democratic Party, and it will hurt Gore if he wants to run again in four years.*

Joe Lieberman was not one of those voices.

"I almost felt as if I were back as Connecticut attorney general," he recalled. "I was saying, 'We've got a grievance, and what you do is you go to court. This is no longer a campaign, we're not reading polls. If we think something unfair happened in Florida and we've got a legal case, we've got to go out and make the case. I thought the other side had decided, they had that five-hundred-vote lead and they were going to hold it come hell or high water. They'd worry about rehabilitating George W. Bush once they got him in the White House." Nonetheless, the caution inside even the inner circles of the campaign demonstrated just how uphill the Gore fight was going to be. Early on, some of them had concluded that Al Gore had simply been the victim of fate. Said one Democratic notable:

"Al Gore is armed with the knowledge that he won the popular vote, and there is compelling evidence that the plurality of Floridians went to the polls intending to vote for Gore. He lost because of the failure of Palm Beach Democrats to handle a confusing ballot, and because the NAACP in Duval County gave bad instructions to black voters to 'punch every page,' not knowing that there were *two* pages of presidential candidates.

"It's like there was a divine plot to keep him from becoming president."

Defeat by a malicious divinity, of course, inspires not a

girding of the loins, but a shrug of the shoulders. It may also provide one more explanation for the lack of Democratic passion: Al Gore himself.

When the Florida outcome was still in doubt, former Reagan Chief of Staff Duberstein was speculating about the potential difficulties a President Al Gore would face.

"He will quickly realize," Duberstein said, "that in spite of all his years in Washington, he's never developed any good relationships on the Republican side of the aisle—and quite candidly, not many more on the Democratic side of the aisle as well." You can dismiss that as a partisan take from a prominent Republican—except that Democrat after Democrat expressed the same view, some of them in much stronger terms.

"He never built any bonds with us while he was in the Senate," a former colleague says. "There was always the sense that he was out for himself." Another looked back with exasperation at the campaign itself.

"How the hell can you take the record he had going for him and turn it into a tie?" Even while pledging to stand by Gore during the fight for a recount, some in Congress argued that Gore's lackluster campaign had cost them a chance to take back the House of Representatives.

Put all these factors together, and what you have is a striking contrast. One side in this fight was convinced it had won, convinced the other guys were out to steal the victory away, standing united behind their candidate who would win back their rightful prize—the White House—from the amoral, sly, frustratingly skilled usurper. The other side in the fight believed it had been victimized not by the other side, but by fate; believed its victory had been lost not through fraud or malice, but through mistakes—including mistakes made by their most enthusiastic supporters. They believed they had a small chance at best of changing the results of Election Day, and they were less than devoted to the leader of their own side.

All things considered, not exactly the prevailing wind you want for the political battle of a lifetime.

On a personal and professional level, I was having the time of my life. For once, we did not have to beat people over the head to get them to think about politics for more than ten or fifteen seconds. On a Saturday in mid-November, when I flew back to New York from CNN's *Town Meeting* in Palm Beach, my fellow passengers wanted to share their engagement with me.

"My son's social-studies teacher is reenacting the Constitutional Convention in class." "I can't believe it. My fourteen-year-old came home from school every day this week and turned on CNN instead of MTV." "Is it legal to have a revote?" I felt the way the general manager of the Palm Beach Sheraton did as he eagerly watched a steady stream of media people checking in and out of his hotel: "This is usually one of our slowest weeks of the year!" Any journalist covering the deadlock was at the center of the universe, and any journalist who tells you he doesn't get a charge out of that kind of story is blowing smoke up one of your orifices. The ratings spike was only one measure of the public's fascination. I've come to believe that when a story gets big enough, it triggers a chemically induced jump in wacko e-mails and phone calls. In volume and in volubility, the pulse was quickening (the hands-down winner: an e-mail charging that Vice President Gore's campaign had gathered up thousands of absentee ballots from Cuba in a hypersonic SR-71 aircraft in order to change the outcome of the Florida vote. Don't ask).

This journalistic picnic, however, did not come without an

infestation of ants. With the Florida vote up for grabs came an inevitable consequence: the Return of the Sock Puppets.

I seized on this phrase one night on *Larry King Live* during the Lewinsky Saga of 1998, after listening to one too many debates on the matter.

"You know, Larry," I said, "all of us could save a lot of time and money by not booking any more guests at all on this story. We should just use sock puppets instead. Because it's the same damn argument *every single night:*

" 'He lied under oath!'

" 'But it was about sex—everybody lies about sex!'

" 'No man is above the law!'

" 'You can't overturn an election because of private misconduct!' "

This was, I know, a late insight at best. In an age of round-the-clock political gab, on cable and on talk radio, original opinions are on the endangered-species list. Campaigns, political parties, and interest groups churn out blast faxes and e-mails by the hour, equipping surrogates with the same set of facts, factoids, and anecdotes. To paraphrase Spiro Agnew's observation about ghettos, when you've heard one precooked, poll-driven sound bite, you've heard 'em all. I became so fed up with the process that before the first Gore-Bush debate, I snapped. After listening to the campaign mouthpieces recite their lines, I asked Gore man Chris Lehane, "Can you say there's something—anything—about Governor Bush, where you have said, 'Not bad'?"

"Well," Lehane began, "I think he's done an incredibly good job of not explaining any of the—"

"No, come on," I interrupted, "I mean seriously. Let's not spin it. Just for once, anything about Governor Bush that you can legitimately say, 'Not bad'?"

I thought I heard a few teeth gnashing, but Lehane did say, well, yes, Bush and Gore did agree that we need accountability in our schools. Ari Fleischer said Al Gore was a good debater. Since that was part of the campaign's lowball strategy, he got no candor points at all.

Now that the battle had shifted away from the ballot box, the sock puppets returned with a different set of offerings. The two sides began to wage an all-out rhetorical war devoted to demonstrating how the other guys were out to commit grievous wrongs against the American voter, the American political system, and common decency. I thought I had run into a brick wall down in Palm Beach when I tried to get the partisans to concede something, anything, from the other camp's argument. Once I went back to my role as analyst-anchor-kibbitzer, I realized that Palm Beach was a small appetizer. As Al Gore might have said to me afterward, "You ain't seen nothin' yet!"

There were times in those first days when I felt as if I had dropped in for a visit with the parents of George Costanza, during their celebration of the "Festivus" holiday. As every *Seinfeld* fan knows, the highlight of Festivus is the Airing of the Grievances. For a while, we were celebrating Festivus every single day.

Two days after Election Day, for example, Bush started holding meetings at his Texas ranch with prospective cabinet and staff members. A prudent bit of contingency planning? Not according to Gore campaign chair William Daley. His grievance?

"Their actions to try to presumptively crown themselves the victors, to try and put in place a transition, run the risk of dividing the American people and creating a sense of confusion."

Gore's campaign, meanwhile, was calling for hand recounts

in selected Florida counties. A move in accord with long-standing Florida election law? Not according to Bush campaign chair Don Evans. His grievance?

"Our democratic process calls for a vote on Election Day. It does not call for us to continue voting until someone likes the outcome. . . . it's important that no party act in a precipitous matter or distort an existing voting pattern in an effort to misinform the public."

When the Florida Supreme Court blocked Secretary of State Harris from certifying the election results until it heard the case for an extension, the grievances grew stronger.

Said Bush spokeswoman Karen Hughes, "The votes in these four selected counties are not being counted accurately or fairly. They are being counted subjectively and selectively. . . . [Today], the vice president essentially said we should ignore the law so that he can overturn the results of this election."

As for the Gore camp, its grievance was always stated more tentatively, in keeping with its fundamental premise: *We don't know who won, but we need to find out what the voters said, and the Bush camp simply is afraid to do that.* Here is how the vice president himself expressed it six days after Election Day, in his own inimitable nobody-here-but-us-fairminded-neutral-observers style:

"I would not want to win the presidency by a few votes cast in error or misinterpreted, or not counted, and I don't think Governor Bush wants that either. . . . While time is important, it is even more important that every vote is counted and counted accurately, because there's something very special about our process that depends totally on the American people having a chance to express their will without any intervening interference."

Hearing Al Gore once again dismiss any notion that he might have a rooting interest in the outcome was enough to trigger another Froggy the Gremlin moment. Here's how I would have channeled Gore's grievance:

"Listen good. I've been running for the presidency in one way or another for twenty-five years. I've spent the last four years working my butt off for this job. I've frozen my mukluks off in Iowa pastures and on New Hampshire street corners. I've gotten up at dawn to shake hands with strangers. I've eaten horrible food, listened to special pleaders, and suffered endless ridicule and smart-ass questions from a mob of reporters who just can't wait to take another shot at me. And now that I've won hundreds of thousands more votes than the other guy, now that I'm just a few hundred votes behind in the count, with God-knows-how-many votes for me sitting somewhere in those piles of uncounted ballots, you want me to just fold my tent and steal away? You want me to give up the White House, the 747, more temporal power than any emperor ever dreamt of, historical immortality, and a chance to change the country, and spend the next four years at some think tank or popping up on cable television and seminars on reforming the federal budget? Take a hike!"

We never got to hear that particular grievance. What we did hear, in telephone calls and e-mails, and in the more ideologically intense columns and arguments, were grievances that took the arguments of the respective campaigns, and repackaged them—with the bark off.

"We're supposed to trust Katherine Harris to set the rules for a vote count? She's the co-chair of the Bush campaign, for God's sake! She wants to be an ambassador. And"—this one offered after the mikes were off—*"you know how . . . close she is to Jeb."*

"We're supposed to worry because a lot of people spoiled their ballots? It happens in every state, every election. Ninety-seven percent of the voters in Florida did it right. A lot of Gore's voters were too befuddled or too old or too dumb to do it right. You know"—this one offered after the mikes were off—*"you know how it is with some of . . . those people."*

When the arguments began to focus on the recounting of votes, the sock puppets got even weirder. Think for a moment about what arguments logically or historically divide Republicans and Democrats. You might list the power and reach of the federal government, the virtues of labor and capital, affirmative action, abortion, welfare. Nowhere in the recorded history of American politics have the parties divided on the relative merits of counting votes by machines or by hand. Yet by the time ten days had passed in the battle for Florida, the argument had taken on near-theological significance. It was as if the parties were preparing to go to war over total immersion, or predestination. In fact, it sounded at times like a debate out of Jonathan Swift. In *Gulliver's Travels*, Swift writes that Lilliput had long been divided by a ferocious argument over whether an egg is to be cracked at the big end or the little end.

Here, for example, are the comments from Bush spokesman Tucker Eskew, who was interviewed in front of the Palm Beach County offices. The canvassing board, acting under an interim ruling of the Florida Supreme Court, was undertaking a manual recount of the ballots. Eskew's reaction?

"Behind me tonight there is another tally going on, a count with a new set of rules adopted just tonight, a count where people are mishandling, manhandling even, those ballots . . . These are fragile pieces of paper that have been through the precision machinery that is supposed to count them. And that process is just fatally flawed. . . . And then, of course, those questionable ballots will be turned over to the three Democrats for them to apply a new and different set of standards in what constitutes a vote. They admitted tonight that they will seek to determine a voter's intent, read voters' minds."

You don't spent a lifetime immersed in politics without developing a reasonably thick skin about this sort of stuff. Nobody expects political debate to be sweetly reasoned. The high-minded folks who wrote the Constitution were in fact not high-minded at all when it came to their understanding about politics. They knew all about "factions" and the heated passion that people bring to their causes. In our own time, the domination of politics by law-trained men and women means that political language is more and more shaped by those skilled in the art of making indefensible conduct reasonable. When you know how to argue that cigarettes don't kill, or that a recidivist drunk driver was simply the victim of a faulty Breathalyzer machine, it is no great trick to argue for the moral superiority of a swinging chad over a hanging chad (or vice versa).

With all the years I've put in covering politics, not to mention a law degree of my own, I'm hard-pressed to explain my increasing impatience with the Return of the Sock Puppets. In retrospect, I think it was because we were now playing on brand-new terrain. This wasn't the usual predebate, postdebate, Big Speech event, where there's a kind of inevitability to the palaver.

"Phil, you're the senator's chief campaign spokesman—rate his performance tonight on a scale of one to ten."

"It was a twenty, Biff. He hit it out of the park, a grand slam. Quite frankly, I think he won the election tonight."

Nor was it the normal Washington policy debate, where the cheerleaders all knew the routines by heart:

"You can spend your money better than those Washington bureaucrats can!"

"Don't balance the budget on the backs of the poor!"

"Protect innocent life!"

"Protect a woman's right to choose!"

No, now we were asking new questions—rather, some very old questions now given new life. How do you balance order and fairness? How should a president be chosen if the process doesn't yield a clear result? Are there "neutral" standards that apply, so that when the fight is over the combatants will agree that the result is fair? Normally, the only time you see questions like these debated is on one of those PBS roundtables, where a group of notables gathers around a table to debate a "what-if" scenario sketched out by a prominent law professor. In these settings, you can watch prominent figures from the worlds of politics, journalism, business, and academia wrestle with the rights and wrongs of an idea: "Where does freedom of the press stop and privacy begin?" "When does private conduct have pubic consequences?" Stripped of a rooting interest in any specific outcome, these notables often surprise the audience—and themselves—with their conclusions.

Every once in a long while, it happens for real. When a question with enough weight lands in the public forum, that question sometimes has the power to change minds. The rise of Hitler and the Soviet Union convinced significant isolationists that the United States had to be a major world player. The civil-rights revolution forced states'-rights advocates to acknowledge that the principle had, in this case, become an instrument of discrimination. The Vietnam War pushed Democrats into a politically painful break with their president. Watergate pushed Republicans into a personally painful break with their own president.

Now? The most charitable response I can find is that we were witness to a series of coincidences that make the Harmonic Convergence look like a daily event. Republican after Republican found the prospect of recounting ballots by hand a threat to the integrity of the vote—even those Republicans who came from states where hand recounts were the norm. Democrat after Democrat argued for the most expansive possible standard in examining those ballots. An army of distinguished conservative legal scholars found no problem with the Florida legislature taking over the process of choosing Florida's electors. An army of distinguished liberal legal scholars found no problem with proposing a new special election limited to Palm Beach County—something unprecedented and almost certainly extralegal.

The more I heard the special pleaders at work, the more I thought the best solution to the outcome had come not from a pundit or legal scholar, but from a man who made his living making people laugh. The night before the election, I asked screenwriter-director-novelist Andrew Bergman to make a fearless on-air forecast. Bergman, whose writings include *Blazing Saddles, The In-Laws,* and *The Freshman,* came up with both a dead-on prediction and an inventive solution.

"They wind up dead even—two hundred sixty-nine electoral votes apiece," Bergman said. "They have to put on a big show to see who wins, like one of those old Busby Berkeley musicals. They fly all the electors into New York, to the Roxy or the Palace. Each candidate puts on a show. The electors vote by applause meter. Whoever puts on the best show wins. A real bang-up finish."

I also began to think that if Diogenes showed up wandering the political landscape in search of a disinterested voice, he'd need a flashlight and a lifetime supply of batteries to go along with his lantern. That was before the spotlight fell on Charles Burton.

● The Palm Beach County Courthouse on West Palm Beach's North Dixie Highway is about ten minutes away from the wealth and glitz of Palm Beach, where so many high-priced stores line Worth Avenue that the parking meters take Krugerrands. This is the Palm Beach of Dunkin' Donuts, self-storage lots, health-service centers for the poor. Charles Burton's modest office is on the ninth floor. Burton is a native of the Boston area, educated at Suffolk Law School, a few miles and several light-years away from Harvard. He's a Democrat by birth and choice, a one-time intern in Ted Kennedy's Senate office. His work as a lawyer did not take him into partisan fields. He was named to the Palm Beach County Court by Governor Jeb Bush in May of 2000, and, as I've already noted, he was named to head the canvassing board because state law requires the boards to be chaired by a judge who was running unopposed in the fall. So when the chairman of the Palm Beach board found himself with a challenger, the job fell to Burton, the most junior judge on the circuit.

His first hint of trouble came when, as previously described, he dropped by the county elections office at 4 P.M. on Election Day and found a distraught Theresa LePore, who handed him a sample ballot and asked him if he could tell how to vote for Gore. He spent the night watching the election tilt back and forth, and stayed until the networks declared Bush the winner. He fell asleep at 3 A.M., woke up to a telephone call from LePore, and went down to the office to find protesters in the street and "a ton of reporters."

Burton is not a man shaped for the public arena by a team of consultants. He runs a bit on the portly side, smokes cigarettes, and is not very good at hiding what he is thinking. When he talks of what he lived through, a small smile sometimes plays across his face as he remembers private assurances abandoned for public spin, and his own naïve belief that interested political parties might be interested in a dispassionate approach to the ballots.

The real problem emerged Thursday night after Election Day, when the canvassing board met to consider a recount. Under Florida's "sunshine law," all such meetings are open to the public. This meeting took place in an office that faced the courtyard of the Governmental Center complex. Outside, cameras peered in through the picture windows that ran the length of the office. The TV picture captured the board members staring at the ballots from sample precincts. (It was a scene later immortalized in a TV commercial for a snack-food chip.) The question before the board? Did the ballots from the sample precincts yield a big enough difference to trigger a countywide manual recount? The overwhelmingly Democratic crowd had no doubts:

"Go count! Go count!" they chanted.

Burton had a different notion.

"We needed to stop and think," he said. He was simply not sure how to proceed, how to count. Do we hold the ballot up to see if any light is peeking through? Do we count ballots where there's an indentation that did not punch through? The most openly partisan board member was calling for a full recount; Burton wanted to know whether it was legal.

So, he asked, "Is there any reason why this board does not obtain the benefit of the knowledge of the secretary of state to provide this board with information?" (Weeks later, he thinks back to the idea of asking Katherine Harris for impartial guidance, and one of those small smiles appears.)

Democrats in the crowd were incensed.

"Who got to Burton?"

Burton held his ground, refusing to vote for a full manual recount until the secretary of state's office weighed in. He was outvoted, two to one. The manual recount began—and Burton began getting more lessons in the way politics works.

"I saw what it means to have as much money, as much firepower as you needed," he says. When the Florida Supreme Court issued its first opinion extending the deadline for certification, they cited a case from Illinois that suggested a liberal standard for ballot inspection.

"Within a day," he says, "the Republican lawyers had *transcripts*, with the judge actually counting the ballots, to show that the court was wrong.

"I saw Democrats stabbing Theresa LePore in the back, on TV, *right* after they'd come into her office privately to tell her they knew she'd tried to do her best. When I voted to delay a recount until after the Florida Supreme Court had ruled, I had the Democratic county chairman say publicly, 'He'll never get elected in this county.' "

And once the Florida Supreme Court gave the go-ahead for a recount, Burton still clung to the idea that something other than full-contact politics would have a role to play. The local board began counting as soon as the state high court issued its ruling, and, to Burton's dismay, Republicans began challenging almost every ballot.

"I want to assure you," he said to the observers, "by all means put aside a ballot if it's questionable. But if you're objecting simply to object, the board is going to have to discuss it."

All those delays—and a one-day Thanksgiving holiday—brought the board up against the deadline imposed by the supreme court. The vote counts were due in Harris's office by 5 P.M. on the evening of Sunday, November 26, or 9 A.M. Monday if the secretary of state's office was not open. As the board moved through the count, Burton realized that it would fall just short of the deadline. Once again, he decided to ask for help from the state canvassing board.

"You want to know how naïve I was?" he asks later. "We had folks working twenty-hour days. We're two hours away. I'd taken all this heat from the Democrats to try and be fair. They'd even taken us to court to demand we use a liberal standard for ballot counting. And here I am asking Katherine Harris's office for an extension. What was I expecting?"

Harris turned down the request. The Palm Beach board submitted its final count anyway, a little after 7 P.M. Sunday. It showed Gore with a net gain of 215 votes in the county—a hundred short of what he needed to change the statewide outcome.

"Would it have made a difference?" Burton says. "No, thank God."

When it ended, Burton had made a lot of enemies. If he chose to run for political office—if he chose to seek reelection as a county judge—he knew there'd be people with long memories out to get him. He knew two other things: First, he had played in the big leagues and played well. He was honest enough to acknowledge that he'd enjoyed it.

"If you had asked me two months ago, 'If you knew what you had to go through, would you turn it down?' I don't know what I'd have said. But yeah, I'd do *Nightline*. I'd do *Larry King*. But I also wanted people to know how hard we'd worked—I wanted people to know I was just trying to do what the law told me to do."

Second, Burton knew that some people had gotten the message. In the few blocks that we walked together from his office to a restaurant and back, he was stopped two dozen times or more by people who told him, *great job, we're proud of you.* Maybe it was a case of "local boy makes world spot-light." Or maybe it was a case of people seeing somebody in that spotlight who was working without an agenda. As the Florida deadlock played out, Burton did not have many com-panions on that list.

● What was it like to be spending every waking moment, seven days a week, in the middle of the biggest political story of the century? There was, of course, a sense of exhilaration, an almost self-conscious sense that can be best summarized by a comment frequently heard during that time: *Do you believe this? Isn't this incredible?* I remember reading a story about Pete Rose, who came to bat late in the sixth game of the 1975 World Series, perhaps the single most exciting World Series game ever played. Rose looked back at Boston Red Sox catcher Carlton Fisk and said simply, "Isn't this great?" Even some of the principals—Joe Lieberman, for example—found them-selves looking up from the combat to shake their heads at the spectacle.

In fact, the emotional climate—among combatants and chroniclers—seemed to change by the hour, and for good rea-son. The fight for Florida was so intense, so compressed, so ut-terly unlike anything anyone had ever lived through that it seemed at times to crystallize everything about our political process into a concentrated, supercharged mass. It was at once high drama and low farce, hugely consequential and breathtakingly ridiculous—a combination, as Andrew Bergman put it, of *The Federalist Papers* and *Celebrity Death Match*. At times, the posturing seemed to reflect perfectly the themes of the campaign and the candidates. At times, the fight threatened to spiral out of control, wrenching the process into something none of us had ever seen before. In the midst of those twelve-to-fifteen-hour days and seven-day weeks, nothing was harder than trying to separate the trivial from the consequential, the sideshow pageantry from the Real Deal.

One of my favorite sources of comic relief was the way in which the campaigns chose to show their candidates to the public. It was almost as if the handlers could not let go of the campaign. How did we see Al Gore? As the relaxed suburban guy, playing a game of touch football with friends and family on the lawn of the vice-presidential home, and double-dating at a movie with Joe and Hadassah Lieberman.

"Overweening, ambitious control freak? Me? Hey, I'm just hangin' around, waitin' to see if ah'm gonna be the president or not, but hey—deep down, I'm just the same kinda regular guy you are. C'mon, kids, you float out by the RV and run a post-pattern. . . ."

How did we see George W. Bush? Conferring at the ranch with his running mate, congressional leaders, prospective cabinet, and staff members.

"Detached, incurious lightweight? Me? Hey, we're talking geopolitical strategic premises. We're talking budget priorities, fiscal and monetary policy, education reform. If I were any weightier, I'd need to inhale helium just to stand up straight."

If such posturing was surrounded by a faint air of foolishness, it was also an understandable impulse, a reflex born out of force of habit. For the better part of two years, these men had rarely spent a waking hour in public that was not calculated for public impact: George W. Bush in a hundred kindergartens, Al Gore at a hundred senior-citizens' centers, Bush at an inner-city community center to demonstrate compassion, Gore at a pro-football training camp to demonstrate *cojones*. Who could expect them to stop now? Besides, no one could say with any certainty *where* this fight would be won or lost. Was it the county canvassing boards, the state legislature, the state courts, the federal courts? When and where would public opinion weigh in? Far better to keep the candidates on "image message" than to risk some unguarded moment.

Besides, for sheer absurdity, nothing the campaigns did came close to matching what the media did on November 30. On that date, 462,000 ballots from Palm Beach County were dispatched to Tallahassee, where the Florida Supreme Court was preparing to decide if it would order a manual recount. Since the ballots were part of the evidence, they were loaded into a yellow Ryder truck and sent on their way. And yes, folks, we were there. Hour after hour, citizens of the world could turn on their TV sets and watch aerial shots of the truck, ground-level shots of the truck. Only prior commitments at football games prevented us from employing the services of the Goodyear, Budweiser, or Fuji blimp to record this historic journey foot by foot. I gave quiet thanks that I was not part of the anchoring team during this time, because I am convinced that I would have abandoned all sense of propriety in an attempt to provide narration worthy of this image:

". . . *and now the truck has increased its speed from fifty-three to fifty-six miles an hour, which would put it at the Tallahassee city limits in approximately . . . Have I got this right? . . .*

yes, in approximately seventy-five minutes. As we've mentioned several times, the truck is being driven by Thomas Cracklebury, a thirty-four-year-old native of Swainsboro, Georgia, who now lives in Orlando with his wife, Patty, and their daughter, Samantha. Cracklebury stands five feet ten and a half inches, and weighs in at one hundred ninety pounds. His hobbies are said to include . . . Wait, wait a minute, I believe—yes, yes, the truck is slowing down! The truck is slowing down, and it appears that Cracklebury is headed for the Mangrove Acres Rest Stop. Sources have told us earlier that he did plan to have a bite, but we cannot confirm that at this time. We can report that Cracklebury's normal routine is to stop midway through his driving route for a meal that usually consists of a cheeseburger, onion rings, and a root beer, but no hard information is available at this time. . . ."

Yes, it was absurd. Yes, every single anchor and reporter made the compulsory allusion to the pictures that had mesmerized the country six and a half years earlier, when O. J. Simpson led Los Angeles police on a low-speed chase up and down the freeways of Southern California. At least that chase had a morbidly compelling element to it. Was Simpson holding a gun to his head? Was he about to take his own life rather than stand trial for his wife's murder? Here, the odds of some political terrorist hurling a Molotov cocktail into the belly of the ballot truck were somewhat remote. Nonetheless, we put it on the air because . . . because that's what we do. Television is a medium that lives by the premise that the visual is compelling shorthand for the broader story. It is our great strength, and our abiding weakness. We *know* that if we can find the right image, we can convey the meaning of the story.

Sometimes this is true. The pictures from an Ethiopian feeding station in 1984, captured by a BBC camera crew and flashed around the world, told us the essence of that story: *Countless innocents are starving to death right now.* Those visceral images did not convey the broader context of the story, or the policies of the Ethiopian authorities that led to those starving innocents, but they told enough of the tale to galvanize people to act—and a lot of lives were saved.

Sometimes, the faith in the image is misplaced. When American hostages were seized in Iran in 1979, much of the American media focused on the emotional response at home, the yellow ribbons around trees, the faces of relatives at prayer. Those pictures overwhelmed any notion that broader national interests might be at stake, or that these captives were not necessarily at the epicenter of American foreign policy. Instead, Walter Cronkite at CBS News ended every broadcast by reminding us that this was "Day one hundred twenty-three of captivity for the American hostages in Iran." ABC News launched a late-night program called *America Held Hostage*— not *Americans Held Hostage,* but *America,* the whole country. (The show morphed into a pretty fair public news broadcast called *Nightline.*) President Carter himself made the hostages the focus of White House attention. The power of the presidency was no match for the power of these images.

And sometimes, as with the mile-by-mile coverage of the ballots, the visual image is ludicrous. As I watched the coverage, I thought back to the summer of 1998, to a flock of camera crews descending on the steps of the Capitol as a hapless cluster of workers unloaded cartons from vans and trucked them into the building. The cartons contained *The Starr Report,* the lubricious compendium of presidential misbehavior that had been prepared for the House of Representatives. Grown men and women were risking disabling injuries for the sake of a marginally better shot of . . . a bunch of cartons. Why? Because that's where the story was. Now, I suppose, the pictures of that truck were supposed to carry with them a portentous message: *Inside that truck are the ballots that could decide the identity of the next president of the United States.* Three weeks earlier, the story was on the streets of Palm Beach; then in a conference room in a government building; then in courtrooms from one end of the state to the other; then in the chambers of the state legislature. The pace and variety of these images was dizzying. The television networks were less the ringmasters of the pageant than its victims. We did not know what was significant because, in the most literal sense imaginable, we had never been here before. We did not know what image might yet stand for something genuinely consequential. So, like the religious fanatics of another time, we shot them all, assuming that God or history would sort it out.

For the partisans, of course, just about every image proved the case to which they were committed. The Bush camp pointed to the pictures of county canvassing board members holding ballots up to the light, squinting to find marks or indentations or light peeking through the hanging chads, and said, "You see? It's impossible for these hand counts to be valid!" (Newspaper articles in the *Washington Post,* the *New York Times,* and the *Wall Street Journal* suggested that the ballot inspection was a lot less contentious than Republican officials were claiming.)

The Gore camp pointed to the crowd of Republican operatives that poured out of elevators and pounded on the doors where the Miami–Dade board was counting ballots over the Thanksgiving weekend, and said, "You see? A partisan mob intimidated the board into stopping its manual recount before the November twenty-sixth deadline!" (*Miami Herald* reporter Tom Fiedler later said, "Politics in Miami–Dade County has long been a contact sport, and this hardly rose to the level of something that would be terribly upsetting to a canvassing board down here.")

From my vantage point, there *was* one image, one picture, that captured the story of what happened in Florida. It was both a turning point in the story and a symbol of why the cause of Al Gore was just about lost from the beginning. It happened on the night of Sunday, November 26, when Florida officials certified George W. Bush as the winner of the state's twenty-five electoral votes.

When the Florida Supreme Court handed down its first ruling on the election on November 21, it told the county canvassing boards, in effect, "You have five days to complete your counts. Get them in by 5 P.M. on Sunday, November 26—or, if the secretary of state's office is closed, then get them in by 9 A.M. Monday."

There was no doubt that Secretary of State Harris would be in her office Sunday evening. Call it devotion to duty, or devotion to the political interests of Governor Bush, but she was determined to get the vote certified as soon as possible. (Would she have done the same if Al Gore had been ahead in the count by a few hundred votes, with the Bush campaign demanding that votes be recounted in Republican counties? Weeks later, at a pre–Inauguration party, she told me, "The only way it could have been tougher for me is if Gore had wound up ahead in the count, because then I would have been a woman without a party, because I would have *had* to certify him as the winner." My hunch is that your confidence in her statement is directly related to your satisfaction with the outcome of the vote.)

In a typical election year, the state election board's certification is surrounded by all the pomp and circumstance of a brown-bag lunch. This time, however, the election board turned it into an imposing public ceremony. At 7:33 P.M. Katherine Harris, Clay Johnson, and Bob Crawford walked into the Cabinet Room of the state capitol in Tallahassee and seated themselves behind a raised table. In front of an audience of journalists and photographers, Harris declared Bush the victor by 537 votes. At that point, the board members began to sign bound copies of the certification documents. As the copies were passed from member to member, and flash cameras began to pop, the room grew quiet; so quiet that, for long moments, the only audible sound came from the scratching of the fountain pens. Harris later said she and the other board members found the silence so awkward that they ended the ceremony early; Bob Crawford had to wait until later to sign the last set of documents.

On television, however, the silence worked to lend an air of solemnity to the ceremony. Television may be, as cliché-mongers like to note, "a visual medium," but it is also a very noisy medium. Programmers fear nothing quite so much as "dead air." That's why a news item about the tragic death of a notable public figure is followed by a three- or four-second fade to black before the denture commercial pops up. On TV, that three- or four-second pause is equivalent to an hour of silence. When television shuts up, you know something significant is going on: live coverage of a memorial service, say, or the investiture of a pope, or Tiger Woods lining up a putt on the eighteenth green for the title. As they signed their certification papers in silence, Katherine Harris and her colleagues looked as if they were putting their signatures on a Middle East peace treaty or a nuclear-arms agreement. It was the most powerful evidence imaginable that the Bush campaign had indeed won.

"The election was close," Governor Bush said that

evening, "but after a count, a recount, and yet another manual recount, Secretary Cheney and I are honored and humbled to have won the state of Florida, which gives us the needed electoral votes to win the election." He announced that he was naming running-mate Cheney to head the transition; that Andrew Card would be his White House chief of staff.

Bob Crawford, the Florida agriculture commissioner who had taken Governor Jeb Bush's place on the state elections board, drove home the point.

"Yogi Berra once said it's not over until it's over," Crawford noted. "Well, it's over, and we have a winner, and it's time to move on."

The Gore argument stayed the same: What count? What recount?

"Until these votes have been counted," said Gore attorney David Boies, "this election cannot be over. There are votes, thousands of votes, that have never yet been counted once." The search for the right metaphor grew intense.

"Sometimes you put a dollar in a vending machine, sometimes it comes out," said Democratic Representative Sherrod Brown of Ohio. "It doesn't mean the dollar's defective. It means the machine didn't read it."

Gore himself preferred the supermarket-scanner metaphor, as he hit the interview circuit in the days following certification.

"Let me ask you this," he said to CNN's John King. "Have you ever gone through the supermarket checkout line, and they run the scanner computer over your items? What happens when it misses one? Do they give it to you for free? No, they do a hand count of that item. And those computers are far more sophisticated than these Votomatic machines. . . . And in fact, those machines are far more statistically likely to be found in low-income areas, with populations that don't have the big tax base to have the fancier up-to-date machines that don't make very many mistakes."

Whatever the merits of that argument, it could not overcome the impact of that certification ceremony. For nearly three weeks, the public had been waiting to find out who its next president would be. Now, Florida officials had provided the answer. Within a day, the polls said, public opinion had shifted dramatically. Before the ceremony, the public was split fifty-fifty on whether the contest should end or go on. A day after, 62 percent said, "Enough, already." Before the certification, 46 percent of the people said Gore should concede. A day after the ceremony, the number had jumped to 56 percent—including a third of Gore supporters. More than half the country now thought Bush had in fact won Florida; only 15 percent thought Gore had won. From the moment Gore called Governor Bush on Election Night to concede, his campaign had been fighting to prevent a sense among the public that he had in fact lost the race, that he was a sore loser who could not concede gracefully. Once those certification papers were signed, that public-relations fight was lost. Nor was it simply a public-relations fight; the campaign's political position was now particularly vulnerable.

In a political sense, Al Gore's post–Election Day problem was impeachment in reverse. From the day the Monica Lewinsky story broke in January 1998 until the Senate acquitted Clinton on February 12, 1999, only one possibility genuinely threatened the president's survival in office: the defection of the Democrats. A party united behind Clinton ensured that there would never be a two-thirds vote in the Senate to convict him. As long as Clinton enjoyed high job-approval ratings from the public, that Democratic unity was certain to hold. (That's why the only real danger Clinton ever faced came in the summer of 1998, after his televised mea-sorta-culpa. Had the sense of anger and betrayal among congressional Democrats turned into hints about resignation, the story might have been very different.)

Al Gore's worry was that public impatience with the contest would translate into impatience among Democratic officials. Senators like Breaux and Torricelli had voiced such concerns within two days of the election. Every day brought new fear that some group of prominent party leaders would publicly call on the vice president to step aside, to be the "statesman." In fact, the party stood behind the vice president, at least publicly. Right after the certification, Senate leader Tom Daschle and House Minority Leader Dick Gephardt flew to Florida in a sign of solidarity. Still, the certification ceremony did have a clear and present impact on the Gore strategy, above and beyond the shift in public opinion. It forced the campaign to rely again on the "reasonableness" case.

"That is all we have asked for since Election Day," Gore said the day after certification. "A complete count of all the votes cast in Florida; not 'recount after recount' as some have charged, but a single full and accurate count." Gone was the talk of winning the national popular vote; gone was the assertion from his side that "we really won Florida." There was no talk that remotely matched the persistent Republican claims that the Democrats were out to steal the election by manufacturing votes—a charge repeated in one form or another by everyone from Bush spokeswoman Karen Hughes to ex–senator Robert Dole. There was no sense that Al Gore was standing at Armageddon and battling for the Lord. Whatever the merits of the argument, "let's be reasonable" does not make for a powerful political rallying cry.

Maybe it would have been different if Al Gore had managed to make a passionate case for himself during the campaign—or for that matter, during his quarter-century-long career as a national political figure. Imagine, for example, if at the end of the 1980 campaign, Ronald Reagan had found himself leading in the popular vote, a few hundred votes behind in a state where the political machinery was solidly in the hands of Jimmy Carter loyalists, urging that questionable ballots be counted. Imagine how his supporters would have rallied behind the man who had championed their conservative beliefs for so long. Imagine how powerful their passion would have been compared with that of the Democratic Party—nearly half of whose voters had wanted to replace Carter with Ted Kennedy.

Al Gore had nothing like that support. *Newsweek* reporter Bill Turque, author of a Gore biography, echoed the private sentiments of many Democrats in an observation he made just before Florida certified Bush as the winner:

"This is a party that has never really fallen in love with Al Gore. I think what you're seeing now is some of the same ambivalence about a Gore candidacy and a Gore presidency that there's been from Day One."

Without that base of devotion, the Gore campaign was constantly looking over its shoulder, waiting for the moment when they would see the backs of important Democrats fleeing the battlefield. They had no confidence that they could sustain a protracted battle. Further, they believed that once the word came out of Florida that Bush had "officially" won, the public cry of "enough, already" would translate into just such a mass political retreat. Time was on the side of the Bush forces; the Gore camp needed to find votes, and the sooner the better.

Now retrace what happened in Florida, and you can understand why many in the Gore campaign came away with a powerful belief in the "malicious deity" explanation for what had happened to them:

One: The Gore forces fought hard in the courts to extend the deadline for the local canvassing boards to recount the votes in their county.

Two: On Tuesday, November 21, a unanimous Florida Supreme Court extended the recount until Sunday, November 26, at 5 P.M.

Three: When local election officials in Miami–Dade County decided they could not complete the recount by that deadline, that same Florida Supreme Court refused to order the officials to conduct that recount.

Four: When the court-ordered deadline passed, George W. Bush was 537 votes ahead of Al Gore; that was the total certified by the state.

Five: Once the Gore campaign launched its "contest" of that certified result, it found itself confronting December 12 as a deadline—a deadline created by a late-nineteenth-century law to protect states from any challenge to their electors.

Six: By the time a narrowly divided Florida Supreme Court ordered the counties to manually examine the so-called "undervotes"—ballots on which no preference for president had been recorded—only four days remained until the December 12 deadline. That looming deadline, and the possibility that Florida's electors were still up for grabs, is what empowered the Florida Legislature to step into the act—beginning the legal moves that would permit it to name the electors. That time frame also propelled Chief Justice Charles Wells to warn of "an unprecedented and unnecessary constitutional crisis [that] will do substantial damage to our country, our state, and to this court as an institution."

Seven: That warning, it is fair to say, was an open invitation to the U.S. Supreme Court to step in and stop the process dead in its tracks on December 9. Its decision three days later has to be seen in light of what would have happened had the high court permitted a manual recount in Florida. (I'll take you through this "what-if?" scenario in a moment. I recommend you keep your seat belts securely fastened for that part of the journey.)

Eight: When the legal fight ended, critics—including some of Gore's own lawyers—began to second-guess the court-room tactics.

"You should never have let the first phase of the fight go on so long," they said. "You should have let the certification take place quickly, and then moved right into the 'contest' phase of the fight. That would have left you plenty of time to make your case before the December 12 deadline became so critical."

That exercise in hindsight misses a couple of crucial points. As that certification ceremony showed, the Gore campaign was right in fearing the consequences of an "official" declaration of a Bush win. All along, Bush's people were doing, in effect, what a basketball team who have taken a one-point lead just as the buzzer goes off should do: Get off the court and into the locker room before the officials have a chance to decide whether the clock really ran out. Had the Gore folks stood aside and let a certification ceremony take place, the public might well have concluded that the election was over. It might well have seen any court contest as the act of a spoiler, no matter what Florida law provided.

Moreover, suppose the Miami–Dade board had pushed ahead with its manual recount. Suppose the Palm Beach County board hadn't taken Thanksgiving Day off, and finished its count in time to meet the 5 P.M. Sunday deadline. Suppose the new totals from those boards added six hundred votes or so to Gore's total. Unless Katherine Harris was willing to risk a contempt citation, she and her colleagues would have had to certify *Al Gore* as the winner in Florida. Suddenly, the central premise of the Bush campaign would have been stood on its head. It would have been Al Gore who was the official victor, who could talk of "finality." It would have been the Bush campaign racing into courts with motions and objections. As we'll see in a moment, this would in no way have guaranteed Al Gore the presidency. But it was surely a reasonable strategy for the campaign to pursue. It just didn't work out that way. Miami–Dade's board never looked at those "undervotes." Palm Beach's board didn't get its look completed in time. And the numbers from Broward County, which included even "dimpled" ballots in its count, were not enough for Gore to overtake Bush in the statewide total.

● The Gore camp's best hope for victory—a recount that would make Gore the certified winner of the Florida vote—was frustrated by bad timing, indecision, and skillful, well-organized political opposition. That could well stand as the epitaph for their entire Florida effort. To turn a New Age aphorism inside-out, every time a door opened another door closed. It was as if the Gore campaign was living through the classic examination dream that has bedeviled generations of anxious students: You show up for an important test, and the door to the room is locked; when you finally enter, all your pens and pencils are broken; when you look at the test, the questions are written in a language you cannot understand.

An overstatement? Look at what happened to Gore on the issue of overseas absentee ballots. Florida law is very clear about what counts as a valid overseas absentee vote: It must be postmarked or dated by Election Day, since no voter is permitted to vote after that date (one major reason why the whole idea of a Palm Beach County recount was never in the cards). But hundreds, maybe thousands, of ballots were pouring into county election boards well after Election Day—a strong suggestion that they had been sent in late. Who were these voters? There was no way to tell. It was a reasonable guess that many of the ballots sent to Duval County came from military personnel, because that northern Florida county is home to several large Navy air bases. They might also be coming from business folks working abroad, or from tourists with the foresight to ask for absentee ballots before they left the country. Whatever their source, most of these votes would likely go to Bush. Back in 1996, when Bill Clinton won Florida, Republican nominee Robert Dole won 54 percent of the overseas absentee ballots.

Al Gore's camp was fully aware of that political reality. That's why Mark Herron, a member of the Gore legal team, had written a memo explaining exactly how to challenge those ballots. Local election boards knew what the law said, too, which is why the all-Republican canvassing board in Duval refused to count any of those ballots that came without a date or a postmark.

Then the roof fell in. The Bush camp somehow got hold of the Gore legal memo explaining how to challenge overseas absentee ballots. By November 18, Montana Governor Marc Racicot was on television, denouncing this effort by the Gore camp for having "gone to war . . . against the men and women who serve in our armed forces." Senator Bob Dole, a hero of World War II, raised hell. So did General Norman Schwarzkopf, commander of the Gulf War forces. It was a brilliant public-relations strike, suggesting that the Democrats, no doubt under the leadership of First Draft Dodger Bill Clinton, were out to purge every GI Joe from the voter rolls. This was not a position that Florida Democrats like Senator Bob Graham and Attorney General Bob Butterworth found comfortable—and they quickly rejected any effort to disqualify absentee votes. Even worse, such an effort ran exactly counter to the fundamental Florida theme: "Count every vote." How could Gore's supporters demand that local boards scrutinize every ballot for indentations, dimples, and strike marks, while demanding absolute compliance with the law for overseas ballots?

The answer was simple: They couldn't. When Senator Lieberman was asked about the issue on *Meet the Press* ten days after the election, he said, "If I was there, I would give the benefit of the doubt to ballots coming in from military personnel generally. . . . Al Gore and I don't want to ever be part of anything that would put an extra burden on the military personnel abroad who want to vote." Who could blame him? What do you do when you turn on your TV and see the wife of an American sailor, thousands of miles away from her husband who is on duty somewhere in the Mediterranean, wonder why the Gore campaign doesn't want her husband to be allowed to vote? Who wins the image battle between an Ivy League lawyer and a nationally famous war hero? Ultimately, canvassing boards in twelve counties revisited their decisions, and George W. Bush picked up a net gain of 176 votes. Had Miami–Dade and Palm Beach Counties completed their hand counts and discovered extra votes for Gore, those absentee ballots could well have made the difference between victory and defeat.

That same trap confounded the Gore camp when it came to some twenty-five thousand absentee ballots in Seminole and Martin Counties, two heavily Republican areas. In both counties, the party organizations had mailed out absentee-ballot application forms to voters, who had only to supply their signatures to qualify. Through a computer glitch, the Republican applications failed to include the voter identification numbers—a fatal flaw. In both counties, election officials had permitted Republican workers to come into their offices, cross-check the ballot applications with the voter ID numbers, and enter those numbers on about 2,500 applications. (In Martin County, the Republicans had actually taken the forms out of the office and then returned them.)

All this was a flat violation of election law. But it was not as if the party workers had handled any of the ballots themselves. The only way to throw out those ballots was to argue that the technicalities of the law were supreme, a notion that the Florida Supreme Court had explicitly rejected when it extended the time for certification. And how could the Gore campaign argue that "every vote must be counted!" while arguing that these valid votes be tossed out? (That contradiction did not prevent the campaign from privately encouraging a wealthy supporter to underwrite the legal challenge to those absentee ballots.)

If the fight over the absentee ballots illustrated the dilemma of the Gore forces, it also illustrated the scorched-earth approach of the Bush forces. One of the consistent themes on the Bush side was that any attempt to revisit the results of November 7 was *by definition* an act redolent of corruption and dishonesty. If canvassing boards were examining ballots by hand, it was not to find votes, but to "create" them for partisan political purposes. If the Florida Supreme Court extended the deadline, it wasn't to protect the rights of voters, but to manipulate the process on behalf of the more liberal presidential candidate. Now, when the Seminole County absentee-ballot case wound up in the hands of Circuit Court Judge Nikki Ann Clark, the Bush partisans instantly jumped to a highly dubious conclusion.

Nikki Ann Clark was a forty-two-year-old native of Detroit, the only African-American woman to sit on a Florida circuit court, and a protégé of the late Lawton Chiles, Jeb Bush's Democratic predecessor. Further, earlier in the year, Governor Bush had passed over her request for a promotion to a higher court. To ideologically rigorous conservatives, Judge Clark's race, gender, and prior political experience apparently proved that she was poised to do the bidding of Al Gore. At one point, when Reverend Jesse Jackson visited Clark's courtroom, *Wall Street Journal* columnist Paul Gigot noted pointedly, "You can bet Judge Clark noticed who was watching her from the gallery." The Bush lawyers repeatedly and unsuccessfully urged Judge Clark to recuse herself. There was plenty of reason for concern. Had Judge Clark thrown those ballots out, Bush would have lost 4,700 votes—putting Al Gore nearly 4,000 votes ahead of Bush in the final statewide count. Still, I wondered whether anyone on the Bush side of the battle bothered to express a sense of regret, or even a second thought, when she refused to toss out the ballots, holding that "neither the sanctity of the ballots nor the integrity of the election has been compromised, and . . . the election results reflect a full and fair expression of the will of the voters."

When this ruling was announced at 2:20 P.M. on the afternoon of Friday, December 8, the Gore camp was looking like a condemned man in one of those old black-and-white death-row movies, watching the clock wind down. Four days earlier, Circuit Court Judge N. Sanders Sauls had thrown out the Gore campaign's effort to contest the Florida results. They had shown no "reasonable probability" that manual recounts would change the outcome. ("Was there anything in the ruling that was good for Gore?" I asked rhetorically that night. "Well, he didn't hold Gore's lawyers in contempt.") The Florida Legislature was meeting in special session, with its heavily Republican majorities in both houses fully prepared to choose Florida's electors should the courts move in Gore's favor. The Florida Supreme Court had been rebuked by the U.S. Supreme Court, which had pointedly reminded the Florida justices that unless they were following the Constitutionally protected desires of the state legislature, their opinion could not stand. Finally, December 12—widely assumed to be the "deadline" for resolving electoral disputes—was only four days away. And not one canvassing board was doing any recounting. Gore's loyalists might well have been reprising the most familiar line from Election Night: *If only the Florida Supreme Court had ordered the local boards to start counting immediately; if only those absentee ballots from Seminole and Martin Counties had been thrown out; if only Al Gore had pulled ahead of George W. Bush any time in the last month.* Such wistfulness was fully understandable. Looking back, I now believe it would have been badly misplaced. Indeed, I now think our nightly *Perils of Pauline* coverage of Florida missed one essential point: Once Election Day had ended, there *were* no "if-onlys" that would have saved the Gore campaign. Once the vote ended in a virtual tie, it was up to the political institutions of Florida to figure out what would happen next. Every one of those institutions was firmly in Republican hands, with the single exception of the Florida Supreme Court—and even that institution would have been unable to salvage a victory for Gore, even if that was its intention. Why? Because there was *no* way for Al Gore to have won a conclusive, final victory in Florida. Every door that might have opened for Gore would have been firmly shut. Watch and see:

- Suppose the canvassing boards in Miami–Dade and Palm Beach Counties had successfully recounted their ballots in time to meet the Florida Supreme Court's deadline of Sunday, November 26. Suppose Al Gore had wound up the winner. Suppose Katherine Harris had gritted her teeth and certified the result. Those results would have been effectively nullified by the U.S. Supreme Court's first decision, which strongly hinted that the Florida justices had not understood that in presidential election matters, the state legislature is the supreme authority. In that first decision, the Florida court had written:

  "To allow the Secretary [of State, Katherine Harris] to summarily disenfranchise innocent electors in an effort to punish dilatory [canvassing] Board members, as she proposes in the present case, *misses the constitutional mark*" (italics mine).

  This seemed a clear reference to Florida's constitution, which makes "the will of the voters" paramount. This line of reasoning would have been fine in a vote for a county sheriff, or even for a mayor or governor. When it came to the presidency, as the U.S. Supreme Court noted, a higher authority governs. Article II of the U.S. Constitution says it is the state legislature's desires that count—*not* the state constitution. The highly skeptical tone of the U.S.

Court's first opinion suggests that it would not have bought into the Florida court's rationale that it was only interpreting the state legislature's will.

• Suppose the U.S. Supreme Court had somehow stayed its hand after Katherine Harris had certified that hypothetical Gore win. What then? The Bush campaign would have launched a "contest" of its own in state court. That contest could easily have extended right up to the December 12 "deadline"— and the state legislature would then have appointed its own slate of Bush electors. Even if the Florida Supreme Court ordered that the Gore slate of electors be certified, that would simply have produced two slates—and a confrontation in the Congress in January. (See below for the gory details of such a scenario.) And what if a federal court had told the state legislature that it could *not* appoint its own slate? That decision would have been appealed straight to the U.S. Supreme Court, a Court strongly disposed toward legislative supremacy.

• Suppose Judge Clark had decided to throw out the absentee ballots from Seminole County. The Bush camp would have appealed that decision to the Florida Supreme Court—the same court that had declared less than two weeks earlier that "hypertechnicalities" should not interfere with the will of the voters. Further, federal courts, which have been rigorous in protecting a citizen's right to vote, would have taken center stage. The battle over such a decision would have been another basis for intervention by the state legislature.

I'd like to think I had a whiff of just how tough things were for Gore when I mused on the night of December 7, "I don't think anybody yet has figured out a scenario, no matter how weird of mind you may be, in which Al Gore winds up as president."

But I didn't—because less than twenty-four hours later, the Florida Supreme Court would throw Al Gore one last lifeline. Only much later did I realize that it was an untethered lifeline. In fact, for all the furor over the decisions of two supreme courts, neither of those decisions would have altered the outcome: George W. Bush was going to wind up as the next president. The only question was: Just how far down the Road to Weirdville would we go before reaching that conclusion?

● One of the joys of modern communications is that you don't have to *be* in any particular place as long as the event itself is being televised. This isn't exactly true, of course. It's probably a good idea to live in Washington if you're going to cover the Congress, and Detroit makes a lot of sense as a base of operations for in-depth coverage of the American auto industry. But if you're watching, say, an impeachment trial of a president, you're going to be watching a television monitor, even if that monitor is in the press gallery of the United States Senate. (If you wanted to hear the senators' off-the-floor comments, a TV set worked just fine; every time the Senate recessed, a flock of senators flew toward the network camera stands like pigeons in a park at feeding time.) If you're an anchor-analyst on a cable-TV network in the midst of a political firestorm, you find yourself talking with people from all over the country. As long as the video and audio work, it makes no difference whether you're in the same studio or a thousand miles away.

On Friday afternoon, December 8, I was in my New York office, monitoring the daylong coverage, and working with the production staff on our 10 P.M. show. Between booking the guests and planning the set pieces, we all spend a lot of time in telephone conferences. During each of those calls, there were moments when everyone stopped talking at exactly the same time. Those were the times when CNN cut to a shot of a rostrum on the steps of the Florida Supreme Court in Tallahassee, Florida. Unlike the Washington Supremes, the Florida high court makes an accommodation to the press. When a decision is announced, it sends out a spokesperson to brief the press on the highlights of the ruling.

That's why a mild-mannered civil servant named Craig Waters became an internationally recognizable figure in the last months of 2000. Sometime in the next several minutes, or hours, Waters would appear to announce the Florida court's decision about Al Gore's appeal. If the court turned him down, George W. Bush was the next president. If the court ruled for Gore, everything was up for grabs.

On days like this one, when there is no way to know when news will break, on-air folks like me walk around with an earpiece clipped to the back of our shirt collars. I'm sure it looks odd to visitors, but it is a vocational necessity if the phone rings and a producer is barking, "Get on set—now!" Since CNN has a camera position fifteen feet from my office, "now!" is measured in seconds. That's about how long it took me to throw myself into position when CNN cut to a shot of Craig Waters taking his place in front of the Florida Supreme Court.

"The court has authorized the following statement," he said. "By a vote of four to three"—*Four to three? The court's*

first opinion was unanimous—"the majority of the court has reversed the decision of the trial court in part. It has further ordered that the Circuit Court of the Second Judicial Circuit here
in Tallahassee shall immediately begin a manual recount of
the approximately nine thousand Miami–Dade ballots that registered the undervotes." *Nine thousand undervotes? Can Gore
make up 537 votes out of 9,000?*

But wait—there was more.

"In addition," said Waters, "the circuit courts shall enter
orders ensuring the inclusion of the additional two hundred
fifteen legal votes for Vice President Gore in Palm Beach
County, and the one hundred sixty-eight additional legal votes
for Miami–Dade."

And my jaw dropped.

I once assumed that that notion was a cliché, not simply
uninspired but anatomically unlikely. But in my time as a
working journalist, I'd experienced it twice before: first, in
1991, when Anita Hill testified before the Senate Judiciary
Committee and claimed that Judge Thomas had made a joke
about pubic hair on his can of Coca-Cola; second, when the Los
Angeles District Attorney announced that his office was "actively seeking" a missing murder suspect named O. J. Simpson.

*The Florida Supreme Court's just said that the votes
Miami–Dade had tallied when it stopped the recount were valid
after all. It's just said that it didn't matter that Palm Beach
County had missed Katherine Harris's deadline. Add those votes
to Gore's total, and Bush's statewide lead is now . . . 156 votes
out of 6,000,000 cast. And there are 9,000 undervotes in
Miami–Dade.*

But wait, there's more.

"In addition, the circuit court shall order a manual recount
of all undervotes in any Florida county where such a recount

has not yet occurred. Because time is of the essence, the recount shall commence immediately. In tabulating what constitutes a legal vote, the standard to be used is the one provided
by the legislature. A vote shall be counted where there is a
clear indication of the intent of the voter."

*Okay. Let's see. The court is telling every Florida county to
check every ballot where there's no preference for president. So
we're not talking about nine thousand votes in Miami–Dade, but
forty-three thousand votes everywhere. It's tried to say to the
U.S. Supreme Court, "Hi, there—we're just interpreting that all-
powerful state legislature, so we're going to use its standard"—
except that's the same standard that was around when Broward
County said, "Count the dimples," and Palm Beach said,
"Don't count every dimple." And what does "immediately"
mean? And who's doing the counting? And what happens when
the Florida Legislature says, "This is not what our law says, so
we're going to appoint our own electors"?*

My first on-air comments reflected the calm, dispassionate,
orderly nature of my first thoughts:

"We have now left the gravitational pull of the Earth."

In retrospect, I was a bit timid. With this decision, all of
the wilder fantasies of we Constitutional Catastrophists now
appeared to be just around the bend. Two slates of electors? If
the hand recount produced enough Gore votes to give him the
lead, that scenario was a near certainty. A presidency hanging
in the balance until the new Congress convened in January?
That was no longer the speculative notion of a melodramatic
writer of political fiction. House Majority Whip Tom DeLay
said that the Florida court had "distorted the judicial process
into nothing more than a mechanism for providing Al Gore
with a victory he was unable to win on November seventh. . . .
This judicial aggression must not stand."

JEFF GREENFIELD | *Oh, Waiter! One Order of Crow!*

Translation: *The House of Representatives will not accept a slate of Gore electors from Florida when it convenes in special session next January.*

Tom DeLay, to be sure, had shown few signs of believing that "a soft answer turneth away wrath." But he reflected a broad conviction among Bush supporters that the Florida Supreme Court was simply an extension of Al Gore's effort to steal the presidency. Consider this reaction from the *Weekly Standard,* a conservative magazine with a strong streak of independence, which had leaned toward John McCain in the primaries:

"As a result of Friday's Florida Supreme Court decision," it wrote, "Al Gore may be sworn in as president on January 20 . . . some of us will not believe that Al Gore has acceded to the presidency legitimately . . . We will therefore continue to insist that he gained office through an act of judicial usurpation. We will not 'move on.' " (Similar thoughts, and similar words, would spring from the Left a few days later when the U.S. Supreme Court weighed in.) There was nothing surprising in those reactions. Both sides had long assumed that the only way the other guy could win in Florida was through devious means—Bush by silencing the voices of the voters, Gore by cooking the books on the vote count. What was surprising were the powerful words of dissent penned by Chief Justice Charles Wells, who had been part of the unanimous majority that had extended the reporting deadline back on November 26. His warning of an impending constitutional crisis drew headlines, as did his conclusion that "this case has reached the point where finality must take precedence over continued judicial process. Further judicial process will only result in confusion and disorder."

Far less attention was paid to another section of his dissent, which may have been the most acute analysis of Al Gore's Florida dilemma:

"The local election officials, state election officials, and the courts have been attempting to resolve the issues of this election with an election code which any objective frank analysis must conclude *never contemplated this circumstance*" (emphasis added).

Florida's election law had been designed with local contests in mind: seats in the legislature and county board, mayors and sheriffs. In those cases, the courts could take weeks, even months, to examine votes and decide who had won the most votes. The law had never contemplated a presidential election, with its own calendar. Lawyers, judges, and academics will argue for years about just *what* the deadline was: Was it December 12, when a federal law apparently immunized chosen electors from challenge? Was it December 18, when the electors gathered in their state capitols to vote? Was it January 6, when the new Congress convened to certify the electoral vote? Whatever the date, there was surely *some* point before Inauguration Day when the contest had to stop. In state and local contests, however, that was not the case. In fact, there were plenty of state cases where officials had been removed months after taking office, when the courts finally determined that the other candidate had won. Now ask yourself: How exactly would this work in the case of a presidential election? Would a clerk from a Florida circuit court show up at the Inaugural platform, armed with a subpoena? Would a team of Florida state troopers storm the northwest gate of the White House sometime in mid-March, waving the results of the final Florida recount? Moreover, if the mathematicians were right— if the margin of error would always be greater than the margin of victory or defeat—how many recounts would it take to achieve genuine finality? (As of mid-March of 2001, the press recounts of the Florida vote were still going on.)

This mundane argument was all but overwhelmed in the sound and fury that exploded all through that Friday evening. Democrats who had been preparing all week for a Gore concession now returned to the central message:

"We ought to take the time to count those votes," said California Governor Gray Davis. "And if a machine couldn't tell what preference that voter had for president, then we ought to look by hand count to determine who that voter wanted to be the next president of the United States."

Republicans renewed their assault on the legitimacy of any recount. J. C. Watts, chair of the House Republican Conference, said, "Today's ruling by the *all-Democratic* Florida Supreme Court sets a dangerous precedent which places Vice President Gore's recount obsession over the rule of law."

As for the media, we were again looking for the images that would convey the greater meaning of the story—this time the story playing out in local government offices across the state of Florida. How soon could those county canvassing boards conclude their examination of the "undervotes" in their areas? Would the totals reveal that Al Gore had in fact overtaken George W. Bush? Would the Bush campaign be able to challenge those totals under Florida's "contest" rules? Could all this possibly happen by December 12—or even by December 18, when the electors were scheduled to cast their votes?

By midafternoon on Saturday, December 9, all those questions were put on hold when the U.S. Supreme Court ordered the recounts stopped, and scheduled a hearing on the case for Monday. Political partisans will be arguing about what the High Court did all through the next congressional and presidential election cycles. Scholars will be arguing about the case for decades. My own hunch is that the Court's decision cannot be understood fully without looking at the alternative. What would have happened had the Court not ended the matter? My best guess is that George W. Bush would have ended up president anyway—but only after a fight that would have put our political system to its severest test in more than a hundred years. Compared to what we almost went through, Watergate and impeachment would have been a couple of walks in the park.

● It was one of the most compelling moments of the entire fight for Florida. In fact, it was one of the most compelling moments of the entire campaign year. For ninety minutes on Monday morning, December 11, the United States Supreme Court heard arguments in the case of *Bush, et al* v. *Gore, et al.* For the first time in American history, a presidential election was in the hands of the Supreme Court. What made it such compelling television? For one thing, there's a reason why courtroom dramas have been so popular for so long. There is something about weighty matters played out in a forum defined by solemnity that demands our attention. Another reason why it was such compelling television: *It was not televised.* Indeed, it took a special dispensation from the Court to let the public hear an audio recording immediately after the argument had ended. (Inevitably, the cable networks spent long moments on a close-up shot of the audio technician as he prepared to press the "PLAY" button on his machine.) All the viewers saw on their screens were still photographs or sketches of the justices and lawyers, and the text of what they were saying. Behind this simple fact, I believe, lies one of the keys to the final act of the struggle for the presidency.

It is beyond commonplace to note that we live in an age of the Omnipresent Camera. Couples marry, divorce, inflict emotional and physical mayhem on each other as the cameras roll and studio audiences bray. Click on the right Web site, and you can find every moment of someone's life—and I do mean *every* moment—captured by the cameras. Watch the end of a major sports contest, and you will be hard pressed to see the celebrating players through the mass of photographers. In the arena of public life, the cameras are ubiquitous. In fact, it's hard to realize that a generation ago, most of our civic life was off-limits. The public did not begin seeing live presidential press conferences until the Kennedy administration. Television cameras did not enter the House until the birth of C–SPAN in March, 1979. The Senate did not follow until June 1986. Now everything happens in full public view—including the proceedings in most state courtrooms.

The U.S. Supreme Court, though, has kept its doors firmly shut in the face of repeated requests from the media for access to its arguments. The only Americans who have ever seen the Court at work are lawyers, journalists, and the occasional handful of tourists. Not one in a thousand of us would recognize a justice if we passed one on the street, unless that justice had been caught in the glare of the cameras. (Most of us might be able to spot Clarence Thomas, thanks to his protracted confirmation hearing, or William Rehnquist because of his role in President Clinton's impeachment.) This anonymity is one of the Supreme Court's most valuable assets. It may even be the principal reason why the public holds the Court in such high esteem. When it comes to public institutions, I believe, familiarity breeds contempt. Watch a president running through the streets in his jogging shorts and it is hard to see him as a candidate for Mt. Rushmore. Click on a blow-dried congressman orating before an empty chamber and every stereotype about bloviating politicians seems validated. The very accessibility of these political players—combined, of course, with what they say and do to curry favor with us—devalues them as objects of admiration or awe. As Groucho Marx might have put it, we Americans refuse to respect any institution that so eagerly exposes itself to our gaze. By contrast, we seem to believe that if the Supreme Court does not care about putting itself on television, it deserves to be taken seriously.

All right—I concede that this may not explain *why* the American public has invested such confidence in the Court. There's no doubt, though, that by the time the U.S. Supreme Court agreed to hear the case of *Bush* v. *Gore,* the public was overwhelmingly willing to let the justices decide the matter once and for all. Even though most people believed the Court had acted politically when it stayed the recount over the weekend, *three-fourths*—including two-thirds of Gore's supporters—said they would accept the Court's ruling as legitimate. What's even more dramatic is that the voters trusted the Supreme Court—*and no other institution*—to make the choice. More than 60 percent said, "We trust the Supreme Court." Only 17 percent said, "We trust the Congress" (which happens to be the final authority on presidential electors, according to the Constitution). Fewer than 10 percent said they'd trust either the Florida Legislature or the Florida Supreme Court.

In part, this view reflected a growing public sense that enough was enough. Two weeks earlier, in late November, the public had been deadlocked on whom it preferred as president—just as it had been on Election Night. Now, more than a month later, Bush was ahead in every poll as the preferred candidate for president. They believed Bush had legitimately won the presidency, even though 60 percent of the public knew full well that Gore had won the national popular vote. Nor was that the worst news for Gore. Little more than a third of the public approved of his postelection conduct—which meant that even some of his supporters had had enough. The Gore campaign hoped the public would see Al Gore as Rocky Balboa, taking punch after punch and remaining on his feet, or perhaps Jefferson Smith, standing alone in the well of the Senate, fighting for truth and justice. Instead, in the words of CNN's Bill Schneider, "Fairly or unfairly, most Americans do not see Gore as a fighter. They see him as a sore loser." If the High Court could make all this go away, fine.

There was, I'm convinced, a more significant message in these numbers, one that transcended the fight for the White House. As I've said, the connection between the public and our national political life had been weakening for years. Somewhere in this mix—the end of the Cold War; the apparently permanent prosperity; the cynicism of politicians, press, and the popular culture; the abundant alternatives to political news—politics had become a sideshow. For reasons good and bad, much of America had decided that whatever all the fighting was about, it wasn't about them.

(I've always believed this indifference was one of the reasons Bill Clinton survived impeachment. I thought that the strongest case against the president was not some lawyerly debate about perjury and oath-taking, but that he had demonstrated contempt for the office—literally and symbolically. This was the place where Lincoln had drafted the Emancipation Proclamation, where FDR had plotted the New Deal, where Reagan had presided over the fall of the Soviet Union. Now,

Clinton had turned the Oval Office into the punch line of a dirty joke. And from the public came . . . a shrug. *Hey, what do you expect? They're all dishonest in one way or another. Besides, it has nothing to do with me.* Most Americans, it turned out, did not see Bill Clinton as a president who had failed to live up to a standard; they had long ceased to believe in a standard, and in any event, it was not going to make much of a difference to them.)

The astonishing spectacle of a deadlock on Election Night, and the battle that followed, had pushed politics back onto center stage. The public seemed briefly fascinated by the mechanics of choosing a president, as well as by the sheer closeness of the vote. Now, however, the holidays were coming. It was time for Charlie Brown and down-home Christmas specials starring dysfunctional celebrities. Above all, it was time to take the power out of the hands of political bodies. Let the political scientists and legal theorists debate about channeling so much power into the hands of nine unelected men and women. *Enough was enough.*

When the tape of the oral argument began to play, I began watching with a serene sense of confidence. *I have a law degree from a big-shot law school; I was an editor of the law review; this is right up my alley.* Within ten minutes, I was hoping for an interpreter. These justices do not sit behind the bench listening to orderly arguments. They interrupt constantly, often bickering with one another. At times, the lawyers are like the wall of a handball court, as the justices bounce questions off them that they hope will reveal the weakness of another judge's thinking. Still, it was clear that the justices were zeroing in on two questions:

First, did the Florida Supreme Court rewrite the legislature's election law by ordering a statewide recount of the "undervotes"? If that's what they did, it would be a clear violation of Article II of the U.S. Constitution.

Second—and here was the issue that absorbed most of the Court's time—what about the standards for interpreting the "undervotes"? If different canvassing boards used different standards to divine the "will of the voter," was that a violation of the Fourteenth Amendment's "Equal Protection" Clause?

"From the standpoint of the Equal Protection Clause," Justice Anthony Kennedy asked Gore lawyer David Boies, "could each county give their own interpretation to what 'intent' means, so long as they are in good faith and with some reasonable basis finding intent? . . . Could that vary from county to county?"

"I think it can vary from individual to individual."

"Why shouldn't there be one objective rule for all counties, and if there isn't, why isn't it an Equal Protection violation?" asked Justice David Souter.

What about the fact that different counties had different kinds of ballots, Justice Ruth Bader Ginsburg asked Bush lawyer Ted Olson. After all, voters using punch-card ballots are far more likely to have their ballots uncounted than are other voters.

"You are certainly going to have to look at a ballot that you mark one way different than these punch-card ballots," Olson replied. "Our point with respect to the punch-card ballots is that there are different standards for evaluating those ballots from county to county."

Repeatedly, Justices Souter and Stephen Breyer pressed Boies on whether he could suggest a uniform standard that all the canvassing boards might use. *If we do let the boards count,* they seemed to be saying, *can't you give us a clear, objective standard?* Boies kept falling back on the language of the

Florida law that pointed to the "intent of the voter." As a practical matter, the Gore camp needed the most expansive possible view of the standard; the looser the standard, the more votes Al Gore was likely to pick up.

Could we tell from the arguments how the Supreme Court was going to rule? I couldn't. All we knew for sure was that one of the assumptions of mid-November was dead and gone by mid-December. The Court, all the experts had said back then, would try mightily to speak with one voice, to preserve the sense that the Court was "above politics." When the Court froze the recount over the weekend, however, it had done so on a five-to-four vote. Justice John Paul Stevens had dissented from the stay, and Justice Antonin Scalia had written that five justices believed that the Bush camp would likely prevail on the merits. Would the Supreme Court really decide the presidency of the United States by a one-vote margin? Could we even speculate about such a possibility?

Later that evening, I saw how prescient speculation could be in the right hands. As soon as the battle shifted to the courtroom, every television network sent out an all-points bulletin for every presentable ex–Supreme Court law clerk we could find. These men and women had spent a year or two out of law school in the most prestigious of jobs: helping the Supreme Court justices with their research, and in some cases, with their opinions. No one was in a better position to know how these men and women went about their work. That night, we turned to John Yoo of Berkeley Law School, a former clerk for Justice Clarence Thomas, and Heather Gerkin of Harvard Law School, who had clerked for Justice David Souter. Yoo had won my heart three nights earlier by predicting flatly that the U.S. Supreme Court would stay the recount. Tonight, he was on a roll again.

"I didn't see a lot of movement between the five and four votes in terms of granting stay," he said of the oral argument. "So I would bet that if you had to put money on it, the Court tomorrow is going to reverse the supreme court, and it'll be the same lineup as with the stay. . . . You saw some of the justices on the left part of the court trying to reach out and suggest a compromise that might attract some of the more conservative justices. But I didn't really see any of the conservative justices really biting on that compromise."

Heather Gerkin sensed the same maneuvering among the more liberal justices:

"I think what happened on Saturday when the Supreme Court stayed the recount gave them a strong indication that [the court would not uphold the Florida court]. So now they're into new terrain, trying to find another way to bring the Court together on an issue, so that they can render, if not a unanimous opinion, at least something better than a five-to-four decision."

If in fact the Court remained divided, I asked, would it really be willing to effectively decide a presidential election by a one-vote margin? Wouldn't it be in its own interest to let a political body like the Congress decide?

"I not only think it's in the Court's own political interest, but I also just have trouble imagining why it is that the Supreme Court should fall on its sword here in order to save the country from following the processes which the Constitution established."

John Yoo had a different view:

"I think what they've done is they've realized they're probably going to take some kind of hit in terms of legitimacy over the short term. And I think some of the justices in the majority just made the calculation that it might be better for the country in the long run to have this decided tomorrow, that it's

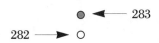

better for the Supreme Court to intervene perhaps, and decide the case than for having this going into Congress . . . this is all child's play compared to what would happen if Congress had to vote and elect the next president."

Twenty-four hours later, I was devoutly wishing that I had John Yoo and Heather Gerkin sitting by my side. Thirty-five days after Election Night, the final act of the story ended just as the first act had—with high drama, and mass confusion.

● Tuesday night, December 12, 9:59 P.M. I was sitting behind the anchor desk in Studio A at CNN's New York bureau, waiting for Larry King to wrap up his show and begin our one-hour program. Suddenly, I watched as King said, "Hold on, we think we have a breaking story, let's go to Bernie Shaw and Judy Woodruff." Shaw brought in Roger Cossack, CNN's legal analyst, from his location *outside* the Supreme Court building. Clad in hat, gloves, and an overcoat, Cossack—along with every other legal analyst now popping up on the monitors— appeared to be confronting a unique challenge: Interpret a Supreme Court decision while fighting off hypothermia. Cossack was also facing a more fundamental challenge: He had not yet seen the decision. Recognizing the problem, Shaw brought in Charles Bierbauer, who was *inside* the Supreme Court.

"Let me get to the bottom line here," he said. "The judgment of the Supreme Court is reversed. . . . Seven justices of this court have agreed that there are constitutional problems with the recount ordered by the Florida Supreme Court that demand a remedy. The only disagreement," he reported, "is what the remedy should be." At this point, Bierbauer was seconds away from delivering a completely accurate account of what the

Court had done in world-record time. He even reported the key paragraph of the majority's decision: that Florida's legislature had intended that the cutoff date for all contests was December 12—this very night.

So far, so good. But didn't the opinion say the case had been "reversed and *remanded*"—that is, sent back to the Florida Supreme Court? Didn't that suggest that the Florida court had more work to do; that the case had not ended? In the first frantic rush to judgment, that's what all of us assumed; one more proof of the old newsroom motto that "assumption is the mother of all f—ups." That "reversed and remanded" language was legal boilerplate. What the Court had really said was something very different. Here's a rough translation into English:

"Listen up, you justices on the Florida Supreme Court: Seven of us think your recount ruling was wrong. You needed to come up with some uniform standard of counting the votes. We seven think that if the votes are weighed by different standards, that violates the Equal Protection Clause of the Fourteenth Amendment. Four of us think you should be given a chance to do that: Devise a uniform standard, and somehow get the count done, and resolve all legal challenges to that count by December 18, when the electors meet. Five of us doubt very much that this is possible, but in any event, it doesn't matter. Your own opinion says the Florida Legislature clearly wanted to protect its electors under the "safe harbor" provisions of federal law. That means the decisions have to be in place by midnight tonight—December 12. So it's over—forget it—no more counting. And by the way, in case anyone else may be tempted in the future to bring an Equal Protection case in a ballot-counting dispute? Forget it. This ruling only applies to this unique case."

Had the U.S. Supreme Court had the same tender regard

for the press as had its counterpart in Florida, all this would have been clear from the beginning. At 10 P.M., a spokesperson would have appeared on the marble steps of the building and offered a quick, shorthand summary of the opinion. The justices themselves might have put "head notes" at the start of the opinion, summarizing their findings and the dissents. That's not how they do it in Washington; the opinions are set down in the press room, and it's everyone for himself and devil take the hindmost. On this night, we at CNN, along with most of our colleagues, were victims of the process. (To give credit where credit is due, the folks at NBC News got it right first.) For long moments, we speculated about what the Florida court might do; our frostbitten colleagues thumbed through the opinion, looking for definitive clues. Anchor Judy Woodruff, unburdened by a law degree, was the first among us to cut to the chase. She went back to the line that Charles Bierbauer had quoted at the very start of our coverage—a line from the majority rejecting Justice Breyer's December 18 deadline as an idea "in violation of the Florida election code."

"It sounds to me," she said, "as if they're saying the remedy proposed by Justice Breyer doesn't work."

Another piece of evidence: White House correspondent John King was reporting from inside the Gore camp that the decision was being greeted "pessimistically . . . not good news."

Many minutes later, when a copy of the opinion reached the anchor desk in New York, I reverted to an old law-school habit of mine, born out of laziness: When you don't want to plow through endless pages of a majority opinion, check out what the dissenters have to say. They are likely to describe the majority's view in stark, often anguished terms. Sure enough, here was Stephen Breyer, writing, "What the Court does today

JEFF GREENFIELD | *Oh, Waiter! One Order of Crow!*

the Court should have left undone, but I would repair the damage done as best we now can by permitting the Florida recount to continue under uniform standards." *Aha!* If Breyer *would* have permitted a recount to continue, and if Breyer was a dissenter, that means the majority is *not* allowing a recount. And here is Justice John Paul Stevens writing, "Although we may never know with complete certainty the identity of the winner of this year's presidential election, the identity of the loser is perfectly clear. It is the nation's confidence in the judge as an impartial guardian of the law." *Bingo!* No Supreme Court justice uses language like that unless his side has lost completely. It was at this point that I subtly signaled to our producers that I had finally figured the opinion out. (I believe I got their attention by setting a small fire in the studio, but my memory may be playing tricks on me.)

"I make no claim to be a legal scholar," I said with rare modesty, false or otherwise, "but it sure sounds to me that the reason why that Gore source told John King this is not good news is because there does not seem to be in this remand any room for the Florida State Supreme Court to conduct a recount."

So it was over. It was left only for the principals to speak their last words on the matter. The next night, they did so in yet another perfect demonstration of their yearlong effort to define themselves. Al Gore, who had always wanted us to think better of him as a person, appeared on camera alone, in a speech touched by grace and good humor. "Just moments ago," he said, "I spoke with George W. Bush . . . and I promised him that I wouldn't call him back this time." He spoke of going back to Tennessee to "mend some fences—literally and figuratively," a self-deprecating reference to the loss of his home state, which in the end cost him the presidency. And he concluded with a good-humored reference to a line from his 1992 acceptance speech. "And now," he said, "it's time for *me* to go."

It was a speech that triggered questions that almost always arise in the wake of a graceful acknowledgment of defeat: *Why didn't he talk that way during the campaign? If he'd been more like that, he might have won.*

There's a simple answer to this: Now, the pressure was off. In a campaign setting, Gore always seemed to be the "Robo-Candidate"—every word weighed for possible damage, every gesture calculated. Now, there were no more votes to be won, there was no more public opinion to be swayed. Now, he could be at ease. Watching Gore now, it was hard to escape the conclusion that the vice president may have been the first candidate since Richard Nixon to have lost the White House because of performance anxiety.

Governor Bush, who had always wanted us to take him seriously as a candidate of presidential weight, claimed victory from the rostrum of the House Chamber of the Texas state capitol—a legislative body controlled by Democrats. "I was not elected to serve one party, but to serve one nation," he said. "Americans share hopes and goals and values far more important than any political disagreements." If the speech lacked the grace notes of Al Gore's concession, it didn't really matter. There were no focus groups, no postspeech polling to be done.

There was, however, plenty of fallout from the Supreme Court's decision. The Gore partisans now spoke just as Bush's supporters had after the *Florida* Supreme Court had come down on Al Gore's side.

"Disgrace!" headlined the *New Republic,* whose owner, Martin Peretz, was a lifelong friend of Gore. It scorned the "healing" message of Republicans as "part of the strategy of the Republican larcenists, in and out of robes, who arranged to suppress the truth about the vote in Florida, and thereby to make off with the election of 2000.

"Constitutionally speaking, this presidency is ill-gotten. It is the prize of a judicial putsch."

Writing in the *Nation* later, Vincent Bugliosi, prosecutor-turned-author, proclaimed the five-person Court majority as "criminal," and wrote that "in a fair and just world," they "belong behind prison bars."

Yale Law School's Bruce Ackerman, a leading liberal scholar, argued that the Democratic minority in the Senate should filibuster *all* of Bush's nominations to the U.S. Supreme Court until 2004, when voters could decide whether Bush should in fact remain the president. The Court worked in the past with six or seven members, he said, and it could do so again.

Even some conservative analysts were left uneasy by the Court's Equal Protection argument.

"By this logic," wrote the *National Review*, "Florida's entire election system, featuring different voting machines, with different levels of reliability from one county to the next, would be unconstitutional." It preferred the approach of Justices Rehnquist, Scalia, and Thomas that the Florida court had rewritten Florida's legislative scheme, which the U.S. Constitution did not permit it to do.

Most pervasive was the conclusion that the Supreme Court had turned itself into a nakedly political body. *Look at the lineup: the three hard-edged conservatives thought the Florida court was completely wrong. Anthony Kennedy and Sandra Day O'Connor thought the time had run out to fix the Equal Protection problem. Souter and Breyer, the moderate liberals, thought the Court should have a chance to fix it. The two most liberal justices—John Paul Stevens and Ruth Bader Ginsburg— didn't see any problem at all with what the Court did. This is nothing but a political argument wrapped up in black robes and legal mumbo-jumbo.*

The more I thought about the decision, the more I went back to the point that ex–Supreme Court clerk John Yoo had made the night before the decision: that the Court majority may have decided "that it might be better . . . for the Supreme Court to intervene and decide this case than letting it go to the Congress. . . . This is all child's play compared to what would happen if Congress had to vote and elect the next president."

What would have happened? There are many alternative paths this fight could have taken. Every one of them, I believe, would have ended up with George W. Bush in the White House. But at what cost? Here are some of the possibilities had the U.S. Supreme Court let the recount continue:

- With the December 12 deadline upon it, the Florida Legislature takes the process over, and appoints a Bush slate of electors. Over the next five days, the partial recounts give the lead to Al Gore. Following a hasty judicial review, the Florida court declares Gore the victor, and orders Governor Bush to certify him the winner. He refuses, citing the Florida Legislature's action. So Democratic Attorney General Butterworth certifies the Gore slate.

  On December 18, both slates of Florida electors convene in Tallahassee. The Bush slate meets in the state capitol. The Gore slate gathers in the attorney general's office. Results from the competing slates are sent to the Congress. On January 6, the

Congress meets in special session to pass judgment on the electoral votes. When Florida's turn comes, objections are raised to whichever slate is presented first. Under the rules, the Congress retreats to its respective houses, where a one-person-one-vote process decides which slate wins.

With the Republicans holding a narrow edge in the House, a party-line vote declares the Bush slate the winner. (It's possible that a handful of conservative Democrats from states that voted for Bush might also defect.) In the fifty-fifty Senate, a party-line vote would produce a tie. Who would break that tie? The presiding officer of the Senate, Vice President Al Gore. (It's also likely that a furious procedural debate would break out on whether the vice president has a vote to cast in such a case.) So unless a conservative Democrat from a Bush-supporting state defects, the Gore slate would likely win acceptance in the Senate.

Now what? The 1887 federal law says that if there's a split, preference will go to the slate certified by the chief executive of the state—in this case, Governor Jeb Bush. But suppose the Florida Supreme Court had declared Governor Bush in contempt for flaunting its order. Would that be a "valid" certification? Who would decide? The Congress? The federal courts? Eventually, this case would make its way to the U.S. Supreme Court, where the Court's traditional deference to the states would likely have meant approval of the Bush slate. By this point, the country would be lucky to have a president by Inauguration Day.

- Another possibility: When the Florida Legislature steps in, the Gore campaign launches a federal court action (as it had planned to do). It argues that under the Civil Rights Act, the legislature *did not have the power* to take over the elector-selection process *once it had given that power to the voters directly.* Suppose a federal court had ruled in favor of the Gore side. Under those circumstances, it is at least possible that Florida would have missed the deadline for submitting its electoral votes. What then? If the Congress somehow decided that Florida had never appointed its electors, then the total number of "appointed electors" would shrink by 25 electoral votes, to 513. With his 267 electoral votes, Al Gore would have a majority of that number, and would win the White House. If the number remained at 538, then neither Gore nor Bush would have a majority.

What then? Under the Constitution, the choice for president would be thrown into the House of Representatives; the choice for vice president would be thrown into the Senate. In the House, each *state* would have one vote. (If a state delegation tied, that state would cast no vote.) When the new House met, 27 states had a Republican majority—so George W. Bush would have been chosen. An evenly split Senate with Al Gore presiding could, at least in theory, have chosen Joe Lieberman as vice president, though at this point some sense of reality would undoubtedly have set in.

For the supporters of Al Gore, the Supreme Court decision was clear proof that the powers-that-be were simply determined to put their choice in the White House no matter what. In their eyes, the votes of thousands of their most loyal supporters in

Florida were never counted, lost to bureaucratic error or through blatant indifference to voting rights in heavily Democratic precincts. The Bush forces never wanted those ballots examined, because in their hearts they *knew* that Al Gore had won. In the end, a narrow right-wing majority of the Supreme Court bent the Equal Protection clause into a pretzel to shut the recount down.

Whatever the truth of that view, there is another way to see it: Our Election Day had produced a tie—not just a tie, but a tie under bizarre circumstances, where the presidency had come down to a handful of votes in one state. Our political machinery lacked the ability to resolve that tie. Hold a runoff in Florida? Impossible. Hold a nationwide runoff? Why, when in the vast majority of states the results were clear? Send the process into the maw of congressional and court fights that could leave the country without a winner for another month or more?

We may never know why the Court did what it did. Historians may conclude in the end that the decision broke faith with the intentions of the founders that political conflicts be resolved in the political arena. But I would not be at all surprised if at least one of those justices looked down the road and concluded simply, *Either we stop this now, or we are heading right for a train wreck. I just can't take that chance. Better we end it now.*

It's nothing more than a hunch. But as hunches go, it's not bad.

Thoughts from an

Inauguration

○ **I N A U G U R A T I O N   D A Y**

is a time of pomp and pageantry; a quadrennial celebration of change and continuity; a time for reaffirmation and rededication; a time for speechwriters and pundits to drag out their books of quotations in search of sentiments even more pretentious than the ones you have just read. On this Saturday morning, as I looked out from our rooftop perch down onto the Mall, then over to the bunting-bedecked West Front of the Capitol, my thoughts were, if more personal, just as powerful and profound:

Thank God I'm indoors for this one.

Washington had turned cold and raw; frozen rain was pelting the streets and the spectators. Had I not found new work as a CNN anchor, that rain would have been pelting me as well. I'd spent the previous three Inaugurals standing on a makeshift wooden platform twenty feet or so above the Capitol. The view was invariably terrific; the climate was invariably terrifying. There is a good reason why songwriters choose "April in Paris" and "Autumn in New York" over "January in Washington." This day, I would be working out of a heated, enclosed tent on the roof of the Department of Labor. The warmth of my surroundings, however, could not disguise the chill in the air— and it wasn't just coming from the temperature.

Down on the street, long lines of spectators were waiting just outside ten checkpoints that ringed the huge expanse of grass. Responding to promises of mass protests, Washington authorities had proclaimed the Inauguration a "National Special Security Event." So, for the first time in history, American citizens could not watch their new president take the oath of office without the permission of the authorities. The sight of armed, uniformed men and women surrounding such public ceremonies never fails to depress me. It's not that I'm indifferent to the need for security; I just hate what it all represents. Every metal detector in a Senate Office building, every new layer to the bubble that surrounds presidents and candidates, is a sign that the Bad Guys have won a round here. By making us fear them, they have made us fear each other. Even that designation—"National Special Security Event"—sounds like something out of Eastern Europe in the 1950s.

If the events on the Mall were dispiriting, the gathering on the Inaugural platform was fascinating. In normal years, the assemblage of notables was a tableau. This morning, it was a psychodrama.

The temptation to imagine the thoughts of this unprecedented gathering was irresistible. Picture each of them looking at the Inaugural stand, each with his or her thoughts focused on the same man.

- George Herbert Walker Bush: *"I was there. I would have stood there twice, if not for that flimflam artist from Arkansas. But now I get to watch my son take the oath. . . . I'm the first ex-president to see that since John Adams."*

- Al Gore: *"I should be up there today. I would be, too, if not for you and your colleagues, Mr. Chief Justice Rehnquist. When George W. thanks you for swearing him in, that's going to be one* heartfelt *'thank you.' And I can't forget you, Mr. soon-to-be-ex-President. If you hadn't done what you did in that room off the Oval Office, I'd be about to become the president. You made me what I'm about to become now—a private citizen."*

- Senator Hillary Clinton: *"The last time I was up there, I was holding the Bible for you, Bill. Maybe four or eight years from now, you'll be holding the Bible for me. I guess I owe you one, Bill. If you hadn't done what you did in that room off the Oval Office, I wouldn't be a United States senator today."*

- George W. Bush: *"I owe you, Mr. President. First off, if you hadn't done what you did in that room off the Oval Office, I wouldn't be about to become the next president of the United States. You let us make a campaign issue out of 'restoring honor and integrity to the White House.' And now, just as you're about to leave, you cop a plea to escape a perjury charge, and pardon a fugitive billionaire literally in the dead of night, after his ex-wife throws hundreds of thousands of dollars at your library. You couldn't have given me a better example of what I mean by 'changing the tone' in Washington."*

As soon as George W. Bush took the oath of office, these random thoughts of mine were blown away: first, by the sound of a twenty-one-gun salute from the cannons hard by the Capitol; second, by the best Inaugural speech in forty years. Speechwriter Michael Gerson has the rare ability to fit a speech perfectly to his principal. Make the Inaugural too conversational, and it lacks heft. Make it too highflown, and no one will believe it could have come from the heart of George W. Bush.

Instead, Gerson somehow found a way to put fresh energy into the sentiments required of every new president. He recapitulated the major themes of Bush's campaign, but in language that transformed the ideas from political to presidential.

Bush spoke of America as "flawed and fallible people, united across the generations by grand and enduring ideals"— a rhetorical recognition of past wrongs. He spoke bluntly of the least well-off when he spoke of "the ambitions of some Americans . . . limited by failing schools and hidden prejudice and the circumstances of their birth." He bridged the debate between Left and Right about the causes of poverty in a single sentence: "In the quiet of American conscience, we know that deep, persistent poverty is unworthy of our nation's promise. And whatever our views of its cause, we can agree that children at risk are not at fault. Abandonment and abuse are not acts of God, they are failures of love." And he used biblical imagery to drive home the point: "Many in our country do not know the pain of poverty. But we can listen to those who do. And I can pledge our nation to a goal: When we see that wounded traveler on the road to Jericho, we will not pass to the other side."

The real message of the speech, however, was not to be found in such high rhetoric. It was found, rather, in a single paragraph.

"Together . . . we will reform Social Security and Medicare . . . we will reduce taxes, to recover the momentum of our economy and reward the effort and enterprise of working Americans. We will build our defenses beyond challenge, lest weakness invite challenge."

What Bush had done in this paragraph was recapitulate the major themes of his campaign. In a speech filled with the language of inclusion, Bush was telling his supporters, "I'm going to do what I said I was going to do."

And here, in a nutshell, was yet more proof that the torrent of speculation about a Bush presidency might very well have been as wrongheaded as those Election Night prognostications.

All through November and December, two themes dominated the media's message about a prospective Bush administration: First, history taught us that presidents who lose the popular vote are doomed to political failure; second, the closeness of the vote, combined with the near deadlock in the Congress, meant that Bush would "have to govern from the center out."

During the thirty-seven-day-long deadlock, the networks

put enough historians on the air to win accreditation as a school of continuing education. All of them pointed to the unhappy presidencies of John Quincy Adams, Rutherford B. Hayes, and Benjamin Harrison as grim portents. Adams and Harrison had lost four years later in reruns against the men they'd beaten. Hayes, whose tainted presidency led opponents to call him "His Fraudulency," didn't even bother to run again. Historians and pundits alike united to explain that Bush's more ambitious plans—for a huge tax cut and entitlement reform—were unthinkable in a season of deadlock.

It was persuasive stuff—until I watched the Inaugural. Somewhere during the hours of pageantry, I realized that George W. Bush had something going for him that his nineteenth-century predecessors never had: a mass medium that would demonstrate his "presidentiality" every day of the week. Whatever his percentage of the vote, he had won one hundred percent of the presidency. There was the Marine Band, in all its glory, playing "Hail to the Chief." They didn't cut the salute down to six or seven guns just because Al Gore had won half a million more votes. Every time Bush climbed aboard Air Force One, every time the photographers snapped his picture in the Oval Office, his "legitimacy" would be "proven" again.

His first days in office suggested that the president and his team understood this in a way that we observers did not. If he entered the White House convinced that his ideas could not work in a closely divided Washington, that premise would doom him to failure. Bush himself knew full well what had happened to his father when his retreat on taxes lost him the affection of the conservative base. That's why he appointed conservative hero John Ashcroft as his attorney general. That's why his very first executive acts imposed new restrictions on the flow of federal money to overseas groups that performed or advocated abortions. That's why he reaffirmed his support for the same tax cut he'd run on during the campaign. Contrary to what everyone had assumed during the post–election battle, Bush was conducting his presidency exactly as he would have had he won 55 percent of the popular vote and 350 electoral votes.

"You dance with the guy that brung you" is still one of the wisest rules in politics.

● When the Inaugural ended, President and Laura Bush escorted Bill and Hillary Clinton to a waiting limousine for their drive to Andrews Air Force Base, for their journey home to New York. One more time, Bill Clinton surprised us. By tradition, the new ex–president says a quick goodbye to his loyalists, then departs the scene. Not this ex–president. As George W. Bush was sitting down to the post–Inaugural lunch with congressional leaders in Statuary Hall, Clinton delivered a lengthy speech to his loyalists in an airplane hangar, and then worked the crowd as if they were New Hampshire voters the night before a primary. As I sat at the anchor desk, I asked the producers one question: *Are the other guys covering this, too? Shouldn't we be staying with the guy we just swore in? Yes,* the answer came back, *they're all with Clinton. Bush is still having lunch. This is just too amazing not to cover.*

This is, after all, what we know—the sensation of the moment, the buzz in the air that tells you: *This is what people want to see right now.* I had another lesson in this later that evening, at a reception at the Phillips Collection, one of Washington's great cultural treasures.

To appreciate it, you need to know something about most Inaugural events, particularly the huge "galas": They have all the charm of a rush-hour New York subway car at high noon in August when the air conditioning has broken down. They are designed principally for the mortification of out-of-towners. Sometime in November or December, John and Susan Partyguys get a lovely, engraved invitation in the mail.

"Look!" they say. "Our hard work and contributions have been rewarded! We're invited to the Inaugural!"

In their innocence, they imagine glittering ballrooms, elegant food, a gathering of the rich and famous and powerful, perhaps a quiet chat with the new president. John buys a new tuxedo; Susan buys a new gown. They book the tickets and the hotel room. And then they arrive in Washington. They find themselves caught in gridlock, marooned by their driver. Their "ball" is a mob scene: The crowd waits for an hour or more on the frozen street to pass through the metal detectors; there is neither food nor drink anywhere. If they are foolish enough to check their coats, they will wait until dawn before they get them back. If they are lucky, they may push close enough to the front of the mob to get a passing glimpse of the First Couple.

For those who are part of the permanent Washington, there is a different Inaugural. There is one dinner, thrown by one of Washington's more prominent hostesses, which looks very much like John and Susan's Washington fantasy. This is where Colin Powell says hello to Dan Snyder, the owner of the Washington Redskins; where the first-name media powers, Tim and Sam and Cokie and Judy and Al, chat with a quorum of senators; and where the belle of the ball is Katherine Harris.

The Phillips Collection, though, was something very different. On this night, it was showcasing a special exhibition called "Degas to Matisse: Impressionist and Modern Masterworks from the Detroit Institute of Arts." The centerpiece: fifty-eight works from the Robert Tannahill collection, including paintings by Cezanne, Degas, van Gogh, Renoir, Picasso, Gauguin, and Seurat.

Amid these masterpieces, the crowd wandered, ate, drank, and talked: *"How badly had Clinton tarnished his legacy? . . . What will it do to Hillary? . . . Who's in charge of foreign policy: Powell, Cheney, Rumsfeld, Rice? . . ."* Every once in a long while, someone wandered up to one of the artworks, looked for the compulsory moment or two, and then went off, in search of a friend, a date, a drink, a morsel of food.

This was not the time for appreciating the lasting power of great art. This was a time to get a fix on who held the reins of power *right now*. We had a president, and he and his circle held those reins, and that was all that mattered.

● By Sunday morning, the cold and the rain were gone; Washington was bathed in a warm sun. I was heading home. My car rode east on Constitution Avenue, then made a left turn on First Street as we headed toward Union Station. I looked up . . . and realized that we were passing the Dirksen Senate Office building. More than thirty-three years ago, I'd come to this building to work in the office of Robert Kennedy. It was the summer of 1967, and everyone I knew was consumed by politics: by the war, by the sight of cities in flames, by a sense of urgency that things were spinning out of control. That year, every speechwriter seemed to be fixated on the line by Yeats: "Things fall apart; the center cannot hold; mere anarchy is loosed upon the world."

Now? Even after the head-shaking events of the last campaign, there was little if any of that apocalyptic sense in the air. Even the talk of reforms seemed cursory. Yes, the networks will be more cautious in their projections next time, and yes, the states will probably spend some money to make sure that their voting machines actually count the votes that the voters mean to cast. As for the rest . . .

Abolish the Electoral College? Fine—except that the smaller states would never allow it to happen. Of course, in a deadlocked race, we'd be arguing not about a few hundred thousand votes in one state, but about all 100 million ballots in every state. And besides, there may be virtue in a system that forces candidates to remember that this is a big country, with a diverse population. Folks in West Virginia and California see the environment very differently; folks in Michigan and Maryland have very different views about guns.

A Presidential Runoff? It looks tempting when you realize that, for the first time in more than eighty years, a third-party candidate changed the outcome of a presidential election. Ralph Nader got 97,000 votes in Florida—had he not run, Gore would have picked up a minimum net gain of 20,000 votes, and with them, the state—and the White House. So it might make sense to say that if no candidate got 50 percent of the vote, the top two finishers would face off a week later. But to have a runoff, you would have to abolish the Electoral College.

Apportion the Electoral Vote? Why would a state like Florida split its delegation, ensuring that the winner of the state would gain three or four electoral votes, instead of twenty-five? States are allowed to split their votes now—and only Nebraska and Maine do it—because they have no clout in the Electoral College anyway.

The truth is, there is nothing but the law of averages to prevent what happened in 2000 from happening all over again. Under the right—or wrong—circumstances, we could again face a deadlocked campaign, with the outcome hinging on a handful of votes in one state.

That's a matter of probability. The harder question is whether the country will accept such an outcome in more tumultuous times. The America of 2000 was "a hotbed of rest"; it could sit back and watch this blend of *The Federalist Papers* and *Celebrity Death Match* with a sense of fascination. Would it be the same if the political climate of my youth returned some day? Would there be genuinely serious consequences to a future deadlock?

Hey—if there's one thing I learned on that Election Night, it's that I don't do predictions.

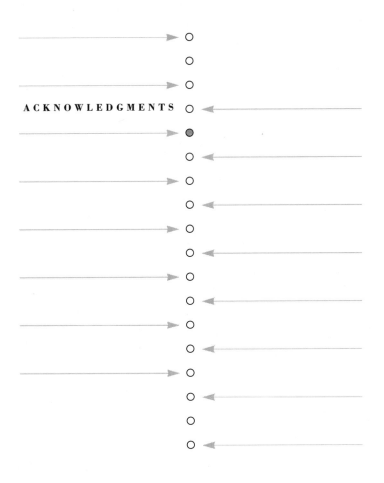

ACKNOWLEDGMENTS

● **WHEN NEIL NYREN,**
Putnam's publisher and editor-in-chief, called me in mid-November, I answered the phone with that sensation of guilt only a writer three years late on a novel can know. When he told me he wanted me to put that work aside and write a memoir-on-the-run about this extra-ordinary election, my relief

was swiftly overcome by stark terror. *I can't do this.* Without Neil's conviction, and his guidance, this book would not have happened. And I'll have that novel done in a day or two.

My colleagues at CNN were invaluable allies all through the campaign year, on Election Night, and in the month and more beyond. The on-camera folks are well known: Bill Schneider, Judy Woodruff, John King, Candy Crowley, and Bernard Shaw, whose twenty-year stint at CNN ended in early 2001. Equally invaluable, though less visible, were the producers and executives. My special thanks go to Sid Bedingfield, Executive Vice President and General Manager, CNN/US, who oversaw CNN's Election Night coverage; to Tom Hannon, CNN political director, who shared his Election Night trauma with me, Shirley Hung of *Inside Politics,* who endured my far-too-frequent much-too-close-to-deadline inspirations, and to Keating Holland, CNN's director of polling, for his counsel and guidence.

During the campaign, I anchored a weekly gathering of "unconventional" voices, in an effort—as President Bush might say—to "change the tone" of public discourse. Executive Producer Bruce Perlmutter and Senior Producer Michael Squadron were largely responsible for getting them on the air, as well as overseeing the nightly specials I anchored during the post–election month.

Producer Bob Ruff and I have worked together at ABC and now at CNN. His creativity, energy, and incredibly high standards provided the best moments of the profiles and essays I did throughout the campaign. He defines the meaning of "pro."

I have a special debt to Rick Kaplan, who brought me to CNN during his tenure as president of CNN/US. At *Nightline,* and again at CNN, Rick was a protean force of energy, inspiration, and creativity. I miss him as a colleague; I value him as a friend.

Frank Lalli was executive editor of *George* magazine during its last year. He was kind enough to invite me to join his staff in a series of conversations with major political figures during the national conventions. Those conversations provided food for thought; the cooking genius of his wife, Carol, will (I hope) continue to provide more tangible sustenance to his ever-grateful schnorrer.

Once again, I must offer special thanks to the "Palmeni Boys," a collection of miscreants with whom I have shared weekly lunches and other diversions for decades. These midday repasts with Andrew Bergman, Jerry Della Femina, Dr. Gerald Imber, Michael Kramer, and Joel Siegel continue to provide me with a constant source of inspiration and heartburn. We take comfort in knowing that, as the years pass by, the conversation remains sparkling, the jokes remain fresh . . . because we can't remember that we have heard each other's stories over and over and over . . .

My thanks and my love to my daughter, Casey, and my son, Dave, for the joy they have brought me, and their energetic efforts to keep me grounded in what really matters.

Finally, I owe more than I can say to two extraordinary women. Beth Goodman has worked by my side since I came to CNN. She began as my assistant; she is now a researcher, scheduler, interviewer, and producer. She excels at everything she does. In fact, I can put it a bit stronger: If Beth Goodman can't do it, it can't be done.

And to Dena Sklar, the love of my life: Thank you for making me believe in miracles.